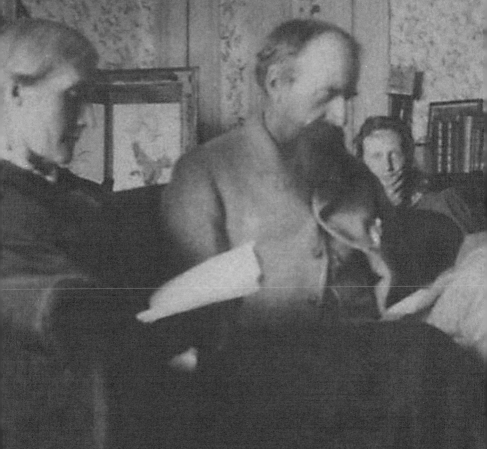

Virginia Woolf

BLOOMSBURY AND BEYOND

VIRGINIA WOOLF

BLOOMSBURY AND BEYOND

ANTHONY CURTIS

HAUS
BOOKS
London

To the memory of VL and NBCL

First published in Great Britain in 2006
by Haus Publishing Limited
26 Cadogan Court, Draycott Avenue, London SW3 3BX

Copyright © Anthony Curtis, 2006
The moral rights of the author have been asserted.
A CIP catalogue record for this book is available
from the British Library
ISBN 1-904950-23-X

Designed in InDesign and typeset in Garamond by Rick Fawcett
Printed and bound by Graphicom in Vicenza, Italy

Cover images Getty Images
*Frontispiece: Julia and Leslie Stephen in the drawing-room of Talland House, St Ives
with Virginia in the background*
Title page: Nocturnal view of the Victoria Embankment 1929
This page: The Stephen and Duckworth families at Talland House, St Ives, Cornwall

www.hauspublishing.com

CONTENTS

Introduction

In 1942, when I was 16, I started to read the work of Virginia Woolf. The headmaster's wife, who taught us French at the grammar school in Midhurst, West Sussex, where I was a boarder, was an early Virginia Woolf admirer. She saw that the school library was well stocked with Woolf's novels and the two volumes of the *Common Reader*. She told us that Mrs Woolf had descended into madness for part of her life but had recovered and had been able to give a remarkable account in one of her novels of what it was like to be mad. Then, in March 1941, sensing the madness was coming back, she had drowned herself in the Ouse, a river in our county.

The nearness of her demise, in both time and space, seemed to give added poignancy to the voice that came so eloquently through the books. Against the background of boarding school life during World War Two with its nightly blackout and the overhead drone of the bombers on their way to Germany, heard as we lay in bed in the dormitory, the thought of Mrs Dalloway sallying forth on a fine summer morning from Westminster to Bond Street to buy the flowers for her party, with not an air-raid shelter along the route, had heart-warming appeal. Mrs Lucas cautioned us against making the headlong plunge into the soliloquies of *The Waves* too soon. She suggested we waited until we were older and more mature before tackling them.

That sent me straight to the book. I found it much easier to read than to understand. Its imagery overwhelmed me as I struggled to find a plot. I reported back to her that I had read it and she asked me to say what I thought was its theme. 'Well,'

Julia, Vanessa, Virginia and Thoby Stephen in front of Talland House

I began hesitantly, 'there are these six people and they all seem to be saying, "Who am I ?"' It was as much as I could manage, but she persisted with the interrogation: 'Yes, go on; what do you think the answer to that should be?' I remained silent. 'They live in each other,' she said. 'They become what they are through seeing themselves in the minds of each other.' I reckon that is as good a description of the binding thread of *The Waves* and, incidentally, of Bloomsbury, as one is likely to get.

By the time I arrived at Oxford to read for an English degree in 1948 (four intervening years were spent in the RAF) a reaction had set in, both in me and generally. Among the dons there was one, Lord David Cecil, who spoke up for Virginia Woolf's work. He had known her and had attended some of the Bloomsbury gatherings. He bracketed her with E M Forster. 'Both are highly civilised persons,' he wrote, 'in whom an exquisite sensibility and an acute, inquisitive intelligence have been developed to the finest point of fastidious refinement.' He quoted the famous passage containing the key Woolfian observation: 'Life is not a series of gig-lamps symmetrically arranged; life is a luminous halo, a semi-transparent envelope surrounding us from the beginning of consciousness to the end.' By that she meant that our experience of life does not take the form of a steady progress like that of a gig, a two-wheeled one-horse carriage with lamps at each side illuminating its onward movement, as earlier novelists suggested through their 'linear' method of narrative. In her view we experience life as a series of disconnected moments in which memories from the past burst continually upon what is happening to us in the present enlightening it. Her narrative method was the attempt to capture these moments in the consciousness of her main characters. He then went on to make out a case for her as a novelist enamoured of the beautiful. It was her strength and her weakness. 'Virginia Woolf was in the fullest, highest extreme sense of the word, an aesthete,' he said. 'The most significant moments in her life were its moments of intense aesthetic experience.'[1] Cecil's was a courageous defence, but it did not do her reputation at that time much good.

Literary criticism should be moral not aesthetic, urged the Cambridge critical journal *Scrutiny*. As for Mrs Woolf and her life-envelope, F R Leavis wrote: 'it may be semi-transparent; but it seems to shut out all the ranges of experience accompanying those kinds of preoccupation, volitional and moral, with an external world which are not felt primarily as preoccupation with one's consciousness of it.'[2] We invited Dr Leavis to come to Oxford to talk to our English Club in 1949. At a packed meeting, his first words were: 'If I had my way the word aesthetic would be banished from the language.'

Outside academia Graham Greene launched an attack, making a similar point to Leavis in simpler prose. He wrote that after the death of Henry James, 'the religious sense was lost to the English novel, and with the religious sense went the sense of the importance of the human act. It was as if the world of fiction had lost a dimension: the characters of such distinguished writers as Mrs Virginia Woolf and Mr E M Forster wandered like cardboard symbols through a world that was paper-thin.'[3]

Angus Wilson, making his name as a writer of abrasive short stories, uttered his strictures on Woolf's novels in a BBC Third Programme radio broadcast on 8th August 1950 in which he poured scorn on her stream-of-consciousness method. John Raymond, the influential literary journalist, wittily attacked both Woolf and Forster in the *New Statesman* for their sheltered view of life. This was taking the attack to her doorstep, as it were. Her husband Leonard Woolf was a director of the journal to which she had been a valued contributor. He made no public comment on the attack but invited Raymond to have lunch with him.

The tide began to be reversed when he decided to publish extracts from the regular journal his wife had kept from 1915 until her death. There were 26 volumes of this in all and, although he felt that most of it was 'too personal' to be published during the lifetime of many of the people referred to, he thought that all the parts where Virginia discussed her work could be published and he brought these together under the title *A Writer's Diary* in 1953. This gave her readers a new

Virginia Woolf. They saw now that among her many gifts as a writer were those of introspection and self-analysis. Attention switched from the work to the woman and then back to the work as posthumous collections of her essays and stories appeared at regular intervals. Her star was once more in the ascendant and among the former detractors Angus Wilson recanted.

At the same time the whole question of what was considered 'too personal' to be published about the living and the dead was rapidly changing. Michael Holroyd's massive two-volume biography of Lytton Strachey in 1967–8, with its detailed account of its subject's serial homosexual amours and those of other members of the Bloomsbury set to which he belonged, made the change of attitude plain for all to see. If we could have Lytton warts and all, could we not have Virginia likewise?

When Leonard Woolf died in 1969, the way was open for a biography that would tell the whole of Virginia's story. It appeared in two volumes in 1972 from the pen of Quentin Bell, the art historian and her nephew. Professor Bell was in the happy position for a biographer of being in possession of virtually almost all the necessary material. He made brilliant use of his opportunity. His biography has never been surpassed; nor, I think, will it ever be. Others have built and will continue to build structures of their own upon the secure foundations he laid. The decision was taken at the same time to publish complete editions of the Diary and of the surviving Letters, of which there were more than 3,000. These appeared throughout the 1970s and into the 1980s in tandem, the Diaries in five volumes and the Letters in six. They were foremost among the major English publishing events of those years.

From the vantage-point of a literary editor of two national newspapers (*The Sunday Telegraph* and the *Financial Times*), as I successively became, I was able to observe this unfolding and to observe the triumph of Virginia Woolf over her detractors, her emergence as being among the most important novelists of the 20th century and, in her polemical writing, as an icon of the feminist movement.

My admiration for her work grew steadily as I learned of the difficulties she had to overcome and the continual renewal of effort and experiment she made. To try to compress the whole of her life and work into one comparatively short book aimed at her and (Dr Johnson's) recipient, the Common Reader, was a challenge I found impossible to resist, and here is the result. It would not have been possible without the existence of the editions of the Diaries and Letters mentioned above. I am most grateful for permission to quote from them. I have learnt much from the many previous biographies and studies of Virginia Woolf and I am grateful to their authors. Finally my more immediate and deep gratitude is to Sarah, my wife, for her assiduous, patient assistance in checking and keying in my text and pointing out to me those passages where she thought I had been unclear, and to Stephen Brown, my editor at Haus Publishing, for similar vigilance. For any obscurities or errors that may remain, I alone am responsible.

A C Kensington, London, August 2005

№22 Hyde Park Gate

—The stream of landaus, victorias and hansom cabs was incessant; for the season was beginning. In the quieter streets musicians doled out their frail and for the most part melancholy pipe of sound... *The Years*

N°22 Hyde Park Gate

Six floors high, 22 Hyde Park Gate, Kensington, rises above the other houses in what still remains today a quiet, secluded, residential London enclave. Its Victorian occupants, Leslie Stephen (1832–1904) and Julia Stephen (1846–1895), added the two top storeys as their family grew in size, careless of the incongruous effect in relation to the architecture of the street. The tall white Kensington house, with its rows of square windows and its small gardens front and back, is still in use, converted now into flats. It has three blue plaques attached to the front wall: the original one, stating 'Sir Leslie Stephen scholar and writer lived here', and two more, unveiled in 2004, commemorating his daughters, Vanessa Bell (1879–1961), the painter, and Virginia Woolf (1882–1941), the writer.

Virginia was born and spent the first 22 years of her life in this house. Here she was educated by her parents, mesdemoiselles and music teachers. Neither she nor her sister Vanessa ever went to school or university. Here she had her first experience of literature. Here she made her first sustained efforts at writing. Those that survive are Diaries, published in 1990, as *A Passionate Apprentice: The Early Journals 1897–1909*, and a family newspaper *Hyde Park Gate News* largely written by her and remarkable for the lively, jokey manner in which she records the busy, convivial family life of the house. If this were the only evidence we had of her childhood, we would conclude that it was a thoroughly happy one. The youngest female (pet-names *Ginia, Ginny, little Goat*) in a family of eight children, some nearing adulthood, she was not spoiled but much loved.

Mother and daughter: Julia with Virginia aged two
Previous pages: The approach to Kensington High Street 1906

It was a comfortably off-household with servants to look after its members, a distinguished man of letters at its head, a deeply caring mother to minister to her children's slightest needs, and a wide, devoted circle of friends and relations, several of them eminent in public life. One of these friends was the expatriate American novelist Henry James (1843–1916), whose London apartment was nearby in De Vere Gardens. In his search for distinction in English life—the highest level of moral and cultural refinement—he might well have described the Stephens as coming close to his concept of 'the Real Right Thing'.

No doubt much of Virginia's childhood was happy. Picture her lying in the long grass on a summer afternoon in Kensington Gardens, just beyond Hyde Park Gate, eating sweets and reading a comic, or sailing her toy boat in the Round Pond, or venturing forth on the top of a horse-drawn omnibus with her stepsister Stella to the Houses of Parliament and Westminster Abbey, or expectantly awaiting the arrival from Cambridge in the vacations of her handsome undergraduate stepbrothers George and Gerald, or celebrating her birthdays, on which each of her grown-up siblings always gave her a generous present, with a tea-party and riotous games in the drawing room, and other festive occasions—not to mention the time she spent each year during the family's long summer break away from Kensington in Cornwall.

But, as no one knew better than Virginia, memories of childhood and adolescence, its joys, sadnesses and agonies, fluctuate violently. As a mature adult she recalled her early life in papers read to a group of Bloomsbury friends, members of The Memoir Club, and in additional material not intended for publication but published posthumously in *Moments of Being*, where she paints with grim humour a harrowing picture. She tells of the constraints imposed on her and her siblings by her celebrated father's relentless dedication to his work (all of it done in the house), of his unreasonableness, irascibility and constant ill health (real and imagined) but life with her difficult father was for many years ameliorated by the presence of her adored, loving mother and an adored, loving older stepsister who acted as a second mother. How cruel then of fate to deprive her of both by the time she was 15! After her mother's death in 1895 from a sudden attack of 'rheumatic fever', followed by Stella's death two years later, Virginia tells of her 'seven unhappy years' at Hyde Park Gate. The causes of that unhappiness were complex, as we shall see.

Her father and her mother had both been married once before. The widower Leslie wooed the widow Julia and after some considerable resistance she consented in 1878 to become his second wife. Julia's first husband, Herbert Duckworth, a rich lawyer, had died in 1870 aged 42, leaving her with three children by him: George, Stella and Gerald. They were in their teens when Virginia was a baby, the boys at Eton. Stella, educated at home, helped and accompanied her mother on social rounds. Leslie had been married first to Harriet Marian (Minnie) Thackeray, the younger of the two daughters of the Victorian novelist, by whom he had had a daughter, Laura. When she was a small child he was told that she was so retarded mentally she would never be able to read or write. Laura lived with the rest of the family at Hyde Park Gate until 1891 when she was placed in a home where Julia and Stella would visit her.

After Leslie's and Julia's marriage there were, at almost yearly intervals, four children born, of whom Virginia was the third. Thoby and Vanessa preceded her; Adrian came last in 1883. Thus it was that during Virginia's girlhood all the members of this joint family lived at HPG. They each had their space, albeit that in Virginia's case it was a shared space with her sister Vanessa. When Stella married, Virginia had at last a room of her own.

Leslie's sacrosanct area was on the top floor, his study whose shelves were lined with the major authors of English literature and history, volumes that Virginia devoured with alarming rapidity once she could read. From its window he had a panoramic view of the Gardens and the spire of St Mary Abbots Church. Here he isolated himself for long hours and did his literary and editorial work. When his day's labour was done, at around tea time, he would join his family in the drawing room and read to them from his favourite writers. In such a fashion Virginia became familiar at a tender age with all the novels of Walter Scott (Leslie read and reread them) and those of other major English novelists.

Leslie told an American friend that he could be as isolated and studious in this house as he was in his rooms in college when he was a don at Cambridge. That had been his original career and when term was over he would go mountaineering in the Alps. As his mind matured and his thought developed, he felt he could no longer honestly subscribe to the Thirty-Nine Articles of the English Church. He resigned his fellowship, for which he had taken holy orders as was obligatory then, and came to London to live by writing. It was a tough decision heralding a precarious existence but if you had a touch of genius, a powerful intellect, determined energy, immense erudition, all of which Leslie Stephen possessed, it was not impossible in those days to support a wife and children on what has been called the Higher Journalism

Victorian society was nourished intellectually by periodicals that were hungry for lengthy, weighty articles on current affairs, literature, art, music, the countryside, anything that might interest readers, many of whom lived remote from London, some in far-flung parts of the Empire. An essay that offered a fresh appraisal of an author was one of Leslie's fortes, even as it would become one of Virginia's. His collected work contains hundreds of such appraisals along with several full-length books, such as his *History of English Thought in the Eighteenth Century*, a landmark study.

Julia's space was the drawing room on the first floor, where on Sunday afternoon she was At Home to a concourse of neighbours and relations, many of whom lived in the surrounding streets and squares. When her first husband died in 1870, Julia was 24. At 32, when she married Leslie, she was an accomplished, gracious hostess. The physical beauty on which everyone who knew her remarked, and to which Virginia did almost excessive justice in her fictional representation of her mother, was undimmed. We can glimpse it in the pictures of her as a young woman taken by her aunt, the pioneer photographer Julia Margaret Cameron, and the drawings and portraits of her by Edward Burne-Jones (1833–1898), George Frederick

Watts (1817–1904) and William Holman Hunt (1827–1910). These Victorian artists belonged to a social group around Sara Prinsep, another of Julia's aunts, at her Kensington residence, Little Holland House. Watts had a studio in the house. Sarah's husband was the lawyer Henry Thoby Prinsep (1793–1878) renowned for his work on the Indian legal code. Julia, who frequently attended her aunt's receptions, was admired by the glittering circle of artists, writers and politicians whom the Prinseps regularly entertained.

Julia Margaret Cameron and Sara Prinsep were two of seven surviving sisters who had been brought up in India where their father James Pattle had been an official of the East India Company. Their sister Maria, Julia's mother, married John Jackson, a doctor and surgeon in Calcutta where Julia was born in 1846. Maria was separated from him from 1848 to 1855 when she returned to live in England taking Julia with her.

The Pattle strain in Virginia's maternal family background is memorable not only for the great aunts' beauty which she and her sister Vanessa inherited, but also for their friendships with and patronage of artists, and their attractiveness to men of creative and intellectual ability, a trait they passed down to their nieces and great nieces. Adeline Jackson, Julia's eldest sister, married Henry Halford Vaughan, professor of modern history at Oxford and Warden of New College. Their son became headmaster of Rugby School and married Margaret (Madge) Symonds, the daughter of Leslie's friend, John Addington Symonds, historian of the Italian Renaissance. Mary Pattle, Julia's middle sister, married Herbert William Fisher, a don at Christ Church, who had been the tutor of the Prince of Wales, and afterwards became his private secretary. Julia remained constantly in touch with both these families for all her life and her daughters were close to them until they married. After Julia's and Stella's deaths, two of Virginia's mother-surrogates were found among her Pattle-descended cousins, Madge Vaughan and Emma Vaughan.

On Sunday, Julia's social day, the Stephen children did not go to church. Leslie had become a confirmed agnostic, one of the first people to admit publicly to that term suggested by Darwin's champion, T H Huxley (at a philosophical gathering in 1869) for those who believed in an unknown or unknowable God. In 1893 Leslie published *An Agnostic's Apology, and other essays* (1893). None of his children by Julia was baptised or brought up to adhere to any religious belief. Julia had lost her Christian faith when her first husband died but not her firm belief in the virtue of charity. Leslie's way of marking Sunday was to go for a walk of ten to twelve miles with a bunch of learned cronies, known collectively as the Sunday Tramps.

Julia's At Homes were well attended. Many of her relations and in-laws lived within walking distance. The Prinseps lived, as we have seen, nearby at Little Holland House. One of her late husband's sisters, Minna Duckworth, also lived in Hyde Park Gate, and Leslie's brother, Sir James Fitzjames Stephen, head of the Stephen family and a legal luminary, lived in the next street. Frederic Harrison, ostensibly a lawyer but almost as prolific a Higher Journalist as Leslie, lived across Kensington Gardens in Bayswater. He and his wife Ethel ran the London Positivist Society. They were followers of the French thinker Auguste Comte (1798–1857), the founding father of a Religion of Humanity that had many active English adherents. Leslie Stephen, 'the godless Victorian' as he has been called, was never a Positivist but he had several friends who were like the Lushingtons (Vernon, a judge; his wife Jane, a close friend of Julia's; and their three musical daughters, who coincided in age with her Duckworth offspring), who lived even nearer in Kensington Square, five minutes away on foot.

We have the testimony of an observant nine-year-old witness to these gatherings. Writing in the *Hyde Park Gate News*, Virginia gives us the following account of the scene on Sunday 6th December 1891, when either the Tramps' peregrinations were in temporary abeyance or they had finished their walk in good time to attend the At Home: 'First came Mr Russel[l] Duckworth [Julia's former brother-in-law] and his wife who conversed affably with Mr Leslie Stephen for a few minutes when they declared they must depart which they accordingly did. Sir Fred[erick] Pollock [an eminent lawyer and a Tramp]

14

and his better half then arrived. We will not however say much about them as they were not very interesting. Dr [Mandell]Creighton [Bishop of London and a Tramp] and Mr Dighton Pollock then made their appearance. Dr Creighton was then most unceremoniously observed by a precocious little girl to greatly resemble a bullfrog.'[4]

Kensington was not the Stephen family's only residence. They also had a place in Cornwall, Talland House, St Ives, where half—the more carefree half—of Virginia's childhood was spent. It was a rectangular white-walled house with chessboard patterns around the windows on a promontory outside the town near the Station. An escallonia hedge bordered the large garden area with its lawn and terraces. Within it was a tennis court, a kitchen garden, a Love Corner and a greenhouse where a rich harvest of grapes ripened throughout the summer. There was a nearby cove for bathing and the house itself commanded a view of the Godrevy lighthouse. Virginia's most famous novel *To The Lighthouse* had its origin here. We get an early hint of it in one of her jottings in *Hyde Park Gate News*, a paper that covered events in Cornwall too. The edition of 12th September 1892 revealed that: 'On Saturday morning Master Hilary Hunt and Master Basil Smith came up to Talland House and asked Master Thoby and Miss Virginia Stephen to accompany them to the light-house as Freeman the boatman said that there was a perfect tide and wind for going there. Master Adrian Stephen was much disappointed at not being allowed to go.'

Leslie, Julia, Stella and the younger children would leave Kensington for St Ives in May and usually stay at Talland House until the beginning of October. Schoolroom lessons for the girls would continue in Cornwall. Leslie would spend much time rambling and botanizing, bringing home uncommon plants and herbs. In the hot weather, moths and butterflies haunted the gardens where there was a bright purple clematis tree, the jacmanna, in the Love Corner. Robust games of family cricket, in which the girls participated, were played on the lawn. George Duckworth had graced the Eleven when he was a schoolboy at Eton. Neighbours' children joined in, among them the sons of the Rugby housemaster, William Brooke, who went with his family to St Ives for summer holidays. His son Rupert with whom Virginia played on the beach became the poet whom the adult Virginia would visit in his later incarnation as a blonde Adonis in Cambridge. On one occasion a cricket ball hit Julia on the head; she was concussed for a time but no serious damage was done.

Julia was an authority on home nursing, a topic on which she published a booklet. Between her engagement to Leslie and their wedding in 1878 she had nursed her uncle Henry Prinsep in his last illness. At bedtime she had a fund of fairy stories to tell her little ones. These appeared in her only other publication, a children's book. Servants accompanied her and her brood to Cornwall, led by Sophie Farrell their cook, who spent her entire working life with members of the family.

In addition to the family's own needs there were those of the continual flow of guests. Their arrivals and departures needed to be carefully scheduled as not everyone could be accommodated in the house at the same time. Some were put up at lodgings in the town and came to the house at tea and dinner-time, as Lily Briscoe does in *To the Lighthouse*. Virginia's Fisher and Vaughan cousins were regular guests. Leslie would sometimes invite young men who were his protégés. One such was Walter Headlam, a fellow of King's College, Cambridge, who had lost both parents when he was a boy. Richard Norton, the son of Leslie's friend Charles Eliot Norton, the eminent Harvard professor, was another erudite young man who came to Talland House for a vacation. (Leslie was one of the earliest English writers to make friends with his American counterparts in academic life and the Higher Journalism. He had been in America during the Civil War and had written about it for the British Press.) Among the distinguished acquaintances of Leslie's own generation who visited Talland House was the novelist and poet George Meredith. He would sit in the garden and read his poetry to Julia.

A favourite among Julia's young female guests was Lucy Stillman, artist daughter of William Stillman, the American art historian, and the stepdaughter of his wife Maria (born Spartali), an artist in the Pre-Raphaelite mould. Lucy painted portraits of both Julia and Stella that do not seem to have survived. More young women guests were the three striking Lushington daughters, Kitty, Margaret and Susan from Kensington Square, whose musical talents were greatly appreciated (there was a much-played piano in the sitting room at Talland House). Their mother Jane Lushington had held a Kensington At Home on Thursdays until she died of a mysterious 'chill' in 1884.

Kitty, the eldest, was then just 18. Julia took all three under her capacious wing. By the time Kitty was 23, Julia was concerned that she was still unmarried. She had been engaged briefly to Charley Howard, heir to George Howard of Castle Howard, Earl of Carlisle, but had broken it off. Julia, who had inherited the Pattle enthusiasm for matchmaking, cast about for a replacement suitor. She found one in the person of a young man of 25 who had political ambitions, Leo, the younger son of Admiral Maxse (RN retired). A graduate of King's, he had been President of the Union at Cambridge. In the summer of 1890 Julia invited them both to Talland House. Leo proposed to Kitty in the Love Corner after dinner one evening (overheard by Thoby Stephen whose bedroom window was open). He was accepted. Kitty Lushington became Kitty Maxse and the Mrs Dalloway of Virginia's later fiction was born. As Mrs Maxse, Kitty would become one of London's legendary hostesses.

Their betrothal and many other happenings at Talland House

were stored in the memory of the child Ginia, melted down in her imagination to emerge transmuted in *To the Lighthouse*. The locale of the novel is described as Hebridean but in all respects it is a description of St Ives seen from Talland House. Virginia Woolf never hesitated to use people, events and objects of her own remembered life at the core of her fiction. In this instance, the real-life Leo and Kitty inspired the creation of the fictional Paul Rayley and Minta Doyle, the couple whose engagement is the climactic moment of the first part of *To the Lighthouse*. Again the fictional Lily Briscoe, with her Chinese features, is not at all like Lucy Stillman to look at and she is painting a landscape not a portrait, but she represents the Artist as Lucy did in real life. Her fluctuating confidence about the picture she is working on and the continual reshaping of it parallel Virginia's struggles in the composition of her novels. August Carmichael, a poet like Meredith, is a very old friend of the family, as Meredith was of Leslie. Mr Bankes, who sits in the sunshine in the garden 'catching words', has no identifiable original but he shares Leslie's botanical hobby. Charles Tansley, like Walter Headlam, is a young don with a tendency to disrupt the harmony of the party. However, this is an instance of where the model and the fictional character diverge. Whereas Headlam's ancestry was academic, one of his forebears being Richard Bentley, the classical scholar, Tansley comes from the working-class; one of his uncles is a lighthouse-keeper. There was a real-life George Tansley, a star pupil at the Working Man's College in Holborn who ended his career as a member of its governing body. I suspect that Virginia knew about him and the name lodged in her mind when she needed to depict someone who had worked his way up from humble origins through outstanding ability.

The eight children in the novel roughly correspond to the eight in real life. James, the most strongly characterised, and with whom the novel opens, and whose longing to go to the Lighthouse is frustrated by the brutal frankness of his father and Tansley, is Thoby as a boy. Even memories of plants and objects are fitted deftly into the jigsaw puzzle of the novel's imagery, like the purple jacmanna tree and Mrs Ramsay's green shawl that had its origin, I believe, in the Curragh shawl the Stephen children gave Kitty Lushington as a wedding-present.

It is the two figures who dominate the novel, Mr and Mrs Ramsay, who owe most to their historical originals, Leslie and Julia. When Vanessa read the novel, sent to her by Virginia before publication, she told her she had given a portrait of their mother 'more like her to me than anything I could have conceived of as possible'.[5] Leslie was, as we saw, the founding editor of the *Dictionary of National Biography*, for which he wrote many of the articles but he retired before its completion. Mr Ramsay is a philosopher whose thinking has reached the letter Q on an alphabetical scale of original thought. Ruminating on his life, he regrets he never reached Z. Virginia here combines the two main aspects of her father's life's work, as dictionary editor and as thinker. She is ruthless in revealing the sense of failure that dogs him and how his children suffer from his domination of their lives and his concern for absolute truthfulness in everything he utters, from a critical judgement to the weather forecast.

What is even more remarkable is the insight Virginia shows into her parents' relationship with each other, the nature of their marriage. They are lovers, to be sure, but it is love second time around (though this is not stated) based upon the wisdom of experience, respect, admiration for each other's nobility, an understanding of each other's anxieties, a love that dispenses with words but is subtly adept at the interpretation of mood, gesture, facial expression. Mr Ramsay takes his wife's love for granted but he never ceases to be astonished by her beauty; nor does Virginia.

Lily Briscoe worships Mrs Ramsay for her beauty, kneeling spaniel-like at her side. Virginia reveals the inward alongside the outward beauty of her mother's nature: like Julia, Mrs Ramsay is acutely sensitive to all forms of life. We observe her in her role as hostess at the serving end of the long, candle-lit dinner table, responding throughout the meal to the needs of all the other characters, gastronomic and psychological, at the end of part one when the novel's entire cast is assembled. This is the last time we see Mrs Ramsay alive.

Little Goat

. . .they were sailing swiftly, buoyantly on long rocking waves which handed them on from one to another with an extraordinary lilt and exhilaration. . . *To the Lighthouse*

Little Goat

The Stephen sons, like their older stepbrothers, were educated at public schools but not at Eton, which Leslie had disliked. Adrian became a 'town' (day) boy at Westminster School, Thoby a boarder at Clifton College near Bristol. In the spring term of 1895 Thoby caught measles. His mother insisted that he came home to Hyde Park Gate so that she could look after him. Virginia had not had the disease, so Julia sent her to stay with her aunt (as she called her) Minna Duckworth who, as we have seen, lived in the same street but in grander style than the Stephens with a butler and her own carriage. Stella was, reluctantly, away from home in Italy with her brother George who had friends among the minor Italian nobility.

Thoby recovered but Julia caught influenza. London was rife with it that year and she had to take to her bed. A few days later, still unwell, she insisted on getting up to preside over Sunday luncheon, in Mrs Ramsay style, and that only made her worse. Leslie became alarmed. Stella sensed that something must be wrong at home from her mother's shaky handwriting. The family doctor, David Elphinstone Seton, was summoned. Kitty Maxse and Margaret Lushington began to make daily visits to Julia's bedside. She who had so often acted as a home nurse now urgently needed a nurse herself. Kitty engaged one for her. George and Stella, fraught with anxiety, returned to HPG at the end of April

As Julia declined further, a second doctor, Russell Reynolds, was called in, on Friday 2nd May. He diagnosed rheumatic fever but Seton, still in charge, said that the immediate cause

Julia Duckworth by Julia Margaret Cameron, her aunt
Previous Pages: Unloading the catch, St Ives Harbour 1900

of the trouble was 'inflammation of the socket of the heart'[6] and gave her two injections of strychnine. Visits to the invalid were strictly limited. Virginia was allowed to go into to see her on Saturday. 'Hold yourself straight, my little Goat,' Julia said. They were the last words Virginia heard spoken by her mother. Julia died at 5.30 on Sunday morning. She was 49.

Virginia described looking out of the nursery window on that terrible morning: 'I saw Dr Seton walk away up the street with his head bent and his hands clasped behind his back. I saw the pigeons floating and settling. I got a feeling of calm, sadness, and finality. It was a beautiful blue spring morning, and very still. That brings back the feeling that everything had come to an end.'[7]

George led Virginia and Vanessa into their mother's room to see her dead body. As they were going in, Leslie was staggering out. 'I stretched out my arms to stop him,' Virginia wrote, 'but he brushed past me, crying out something I could not catch; distraught. And George led me in to kiss my mother, who had just died.'[8]

Virginia, 13 years old, rejected, as it were, by her father and bereaved of her mother, suffered the first of her mental breakdowns. In trying to recall this period a censorship of the nature of her madness affected Virginia's adult memory. As her nephew Quentin Bell put it in his biography of his aunt: 'She did not, could not, admit all the memories of her madness. What she did recall were the physical symptoms; in her memoir of this period she hardly mentions the commotions of her mind and although we know that she had already heard what she was later to call "those horrible voices," she speaks of other symptoms, usually physiological symptoms. Her pulse raced— it raced so fast as to be almost unbearable. She became painfully excitable and nervous and then intolerably depressed. She became terrified of people, blushed scarlet if spoken to and was unable to face a stranger in the street.'[9]

Part Two of *To the Lighthouse* describes the effect Mrs Ramsay's death has on her family and her circle. Her image haunts them like a living presence. In reality the family under Leslie never returned to Talland House after Julia died; but after his death, Virginia, Vanessa and their brothers went

Married to a mountain-climber: Julia Stephen looks out of a window at the Bear Hotel in Grindelwald. This was Vanessa's favourite image of their mother

on a holiday to St Ives, observed the house now occupied by others, and talked to local people who remembered Julia. The concluding part of the novel is an imaginative projection of what it would have been like for the survivors of the house party in part one to return to Talland House after World War One. In the mind of Lily Briscoe, who mainly sustains this part and has the greatest sense of the absent presence of

Mrs Ramsay, we are given a meditation on the act of artistic creation. The creative process and its outcome, a work of art, is something that endures in spite of the most heart-rending bereavement. After the artistic experience of writing this novel Virginia finally became reconciled to her loss in childhood of her mother through having re-created her. 'I have had my vision,' Lily says in the book's closing words, speaking for herself and for the author.

Leslie consoled himself in the only way he understood, by putting pen to paper. He wrote a history of his second marriage in the form of a long letter to be read by his children after his death. The manuscript, known as *The Mausoleum Book,* was published in 1977. He survived for almost another decade and the family continued to live at 22 HPG, Stella taking over its administration. Her duties included helping Virginia recover from her breakdown. Leslie depended now on Stella as completely as he had on Julia. She was as much, if not more, of a dutiful daughter to him than if she had been one by blood. Seton recommended a regime of fresh air and exercise to aid Virginia's recovery, which now gradually occurred. It was Stella who usually accompanied her on daily walks in Kensington Gardens, but sometimes Leslie. In January 1897 there was a period of freezing weather in London; people skated on the Round Pond although they were advised not to. For her birthday she requested a pair of skates. Virginia drew upon her memory of this cold snap in the Great London Frost episode when she came to write *Orlando.*

One of Virginia's walks with Stella took them across to Bayswater where they visited an acquaintance who lived at 31 Kensington Park Gardens, Sylvia Davies, the daughter of the *Punch* artist, George du Maurier. She had married the barrister Arthur Lewelyn Davies in 1892 and during their honeymoon they had visited the Stephens at Talland House. It was the Scottish novelist and playwright, J M Barrie, who, while exercising his dog in the Gardens, became friends with her five sons and told them stories about Peter Pan. The play he made out of these stories first took to the stage in 1904. Gerald took Virginia to see it in the following year.

Gerald was a keen theatregoer and although Virginia's childhood visits to the theatre were mainly restricted to Shakespeare performances—she saw *As You Like It* twice—she would have heard George, Gerald and Stella discussing what they had seen, especially Ibsen's plays, then being given their first exposure amidst a storm of abuse from many of the leading dramatic critics. Gerald took a party to see the American actress Elizabeth Robins, who championed the cause of Ibsen, as the heroine in *The Master Builder*. Stella did not think much of the play but she became friendly with the player. Virginia's contact with Robins, a passionate feminist, would come later in their lives.

When not attending to her stepfather and stepsister, Stella had a life of her own and a subdued beauty that appealed to several young men whose advances she steadfastly resisted. Dick Norton had fallen in love with her when he stayed at Talland House. 'I'm afraid he likes me better than I do him & that's a great deal,' Stella wrote in her diary.[10] Her cousin James Kenneth Stephen, who lived with his father in De Vere Gardens, was in love with her too. Unhappily, this gifted young man became violently insane following a head injury. Whenever he called at HPG Virginia was told to say that Stella was away with the Lushingtons at their country house in Surrey. Another suitor was John Waller (Jack) Hills, a lawyer who worked for a London firm of solicitors. Later in life he became a Tory MP. He came from a family headed by a retired judge who lived at Corby Castle in Cumberland. Jack and his brothers Eustace and Edmond had attended Julia's At Homes and were Old Etonian friends of George and Gerald.

Jack had first proposed to Stella at Talland House where she turned him down. That should have been the end of the matter but Jack had a streak of persistence. He returned again in the summer of 1897 when the Stephens were on holiday at Hindhead in Surrey, in a house lent them by one of Leslie's contributors to the *Dictionary*, and this time he was accepted. Leslie, in giving his consent, said that he did so on the understanding the couple should live with him at No 22 when they were married. After much discussion this preposterous proposal was set aside but they agreed to live as near to 22 Hyde Park Gate as they could, in the same street, so that Stella would always be within calling distance if Leslie urgently required her presence.

George and Gerald came down from Cambridge and began careers, Gerald as an apprentice publisher with J M Dent, George assisting Charles Booth, the shipping magnate, on his survey of London's poor. Virginia and Stella went to see George one day in his office in the depths of the city. *The Voyage Out* has a ship-owner 'who loved his business and built his Empire'[11] in command of his own ship, traversing a route frequented by ships of the Booths' shipping line.

Leslie's present to Virginia for her 15th birthday in January 1897 was Lockhart's life of Scott in ten beautifully bound little volumes. Delighted by the set, she soon read them and requested fresh reading matter from him. He gave her, from his own collection, *Essays in Ecclesiastical Biography* by Sir James Stephen, Virginia's lawyer paternal grandfather. She discovered something of her ancestry in this learned work, her forebears on Leslie's side among the evangelical Clapham Sect. She was given next the poems of James Russell Lowell, a friend of Julia and Leslie when he was American minister (as the official who discharged the duties of ambassador was then called) in London and Virginia's secular godfather at her birth. One of the poems was addressed to her: 'Verses intended to go with a posset [a drink made of hot milk spiced with spirit] dish to my dear little god-daughter, 1882.'

She was making such good progress towards a complete recovery that Seton said she could start some scholastic work again. She appeared with Vanessa in the schoolroom every morning where their father made them construe passages from Livy. They also began to learn German. More exhausting and exciting than schoolwork and her orgies of private reading, were the preparations, now under way, for Stella's wedding. Despite Leslie's agnosticism Stella was to be married in St Mary Abbots church, Kensington, a walk away from home. The Stephen children thought they ought to make an exception to their non-churchgoing to hear Stella's and Jack's banns read out.

Virginia, therefore, attended morning service on Sunday 28th March. 'Our prayers and psalms were rather guess work—but the hymns were splendid,' she told the Diary she had begun to keep.[12] Her compliance had its limits: she refused to kneel.

The great day came and went. 'Goodness knows how we got through it all,' wrote Virginia. The married couple departed to Italy for their honeymoon. On Sunday, George, Gerald and the Stephen children went to Highgate Cemetery where Julia was buried. They placed their carnations and some white roses from Stella's bouquet on their mother's grave.

Then Leslie and the children went to blustery Brighton-on-sea for an Easter break. Virginia thoroughly disliked the town and tried to shut it out by staying indoors reading Lord Macaulay's *History of England*. Several of her Fisher and Vaughan cousins were there. One of them, Adeline Fisher, who was being courted by the young musician, Ralph Vaughan Williams, revealed the details of Kitty Maxse's broken engagement to Charley Howard. Virginia listened avidly to such gossip and never forgot it.

On their return, Jack and Stella moved into No 24 Hyde Park Gate, true to their promise to Leslie. Vanessa and Virginia had filled it with flowers to greet the newlyweds on arrival but Stella hardly had time to notice before she went to bed in pain with 'a chill on her innards,' Virginia was told. She was pregnant.

Dr Seton was called and he diagnosed peritonitis. A week elapsed before Virginia was permitted to see Stella. She found her less unwell than she had feared and sat at her bedside and talked to her until the nurse told her that it was time for 'Mrs Hills' to go to sleep. Stella turned 29 on 30th May, the birthday she shared with Vanessa, who was 18.

In the summer of 1897 Queen Victoria celebrated her Diamond Jubilee ('sixty glorious years') with a procession of massed troops and bands through the centre of London. Frederic Gibbs, a wealthy bachelor lawyer friend of Leslie's, purchased three places at St Thomas's Hospital, near Westminster Bridge, for Virginia, Vanessa and Thoby to observe the parade. 'The Queen was lying back in her carriage,

& the Pss. of Wales had to tell her to look up & bow. Then she smiled & nodded her poor tired head, & the whole thing moved on,' wrote Virginia in her Diary.[13]

Now Virginia became ill as well, not mentally this time but physically. She started to ache all over and became feverish. Stella, whom Virginia had been visiting every day, was confined to a bath chair when not in bed. Indifferent to her own illness, she became concerned about Virginia. History was starting to repeat itself. Stella's concern for Virginia while seriously ill herself echoed Julia's concern on her deathbed for Thoby. Stella wrote Leslie a letter (no telephones yet in these houses) saying that she thought Virginia was not well enough to venture out for the daily walk and she requested Dr Seton, when he came, to look at her. He was so concerned that he sent Virginia at once to bed in Stella's house.

The next day Stella got out of bed in her dressing gown and went in to Virginia. She noticed signs of overexcitement ('I had the fidgets very badly,' Virginia confessed), which threatened another nervous collapse. Virginia's anxiety was no doubt brought on by Stella's worsening condition: she became unable to leave her bed and could only call out to Virginia lying in a little room opposite hers. On Saturday 17th July the doctors said that Virginia ought to return to No 22 to be put to bed there. She was wrapped in a fur cape of Stella's and George lifted her out of bed—Stella called out 'Goodbye' as they passed her door—and carried her along the road back home.

On Sunday evening a surgeon came to join the medical team at No 24 to perform an operation on Stella. They operated at about 7pm. At half-past they said it was successful and that everything was as satisfactory as possible. Virginia went to bed. At three in the morning, George and Vanessa went into Virginia's room and told her that Stella was dead.

There is no entry in Virginia's Diary for the next day, Tuesday, but on Wednesday she recorded that: 'Stella was buried by mother's side in Highgate. None of us went.'[14] The loss was grievous but it was a slightly lesser grief than the sense of total desolation that had overtaken Virginia when she had become motherless. What she suffered from most of all in the immediately following days were the ministrations of family and friendly well-wishers who came to condole.

'Cousin Mia has gallantly held aloof—Ala—others have not been so generous. Helen Holland discusses Religion for hours with Nessa—A[un]t. Minna & Mr Gibbs haunt the place —Sally Norton [sister of Stella's American admirer] & Flora Baker are here a great deal—It is all very strange,' she wrote in her Diary.[15]

Julia and Stella in the garden of Talland House

Only Kitty Maxse, among the most persistent visitors, who was a woman of great sensitivity, seemed able momentarily to alleviate the two sisters' misery.

Jack behaved with admirable stoicism and became for a while like an additional older brother for them. He went through Stella's clothes and gave them some of her jewellery, and then on 24th July took them to Highgate Cemetery to see where Stella was buried. 'We went by bus & tram. The grave is next [to] mother's—near as you go in. It was covered with dead flowers—We sat down & talked for a long time, & then came home and had tea with Jack on his balcony.'[16]

Once again the inhabitants of No 22 regrouped, with Vanessa now in charge of their domestic routine. But for the present they wanted nothing more than to get away from the house that reverberated everywhere with memories of Stella. Fortunately they had a holiday already planned at Painswick near Stroud in Gloucestershire, where they had rented the Vicarage, a two-mile walk from the house of Frederic Maitland, one of Leslie's Tramps and owner of the surrounding farmland. His wife Florence was the daughter of Virginia's Aunt Mary; Julia as matchmaker had brought the couple together. Fred was a Cambridge don, author of a seminal *History of English Law*, a scholar of whom Leslie thoroughly approved and whom he entrusted with the custody of his papers to be read after his death.

The holiday provided just the complete change of scene Virginia needed with some fine weather. She buried herself in novels by Dickens, Charlotte Brontë and Charles Kingsley which were on hand to read, and tried with some success to forget her sorrow by joining in the life of an English country village with a ride in a pony-cart to Cheltenham and 'sugaring' executed by her brothers to observe. This was an entomological pastime the Stephen children had learned from Jack and often practised at St Ives. It consisted of smearing the bark of a tree with a dollop of treacle and then returning to discover what insects had been trapped in it.

Jack, Stella's young widower, was still much in attendance. He was, in spite of his sorrow, drawn amorously to Vanessa, who was by now a beautiful young woman. He came to Painswick and invited the sisters to stay at Corby Castle on the Cumberland estate of his parents. Leslie gave his consent and Virginia had a new dress made for this visit. Kitty Maxse and Margaret Massingberd accompanied her to the dressmaker's. They were mother-surrogates in Kensington for Virginia and Vanessa and they were happy to fulfil that role, remembering how Julia had mothered them when they were in a similar situation ten years before.

Kitty's presence at No 22 was especially welcome because Leslie had become enamoured of her. His bouts of bad temper and peevishness were always in abeyance when Kitty came to visit, as she often did even though her life in London was a busy one. She had embarked on her career as one of the great party-givers of the period, at her house at 23 Montpelier Square in Knightsbridge, to which she and her husband Leo had moved. Because of the severe migraines from which he suffered, he had given up trying to become an MP and instead he was now the proprietor-editor of *The National Review*, an influential monthly journal with right-of-centre political and foreign affairs content, much of which Leo himself contributed. Leslie wrote a series of articles about Cambridge for it.

Kitty's contributions to the publication were the frequent parties she held at 'Montpiel' (as their house became known to her friends), to which contributors, leading politicians, foreign ambassadors, visiting statesmen, writers and artists were invited in order to mingle and drink champagne. Leo would tackle them on the burning issues of the day while Kitty would entertain the gathering with an impromptu recital on the piano. Virginia might just have attended one of these parties when she was old enough; Vanessa would certainly have done. The gatherings became immortalised in *Mrs Dalloway*, in which one such party occupies much of the novel. In *Mrs Dalloway* the preparations for and holding of a grand London party is viewed as a creative act comparable for the hostess to Lily Briscoe's work on a painting or Virginia's on a novel.

Vanessa adored Kitty and fell completely under her spell during this period. Virginia was much more ambivalent about her. She had to admit that at heart Kitty was a good woman, but she found her brittle, off-hand manner, her courting of the aristocracy, her sartorial standards (white gloves always to be worn when going out) and her fashionable lifestyle antipathetic. Kitty's irresistible charm for almost all men, her stylish soothing presence with her halo of bright, fine-spun golden hair and her dimpled cheeks made Kitty a person Virginia could not ignore, but one she declined to emulate.

Virginia found the grandeur of Corby Castle, when she and Vanessa stayed there in September 1897, oppressive and it brought back her sadness at the loss of Stella. She could not think of anything to say to Mrs Hills during the interminable evening dinner with its many courses. Luckily Susan Lushington, Kitty's youngest sister and the other guest, was an uninhibited talker and made up for the silence of the Stephens. After dinner she smoothed things over by playing on the spinet.

At the close of 1897 Virginia's Diary comes to an end and is not resumed until August 1899, when the entries are longer and the sentences more fully formed. During this period, instead of the annual visit to Cornwall, Vanessa and Virginia spent part of the summer in Cambridge with their Stephen Aunts. A visit Virginia enjoyed was the seven weeks in 1899 they spent at Warboys, in what was then Huntingdonshire, at the behest of Dorothea Stephen, the youngest daughter of Leslie's older brother, James Fitzjames, and her enjoyment is reflected in her need once more to record her experience of the day before going to bed: 'Then we came to Warboys Station, found our primitive Omnibus, & drove off the mile to the Rectory. It had been raining all the afternoon (the first rain I have seen for weeks) & the sky was all clouded & misted as for steady showers. However as we drove along the sun shot a shaft of light down; & we beheld a glorious expanse of sky—this golden gauze streamer lit everything in its light; & far away over the flat fields a spire caught the beam & glittered like a gem in the darkness & wetness of the surrounding countries. Let me remark that the village of Warboys runs along the street for a mile to the gates of the Rectory; there are few shops, but we passed 4 windmills (attractive shaped things) & *Nine Public Houses.* Room for Dorothea's Band of Hope [a temperance society of which her aunt was an energetic member] here! The house & garden I cannot describe now; how we snorted the air with our soot sated nostrils, & revelled in the country damp, cool & and quiet. Our sensations were so exquisite, so crowded & so jubilant that music alone could keep pace with them or express a tenth part of their vividness.' Surrounded by Stephen relations, Virginia wrote a description of the species in her Diary: 'They are immensely broad, long & muscular; they move awkwardly, & as though they resented the conventionalities of modern life at every step. They all bring with them the atmosphere of the lecture room; they are severe, caustic & absolutely independent & immoveable. An ordinary character would be ground to pulp after a weeks intercourse with them. They are distinct & have more character than most of the world, so for that we will bless them & thank them sincerely.'[17]

Alongside writing her Diary, Virginia became from this time a compulsive letter-writer. Violet Dickinson, a very tall woman who had lost her own mother when she was a girl, had been taken up by Julia and had been a close friend of Stella's, was Virginia's main recipient. She was well placed for the role, with plenty of leisure at her disposal, sharing a spacious house at Welwyn, Hertfordshire, with her brother Oswald and staying occasionally at a base she had in London. Virginia addresses her as 'Woman' or 'My woman,' signs herself as 'Sparroy' (chirping sparrow?) and inquires after 'your husband'—a laborious joke. Violet did not have a husband, either then or at any other time. She was Virginia's current substitute for Stella, with the advantage that she read books. (She was a niece of Emily Eden, the novelist famous for her letters from India published in 1866 as *Up the Country*, whose other letters she later edited.) She was happy to discuss literature with Virginia and to cast a critical eye over pieces of writing Virginia was starting to show her.

Teachers away from home now began to develop Virginia's mind. She was considered robust enough to take lessons in Greek, which she loved, and history at a college in Kensington and she also had instruction from women tutors whose houses she visited. Vanessa became a student at the Royal Academy, where she studied under the American portrait painter, John Singer Sargent. Kitty, a friend of his, had taken her to his London studio. Thoby left Clifton in 1897 and went up to Trinity College, Cambridge, where Adrian would follow after he left school in 1902. Gerald founded his own publishing business, Duckworth and Company, in 1898. George relinquished his work researching the London poor with Charles Booth to become the unpaid private secretary of the politician Austen Chamberlain. Leslie continued to write essays and to lecture.

Virginia's first ball was when she was 18, during May week 1900 (the final festive week of term when the exams are all finished) at Trinity, Cambridge, at the invitation of Thoby. She danced one dance but she described in a letter to Emma Vaughan how 'I sat on a kind of platform most of the time from which we could watch the dancing, without being disturbed.'[18]

A year later she tells Emma, who was her most frequent confidante after Violet: 'Our London season of which you ask, was of the dullest description. I only went to three dances—and

I think nothing else. But the truth of it is, as we frequently tell each other, we [Virginia and Vanessa, who was almost three years older than Virginia] are failures. Really, we can't shine in Society. I don't know how it's done. We aint popular—we sit in corners and look like mutes who are longing for a funeral.'[19]

In her Diary at this time Virginia adopts a new persona. She refers to herself as 'Miss Jan'—homage, perhaps, to Miss Jane Austen, whose ironic manner in describing her own social exploits she adopts—though Austen always loved dancing. The Stephen sisters distaste for it weakened as they became involved with Thoby's Cambridge friends.

When Virginia became a professional writer, she returned to this period of her life and revealed traumas she did not confide to the Diary. The most notorious of these episodes was when she and George had returned home after a ball, followed by a visit to the Holman Hunts in Melbury Road, Kensington: 'Sleep had almost come to me. The room was dark. The house silent. Then, creaking stealthily, the door opened; treading gingerly, someone entered. "Who?" I cried. "Don't be frightened", George whispered. "And don't turn on the light, oh beloved. Beloved—and he flung himself on my bed, and took me in his arms.

Yes, the old ladies of Kensington and Belgravia never knew that George Duckworth was not only father and mother, brother and sister to those poor Stephen girls; he was their lover also."[20]

Many interpretations have been offered of the above quotation from evidence of a full-scale rape to an affectionate, fraternal fondling when drunk. Virginia often embellished real-life episodes when she recounted them to friends and the paper from which this quotation comes was read in about 1920 to the Memoir Club, a weekly gathering of her closest Bloomsbury friends. When it was Virginia's turn to entertain them, she did not like to disappoint. By then her stepbrothers, both of whom died in the 1930s, represented a patriarchy in her past she felt compelled to rebel against. The one verifiable fact, the description of the Holman Hunts' house, happens to be incorrect: she confused it with Lord Leighton's, also in Melbury Road. But whatever the precise truth of the incident, there is no doubt that Virginia felt sexually threatened by her stepbrothers. In another sketch she gives an account of Gerald's behaviour when she was very small at Talland House: 'I can remember the feel of his hand going under my clothes; going firmly and steadily lower and lower. I remember how I hoped that he would stop; how I stiffened and wriggled as his hand approached my private parts. But it did not stop. His hand explored my private parts too. I remember resenting, disliking it—what is the word for so dumb and mixed a feeling? It must have been strong, since I still recall it.'[21]

These traumas of Virginia's did not disrupt the routine of her life at HPG. That life was centred more than ever on Leslie, who was diagnosed as having cancer of the intestines in 1902. He survived in acute pain for two more years under constant medical supervision and with a succession of visitors to commiserate with him, of whom Kitty Maxse was the most frequent. In the Coronation honours list of Edward VII, in 1903, he was awarded a knighthood in recognition of his life's work, but he was not well enough to go to the Palace to receive it. A representative of the sovereign delivered it to HPG.

Watching her father sinking in agony, but with his mind alert until the end, Virginia wrote almost daily bulletins to Emma and Violet. Sir Frederick Treves, the leading surgeon of the time, who performed an operation on Leslie in a nursing home, was amazed at how long he lasted.

The children discussed what they were going to do when father was no more. Laura, now being cared for in a residential home, had ceased to be a problem. It was clear to all of them that the era of Hyde Park Gate was coming to an end and that they would have to find somewhere else to live. They considered moving to one of those squares near the British Museum, the district known as Bloomsbury. Kitty, who was privy to their discussions, was appalled at this idea. Bloomsbury was far too far away from Knightsbridge for her to visit Vanessa and it was quite beyond the pale socially, she said. On 22nd February Leslie died at home. Kitty was one of the last people to see him alive.

On their own

...the strangeness of standing alone, alive, unknown, at half past eleven in Trafalgar Square overcame him. What is it? Where am I? *Mrs Dalloway*

On their own

Leslie's body was cremated at Golders Green cemetery on 24th February 1904. Then in March George and the four Stephens went away to Manorbier on the Welsh coast between Tenby and Pembroke. 'I havent seen such splendid wild country since St Ives...'[22] Virginia wrote to Violet. Thoby spent his time watching birds and chasing foxes; the sisters roamed the cliff tops. Virginia felt remorseful that she had not spent more time with her father during his last illness. 'I cant believe,' she told Violet, 'that all our life with Father is over and he dead. If one could only tell him how one cared, as I dreamt I did last night.'[23]

Soon after they returned to HPG, George discussed the disposal of the lease with estate agents, and the Stephen quartet went off again on holiday, this time with Gerald, to Italy. Apart from one childhood visit to northern France, Virginia had not been abroad until now. They descended on Venice and had to spend their first two nights in 'a dirty little place off the Piazza S Mark' before moving to the expensive Grand Hotel. They were enchanted by the city and wished to explore the alleys and bridges on foot, but Gerald insisted on taking gondolas everywhere. Thoby and Adrian were 'rampant with excitement' while Virginia felt like 'a bird in a cage'.

After a few days Virginia came to the conclusion the Italians were degenerate and thanked God she was 'an Englishwoman' (as she told Emma Vaughan), but she had to admit that until she saw the great canvases of Tintoretto she did not know 'what paint could do'. Then they went on to Florence, where they

Virginia and Leslie: "If only one could tell him how one cared."
Previous Pages: Workmen laying Quebracho pavers around Trafalgar Square 1904

found a number of their relations and acquaintances including the Prinseps and Aunt Minna. Violet Dickinson joined them in Florence and Virginia was happier there than she had been in Venice. Each sister had her comforter: Violet was Virginia's, Kitty Maxse was Vanessa's.

Their next stop was Paris. Here two of Virginia's worlds coincided, the world of London Society and the world of Thoby's Cambridge that she had begun to enter. Beatrice Thynne, a daughter of the Marquis of Bath, was in Paris. Virginia had met her the year before at the house of her sister Katie, second wife of the Earl of Cromer, and had become a close friend of these two formidable female specimens of the English aristocracy. She enjoyed the sight of them. 'We spent the whole afternoon under a tree in the garden. Katie lay stretched on a long couch, in the carelessness of perfect grace. She doesn't think how she looks—she just flings out her superb limbs—like a child resting after its play. Indeed the whole atmosphere of the place was one of careless ease,' she wrote.[24]

The Stephens took Beatrice Thynne to dine at a café restaurant with a friend of Thoby's from Trinity, Clive Bell, who was then living in Paris. He came from a wealthy Wiltshire family and shared with Thoby a love of outdoor life, especially riding to hounds; his other passions were women and art. Also present at the dinner was the young Irish artist Gerald Kelly, a friend of Bell's from Cambridge and a dedicated Wagnerian. They talked excitedly about the latest fashions in painting, sculpture and music; after the meal was finished they smoked six cigarettes each and continued the discussion until midnight. It was 'a real Bohemian party' Virginia told Violet.[25] She probably overcame her shyness to enter into the discussion from time to time. Her role became that of a referee when at one point, during an exchange about Wagner, Kelly shook his fist at Lady Beatrice, who became so agitated that Virginia had to hold her down. The next day the Stephens went with Bell to visit the studio of the artist Rodin and that of Kelly. Meanwhile, Clive had begun to fall in love with Vanessa.

By the time the Stephens left Paris, the intellectual excitement

A family group in Cornwall: bottom l. to r. Vanessa, Thoby, Virginia, Adrian.
Above: l to r. man in bowler hat, Horatio Brown, a guest, Julia, George and Gerald.

and stimulation had given way in Virginia's mind to a sense of
desolation. She felt utterly lost when she returned to London.
The paternal prop to her existence, often resented, but providing
security, had been pulled away. She suffered the second of her
breakdowns. 'All that summer she was mad,' wrote Quentin Bell
in his biography.[26] The madness took the form of wild, incoherent,
unstoppable torrents of speech combined with physical violence.
Three nurses were needed to restrain her and there was no
question of her being able to write anything. Her Diary does
not re-start until January 1905 and her next letter, after the one
about the bohemian dinner party also to Violet, is in September
1904. Thus we do not have any record from Virginia herself of
this period of her madness and her recovery from it.

Violet came to her rescue. Virginia was taken to Violet's
house at Burnham Wood in Hertfordshire and put to bed with
Nurse Traill, Leslie's nurse, to look after her. Vanessa went

too. While they were there Virginia made her first attempt at suicide by jumping out of her bedroom window. Dr George Savage, a leading London specialist in diseases of nervous disorder and a family friend, one of Leslie's Tramps, was in charge, with a local doctor on hand to make regular visits. Savage was a great believer in treating the problems of highly-strung young women by taking away intellectual stimulation: the rest-cure. We shall meet him again as the model for Sir William Bradshaw that no longer young, weary-looking 'priest of science...would travel sixty miles or more down into the country to visit the rich, the afflicted, who could afford the very large fee which Sir William very properly charged for his advice,' in *Mrs Dalloway*.[27] David Ferrier, professor of neuropathology at King's College, London, was also consulted.

Vanessa gave an account of her sister's progress towards recovery, and of their search for somewhere to live, to Kitty Maxse:

'My darling Kitty,

Ginia has been getting on very quickly this last week but she is at a rather difficult stage now—at times she talks so sensibly that one wouldn't know anything was the matter—and then she gets on to some subject which worries her and one can't get her off it—I suppose that by degrees she will get back her balance and power of control. She has luncheon and tea with us now and leads as ordinary a life as possible. Her mind is working much more than it was which is a good thing of course—but until it gets back its balance it is difficult to know quite how to manage. The doctor here wrote and described her state to Ferrier who thought it very good and said we were to go on in just the same way.

Thoby & I went to look at some houses in Bloomsbury. There are a great many to let there—and there is one in Gordon Square which is one of the quiet small squares that would be the right size for us and was quite nice.'[28]

Bloomsbury was affordable. Unlike their Duckworth stepbrothers, who had substantial private incomes from their late father, the Stephens' finances limited their choice of where to live. Stella had not made a will and the substantial income from her marriage settlement had, therefore, gone to Jack as her husband. He had done the decent thing and offered it to Leslie who had accepted it. 'I felt it right to accept his offer' he wrote in *The Mausoleum Book* '…as I know [Stella] would have been desirous that this should be done to enable me to keep up this household for the good of her brothers and sisters.'[29] On Leslie's death the income was shared between his Stephen children. Leslie added that Jack had the right to discontinue the arrangement 'if circumstances alter'. Jack stopped it in 1931 when he married but for the present the money went to the Stephens in addition to bequests from Frederick Gibbs who had died. However, none of this was enough for Vanessa and Virginia to live on without eventually being supplemented by earnings and/or the income provided by a husband.

Gerald wished to live an independent life as a publisher and he moved to a place of his own. Virginia was glad to see him go but she did not hesitate to make use of him when she became a novelist. Her two earliest novels would appear under his imprint. It had got off to a promising start. Books by Leslie (his Ford lectures), Henry James (*In The Cage*) and John Galsworthy (under a pseudonym) were highlights of Duckworth's first list. Gerald had also become the honorary treasurer of a society formed by the American feminist actress Elizabeth Robins, now settled in England, to put on plays likely to fall foul of the Lord Chamberlain's censorship. He published John Galsworthy's plays, but turned down *The Man of Property*, volume one of *The Forsyte Saga*.

The Stephens relished the thought of moving to a house where they could all have a large room of their own as well as communal rooms and bedrooms, but it seemed they would have to share such a house with George who appeared to wish to stay with them. Before anything was finalised, their dilemma was solved in the happiest fashion. George married Lady Margaret Herbert, fourth daughter of the Earl of Carnarvon, who would bear him three sons. When Virginia's recovery was complete, it was only the four Stephens who moved into 46 Gordon Square, Bloomsbury. For the first time Virginia was wholly free of the Duckworth step-fraternal presence in her daily life and she had a workroom she could truly call her own.

Into print

—The bus took us all the way to nearly the top of Gracechurch St. and after a little bungling we discovered Talbot Court and Charles Booth's offices on the second floor... *A Passionate Apprentice*

Into print

At 46 Gordon Square Virginia worked hard at Greek. Janet Case, one of the first women to take the Tripos, the final honours examination for a BA, in Classics at Cambridge and a campaigner for women's right to vote, was her teacher. Immersing her mind in ancient Greek literature was but a part of Virginia's new, free life. Her ambition was to complement her private income and support herself by her pen as her father had done. His death had destabilised her; now, as it receded, it was beginning to emerge as a liberation. While he had been alive she had felt unable to compete with him at his own game, but in his permanent absence the literary field was wide open to her.

In Cambridge during her convalescence with her aunt, Caroline Stephen, a devout Quaker, Virginia was asked by Frederic Maitland to help him go through her father's and mother's letters, earmarking those she thought suitable for him to use in the biography of Leslie he was preparing. He also requested Virginia to write a recollection of her father for him.

Virginia's three pages, out of more than 500, in *The Life and Letters of Leslie Stephen,* published in 1905 by Gerald, are given as 'by one of his daughters'. She describes how when he recited 'he lay back in his chair and spoke the beautiful words with closed eyes, we felt he was speaking not merely the words of Tennyson or Wordsworth but what he himself felt and knew. Thus many of the great English poems seem to me inseparable from my father; I hear them not only in his voice, but in some sort his teaching and belief.'[30]

Before these words of hers were in print, she had begun to

Virginia in her youth by Charles Beresford
Previous pages: Threadneedle Street and The Royal Exchange 1900

publish work in the periodical press. Violet, Leo and Kitty helped her talent to blossom. She wrote an essay entitled 'Street Music' which she showed nervously to Leo. He liked to leaven the political matter in the *National Review* with lighter fare. He thought her piece was 'charming' and included it in the March number, 1905, above the signature 'Miss Virginia Stephen'. Her theme was the buskers roaming the streets of London. There were notices on railings warning them to keep away but, wrote Virginia: 'No artist…pays the least attention to criticism, and the artist of the streets is properly scornful of the judgement of the British public.'

By treating the buskers ironically as artists in contention with a hostile public, Virginia gave herself opportunities for reflections on the role of art in British life. She continued with some extravagant flights of fancy, suggesting that the buskers incarnated the spirit of the ancient gods banished at the dawn of our era. Above all, they awakened in us a sense of 'rhythm'—that elusive rhythm underlying our existence which much of her subsequent writing would aim to catch. The essay was an assured performance for someone of 23 to have written.

There was another on a visit she had made to the Brontës' parsonage at Haworth that appeared in the *Guardian* at the end of December 1904. This newspaper (not the one we know today) was directed at the clergy and their wives. It had a Saturday Supplement with a spread of cultural pages and book reviews edited by the Hon Margaret Lyttelton, a friend of Violet Dickinson. Violet recommended Virginia to her as a potential book-reviewer. Mrs Lyttelton thus became the editor who first discovered that Virginia was one of nature's book-reviewers and gave her the earliest opportunity to develop her skill. Most of the novels she reviewed for the *Guardian* have disappeared from view but they kept her contentedly busy and occasionally she was able to spread herself on an important subject like *The Letters of Jane Welsh Carlyle,* an appreciative assessment that still reads well, but with which she was far from satisfied when she saw it in print. 'Do you feel convinced I *can* write?' she asked Violet.[31]

Another outlet was *Academy & Literature*, for which she wrote an essay on the Essay (a form she was practising in her Diary). Pearl Craigie, the daughter of an American millionaire settled in England, and who wrote novels under the name of John Oliver Hobbes, edited this weekly. Before her death in 1906 she printed several more pieces of Virginia's. As an early feminist she must have felt Virginia deserved encouragement.

The journal *Literature,* originally owned by *The Times* and bought from them by Craigie's father, was the precursor of what became *The Times Literary Supplement.* It failed as a separate publication but was reborn in 1902 as a part of the Friday issue of *The Times* and it became Virginia's next employer as a book-reviewer. The helping hand of Kitty Maxse is in evidence in Virginia's introduction to its editor. Kitty's friend Valentine Chirol, a foreign affairs specialist on the staff of *The Times,* arranged for Virginia to meet his colleague, Bruce Richmond, who had known Leslie and had been appointed editor of the *Literary Supplement.* Virginia was just the kind of contributor he was looking for, capable of reliably turning out a review on almost any book he sent her. In 1905 he used her for fiction and non-fiction and before the year was out she had nine reviews printed in the paper. She wrote ten; one he rejected because he felt she had been unfair to the book.

All this hard work was combined with Virginia's now full social life. The beauty of Gordon Square without the constraints of HPG was that the Stephens could freely entertain their own friends there. They gave a house-warming party to which Kitty, Violet, Gerald and Jack were invited alongside new Cambridge friends like Clive Bell. In retrospect, it must have seemed like a valediction. They were saying goodbye to one world and entering into another.

At the end of March Virginia took time off to go on holiday to Spain and Portugal with Adrian, now down from Cambridge and studying law like his brother. The engine of the ship they went out in failed and they drifted under sail for seven hours before it was repaired and they reached Oporto. Then they went by train to Lisbon where they visited the English

Cemetery and saw the tomb of Henry Fielding before going on to Seville and Granada.

'Adrian is very happy,' she told Violet, 'and takes great care of me, and does my hair at night, and fastens my dress.'[32] She was becoming a seasoned traveller and on the way back declared: 'We have managed our journey quite successfully, though we discovered on the voyage out that we ought to have booked passage on the return boat, which is very full.'[33] She used there the phrase 'the voyage out' that would become the title of her first novel, concerning an ocean voyage that was interrupted by a stop at Lisbon.

In 1905 Virginia began teaching at Morley College, the adult education institute in Lambeth. Mary Sheepshanks, the deputy principal, who appeared at their first meeting to be 'a large kindly & rather able sort of woman'[34] was another feminist. After a while 'the Sheep', as Virginia called her, began to think Virginia's gift was more for spreading influence than direct teaching and put her in charge of the library. But Virginia struggled on with her students: 'I gave a lecture to 4 working men yesterday—one stutters on his ms—and another is an Italian and reads English as though it were mediaeval Latin—and another is my degenerate poet, who rants and blushes, and almost seizes my hand when we happen to like the same lines.'[35] By the end of 1907, with an ever-growing pile of books to review, she had had enough and gave it up.

Beatrice Thynne and her sister Katie Cromer came to see her in her new abode and so did Lady Eleanor Cecil, the wife of Lord Robert Cecil, a friend of both Violet and Kitty. Eleanor—Nelly as she was known—was the most literary of the Cecils until her nephew Lord David, the future Oxford don and author, grew to manhood. She was a reader for the publisher John Murray and, in spite of being very deaf, had a gift for friendship. Virginia took to her as someone to whom she could talk seriously about literature, though she found speaking through Nelly's ear-trumpet exhausting. It was from Nelly Cecil that Vanessa received her first commission—that of painting her portrait. Vanessa's career was moving forward as rapidly as Virginia's. She had become Secretary of the Friday Club, which she had founded with some friends to discuss the fine arts, and was preparing for an exhibition of her work.

A slim volume appeared that summer, privately printed with the title *Euphrosyne*, containing poems by a group of young men who had been contemporaries of Thoby Stephen at Cambridge: Clive Bell, Saxon Sydney-Turner, Lytton Strachey, Walter Lamb and Leonard Woolf among others. These would-be poets were the Stephen sisters' new friends, the people invited by Thoby to their Thursday evening At Homes and the earliest members of what became the Bloomsbury Group. As Thoby matured into a handsome, commanding extrovert, looked up to by his contemporaries, he became in the eyes of Virginia, her mind fed on classical mythology, like a Greek god; but at Trinity Lytton Strachey had nicknamed him 'the Goth', a label that stuck among his Cambridge set. By the same token they called his two beautiful sisters the Visigoths (related to the Goth and equally handsome). All those invited to Gordon Square by Thoby to meet these sisters at Thursday evening At Homes, fuelled by hock and whisky, had studied at Cambridge, and were either his direct contemporaries or slightly older with careers already under way.

Of his own set, Leonard Woolf was the first to begin a career in earnest. Unlike Clive Bell, who had a wealthy father to support his interest in art, Leonard could not afford to remain unemployed after Cambridge. He was the son of Sidney Woolf QC, a London barrister who had died in his 40s when Leonard was a boy of 11. The Woolfs were Jews who did not greatly participate in the observance of their religion. After Sidney's demise the family's income was severely limited. From an early age Leonard learned care with money. He was tall, bony, aquiline in profile, deliberate in utterance, and had an involuntary trembling of the hands, a congenital trait he had inherited from his father.

Leonard had won a scholarship to St Paul's School where he was a model student in classics and then a scholarship to Trinity but he did not achieve exceptional distinction in the Classical Tripos (a first in part one, a second in part two).

After Cambridge he had settled for work as a Colonial Civil Servant with a posting to Ceylon (now Sri Lanka). He spent the summer of 1904 preparing for it by learning to ride in Hyde Park's Rotten Row. In December he arrived in Colombo to begin what became a seven-year spell of duty on the island. Thus his acquaintance with the Stephen sisters at this time was a brief one. He played no part in the earliest Bloomsbury gatherings, those hosted by Thoby Stephen. His knowledge of these gatherings was through the accounts that came to him in frequent letters from his great friend Lytton Strachey, missives seasoned with scandal. Their friendship was cemented by the profound admiration they shared for Voltaire. Leonard had shipped the Frenchman's correspondence, all 70 volumes of it, out with him to Ceylon.

Giles Lytton Strachey had a broken school career because of ill health, culminating in a year studying English at Liverpool University before he went up to Trinity. His father, Lieutenant-General Sir Richard Strachey, had been an administrator in India before retiring to a large house at Lancaster Gate (the other side of Kensington Gardens from HPG) where he lived with his wife and ten children. The Stracheys were a family noted for their abundance of ability, eccentricity, and a peculiar high-pitched Strachey voice that once heard was never forgotten, all of which Lytton inherited. After taking his BA, he embarked on a dissertation on Warren Hastings, under whom his forbears had served in India, in the hope that it would gain him a prize fellowship at Trinity and he would be able to spend the rest of his life as a don, an ambition that was, as we shall see, unfulfilled.

When they were not entertaining, Virginia and her brothers and sister liked to sit on the balcony of their new house after dinner of a summer evening, drinking coffee, observing the giggling, courting couples parading in the Square below. There is something symbolic about that. Virginia loved to try to get inside the skins of 'ordinary people' but always remained at a distance from them.

Both her brothers were adventurous young men who enjoyed the traditional pursuits of the English country gentleman,

Vanessa by Charles Beresford

such as riding to hounds and shooting, tastes they shared, as we saw, with Clive Bell and Jack Hills. They yearned now for experience of travel in foreign parts of which so far they had enjoyed but little. And was it not time Virginia went to Greece to see the country for herself, not merely read about it in its ancient poets?

The four of them arranged a holiday excursion to Greece and Turkey in the autumn of 1906; Violet went with them. At first they split into two groups: Thoby and Adrian went to Albania where they obtained horses on which they rode through desolate mountainous country to Greece. Violet, Vanessa and Virginia left London on September 8th and met the brothers at Olympia. Virginia absorbed this experience with rapture, recording her impressions of what she had seen during the day in lengthy passages in her Diary each evening. Her account of the whole tour may be read in *A Passionate Apprentice*. With 'the taste of Homer in my mouth' she climbed up to the Parthenon by moonlight (as would the eponymous hero of her 1922 novel *Jacob's Room*).

Unfortunately, the tour was bedevilled by illness. Vanessa was so unwell in October that she remained in bed in Athens with Violet to tend her while the others went to Achmetaga in Euboea. Their friends, the Noels, had a villa there and they stayed with them for several days. Thoby returned to England in advance of the others who visited Turkey. Virginia described going into a mosque during a service. On their way home Vanessa collapsed with exhaustion and had to rest in bed in Athens for a fortnight before she was well enough to take a boat for Constantinople (now Istanbul) where they caught the Orient Express. It was when they were safely back in England that illness struck most malevolently. Both Thoby and Violet had contracted typhoid fever and took to their beds, she at her house near Welwyn seriously ill, he in Gordon Square, where Vanessa also needed to remain in bed to regain her strength.

The Bloomsbury invalids did not lack visitors. Kitty was one of the first and stayed for an hour with Thoby. Her attachment to Leslie had now transferred to his elder son. George and Gerald both showed concern by calling. Beatrice Thynne

Leo Maxse, editor of the National Review. *Kitty, his wife, was the main model for Mrs Dalloway*

was a regular caller as was Clive Bell. By now Clive, after a lengthy affair with a married woman back home in Wiltshire, had twice proposed to Vanessa and twice been turned down. Vanessa made a slow, steady recovery but Thoby continued to worsen and, after an operation, died on 20th November 1906.

Virginia feared that if she told Violet the dreadful news, it would undermine her chance of shaking off the disease and so in her daily letters to her, Virginia fantasised that Thoby was making good progress towards recovery. She was also engaged in an exercise in denial on her own behalf, refusing to accept the unthinkable. Five days after Thoby's death she writes: 'And now that Thoby is out of danger things will go swimmingly: only my dear old furry one [Violet] must heal up—and come to a festal dinner.'[36]

Thoby's death coincided with the publication by Gerald of Frederic Maitland's *The Life and Letters of Leslie Stephen*. Leo Maxse printed a long notice of it in the December number of *The National Review*. A footnote added: 'The book appeared almost on the very day of the untimely death of Sir Leslie Stephen's eldest son, Mr Thoby Stephen, at the age of 25.' It was only when she read this, almost a month after Thoby's death and Vanessa's acceptance of Clive, that Violet realised what had happened.

A remorseful Virginia wrote on the 18th December:

'Beloved Violet,

'Do you hate me for telling so many lies? You know we had to do it? You must think that Nessa is *radiantly happy* and Thoby was splendid to the end.

'These great things are not terrible, and I know we can still make a good job of it—and we want you more and more. I never knew till this happened how I should turn to you and want you with me when no one else could help.'[37] She was turning to Violet as a last resort in what in her despair seemed to her then a double loss, Thoby into the arms of death and Vanessa into those of Clive. In a second letter to Violet of the same date we can observe Virginia willing herself into acceptance of her sister's choice of husband:

'I feel *perfectly happy* [Virginia's emphasis] about her. When you see them together you realise that he does understand every side, and all that is best in her. I never saw anything so beautiful as she was. He is very considerate and unselfish, and he is really interesting and clever besides.

'You know what she has in her, and all that seems now called out; she is a splendid creature, and makes me hope all kinds of things'.[38]

They were married at St Pancras Register Office on 7th February 1907, just two weeks after they announced their engagement. After the wedding they took over Gordon Square and Virginia and Adrian moved to nearby 29 Fitzroy Square.

If work is the most effective medicine for grief, Virginia had plenty of that. She was continually in demand for reviews and longer articles. The editor of the *Cornhill* magazine, Reginald Smith, was her latest employer. The arrangement with him was that she and Nelly Cecil should alternate each month in writing a considered piece of several thousand words on a newly published book. It brought her into closer contact with Nelly, whom she visited at her houses in St John's Wood and at Chelwood Gate in East Sussex; and she had some lively arguments with Smith over the choice of book. As editors always do, he wanted her to write about books with a wide appeal, especially biographies, whereas she would have preferred something more literary such as a volume of new poetry. She was not yet in a strong enough position to have her way and she submitted to her editor's decisions. She was extending her range as a critic and at the same time had the enormous satisfaction of adding to her income through her literary labours. But though she enjoyed criticism and took immense trouble over it, it was in her eyes but a prelude to the task she saw as paramount, the writing of a novel, and she began to take her first hesitant steps in that direction.

She had experienced a lot since that Sunday morning when she saw Dr Seton walking away from the house in Hyde Park Gate where her mother lay dead but she was still, outside of the world of books and the imagination, essentially an innocent abroad compared (say) to Kitty Maxse or even to Vanessa, now pregnant with her first child. She would explore her own innocence in a novel in the form of a sea voyage. Its heroine would be a young woman dependent on a mother substitute, confronted first by self-assured people like Kitty and Leo who had already made their mark in the world—the Dalloways she would call them; they would come on board for a while—and then by a wider, heterogeneous circle of people, including young men of her own generation with powerful intellects who were like Lytton Strachey, Saxon Sydney-Turner, Clive Bell and the others who came to Gordon Square on Thursday evenings, the gatherings initiated by Thoby. A vague preliminary shape of *The Voyage Out* had begun to form in her mind.

Apostolic attitudes

—Strolling through those colleges past those ancient halls the roughness of the present seemed soothed away... the mind freed from any contact with facts... was at liberty to settle down upon whatever meditation was in harmony with the moment... *A Room of One's Own*

Apostolic attitudes

Virginia's mind had been tested in conversations with these men. She was shy initially and there were frequent lulls in the Thursday talk but once it got going it was the kind of conversation several of them had practised as members of that exclusive intellectual Cambridge elite, the Apostles Society. Neither Thoby nor Adrian had been elected to it nor, to his chagrin, had Clive Bell. But Leonard Woolf, Lytton Strachey and Saxon Sydney-Turner, among Thoby's set, were Apostles and the Apostles' spirit of inquiry into everything under the sun, with an emphasis on ethics, sexuality and art, permeated Bloomsbury gatherings and became their hallmark.

Among Virginia's and Vanessa's new friends were Apostles of an earlier generation such as Roger Fry, of the Quaker Fry family. He had been elected in 1887 when he was up at King's reading for the Natural Sciences Tripos, in which he took a First. To the dismay of his father, a judge, he then decided to become a painter and now combined his painting with art criticism and lecturing.

Edward Morgan Forster of King's College (not yet a friend of Virginia) was of a more recent Apostolic vintage, having been elected in 1901. His novel *The Longest Journey* (1907) dedicated 'Fratribus' ('for the brethren,' that is, the Apostles) begins in a Cambridge college where a group of young men are discussing the philosophical question of whether the cow is in the field when no one is looking at it. The episode is said to give the flavour of a gathering of Apostles. The society has existed uninterruptedly since it was founded in 1820.

Clive Bell with Julian, Quentin, and Angelica, painted by Vanessa Bell
Previous pages: King's College Chapel, Cambridge 1926

Membership is by invitation. One of the 'brethren' (the first woman member was elected in 1970) reads a paper, often in the form of an either/or question, and a vote on it is taken at the end of the meeting. A paper that became famous among the brethren was, 'Violets or Orange Blossom?' by the philosopher John McTaggart (Apostle No 212), concerned with friendship and love. Bertrand Russell (Apostle No 224) read a paper in November 1894 entitled 'Cleopatra or Maggie Tulliver [heroine of George Eliot's *Mill on the Floss*]?' posing the question, Passion or Duty?

When Leonard Woolf and Lytton Strachey were made members the latter wrote to his mother:

'...I am now a Brother of the Society of the Apostles.—How I dare write the words I don't know!—I was apparently elected yesterday, and today the news was gently broken. The members —past-present—are sufficiently distinguished. Tennyson was one of the early ones. But I shall know more on Tuesday when I visit the Ark—or chest in which the documents of the Society are kept. It is a veritable Brotherhood the chief point being personal friendship between the members. The sensation is a strange one. Angels are Apostles who have taken wings—viz. settled down to definite opinions, which they may do whenever they choose. I feel I shall never take wings...

Your loving

Lytton'[39]

Paul Levy in his book *Moore: G E Moore and the Cambridge Apostles* writes: 'In its rites, secrecy and neo-Kantian [a school of German philosophers in the late 19th century] argot that made the society "real" and the rest of the world 'phenomenal', the Apostles were a typical undergraduate debating club and typically silly. However, through most of its history, this group was distinguished from all other such societies by the outstanding intellectual capacities of its members.'[40]

From time to time an outstanding member's papers have had a permanent influence on the lives of his apostolic generation. In the early 20th century those of the philosopher G E Moore (1873–1958, Apostle No 229) were of this kind. Moore redefined the nature of goodness in a series of papers read to the society and to other learned bodies, culminating in his *Principia Ethica* (1903), a work that that has been called the Bible of Bloomsbury. The argument, one that Moore continually revised, is too complex for a brief summary, but a salient point is Moore's destruction of what he called the 'naturalistic fallacy' of goodness, goodness thought of as an attribute of something other than itself: a good meal, a good book, a good man, and so on. Moore came to the conclusion that good was indefinable but that certain activities were in themselves good, notably, 'the pleasures of human intercourse and the enjoyment of beautiful objects'. Those who attended Virginia's and Vanessa's Bloomsbury gatherings construed this to mean finding the good life through personal relations (including sexual relations between persons of the same gender) and the practice and enjoyment of art.

When the *Principia* was published, Strachey wrote to Moore: 'I think your book has not only wrecked and shattered all writers on Ethics from Aristotle and Christ to Herbert Spencer and Mr Bradley, it has not only laid the true foundations of Ethics, it has not only left all modern philosophy bafouée [scorned]—these seem to me small achievements compared to the establishment of that Method which shines like a sword between the lines.'[41]

Virginia felt obliged to read the book and found it stiff going. She limited herself to ten pages a night. When she had eventually got through it she told Vanessa: 'I finished Moore last night...I am not so dumb foundered as I was; but the more I understand, the more I admire.'[42] In later life Virginia tended to play down the influence of the Apostles on her work but she found in her contact with the brethren and would-be brethren a confirmation of her belief that Reality consisted in the exercise of the intellect in the pursuit of the truth and that the rest of life was merely Phenomenal. This conviction—it took the place for her as it did for her Apostle friends of a religion—was further strengthened when she married an Apostle in Leonard Woolf.

That was still some way off. He was currently in Ceylon coping with such Phenomena as outbreaks of rinderpest among cattle, or sitting in a village courthouse trying offenders and learning to speak the local languages. Leonard was proving himself to be a highly effective instrument of paternalistic government. While he was away Virginia had several suitors who wished to marry her. A most unlikely one was Lytton Strachey. His proposal was withdrawn almost as soon as it was made. Both realised that though they would always be friends, soul mates indeed, they could never be lovers. His dissertation had not won him the coveted fellowship and he was now reconciled to adopting the literary life as his profession with book reviewing as the immediate prospect before him. St Loe Strachey, his cousin, the editor-proprietor of the *Spectator*, employed him as a critic. Like Virginia, Lytton discovered his métier through reviewing. He had revealed himself in his circle as homosexual in his amours; or as Vanessa and Virginia now described it in their new bawdy Bloomsbury, no-gloves vocabulary, he was a 'bugger'. Lytton was also writing erotic poetry of unremitting frankness which circulated privately among his Bloomsbury friends. Vanessa, shaking off any residual Victorian prudery, read these scatological poems and adopted their bawdy vocabulary with great zest.

Strachey had fallen in love with his cousin, the young painter, Duncan Grant. The son of an Indian army major, Grant had lived with the Stracheys in London while he was a dayboy at St Paul's School. Strachey's mother was his aunt. Thanks to her Grant was allowed to leave school early to study art and to become an artist full-time. He soon joined the Bloomsbury circle and became a fixture in it.

Another admirer of Virginia's was the Cambridge classics don Walter Headlam, now in his 40s. She remembered him from a decade before as her father's guest at Talland House. He had been infatuated by Julia and had made a fool of himself trying to kiss her during a walk. Portraits of Julia and Leslie were prominently displayed in his rooms at King's. Now he made protestations of love to Virginia that she did not discourage. He came to tea and wrote fulsome, praising letters; one was signed off with a pun in Greek, hailing her as his mistress. He asked her if he could dedicate his great scholarly project, an edition of the *Agamemnon* with his own English verse translation, on which he had been at work for almost 20 years, to her instead of to the poet Swinburne to whom he had already offered it. She seems to have refused as it is Swinburne's name which appeared after the title page when the work was published posthumously. Their relationship was not wholly flirtatious. He had told her how much he admired her critical essays and she was glad to find approval from a mind she respected, nurtured on Greek literature. She sent him some of her unpublished manuscripts, imaginative writing, the tentative beginnings of a novel for his reaction. But it all came abruptly to an end when he died suddenly in 1908. A year later Gerald published a memorial volume on his life and work.

Virginia also showed her novel in progress to her brother-in-law, Clive Bell. He, like her, had found work in the periodical press, to supplement his healthy Bell private income. He had become a regular writer on art and books (anonymously) in the *Athenaeum*. He had the gift of communicating his likes and dislikes with vehement Bloomsbury candour and he was candid with Virginia in his criticism of her manuscript. He had many points of detail to take up but there was no doubt in his mind of 'the thrilling real beneath the dull apparent…I believe this first novel will become a work that counts.' That was probably in October 1908. When she showed him the next draft in February, he responded, amid further quibbles: 'I can now say, with a clear conscience, what I really think about your novel—that it is wonderful.'[43]

While her sister was undergoing her pregnancies and producing two sons, Julian (born 1908) and Quentin (born 1910), Virginia embarked upon a prolonged flirtation with Clive. She was partly responsible for her sister's marriage falling apart, as it duly did. While depicting the innocence of her heroine in the novel she was writing, Virginia seems to have decided to lose her own. Whatever her motives may have been, Clive fell in love with her and she encouraged him. It was inexcusable behaviour on both their parts. The heavy flirtation lasted for more than a year. Vanessa, when she realised what was going on, unsurprisingly regarded it as a betrayal. Her marriage became one of shared parenthood and companionship rather than of mutual passion. The bond between the sisters, though dented, stayed in place. Clive reverted to his former mistress in Wiltshire; Vanessa fell in love with Roger Fry and he with her. Fry's wife Helen, by whom he had two children, suffered from schizophrenia and was confined to an institution.

Roger had failed in an attempt to become Slade Professor of Art at Cambridge. He failed, too, initially in his attempt to become Director of the National Gallery in London and when that job did come his way, he had already agreed, after much negotiation, to work for the American millionaire, Pierpont Morgan, at the Metropolitan Museum in New York. Morgan was its donor-President. A large part of Fry's job as curator consisted of acquisition, enabling him to spend a considerable part of the year in England and on the Continent. Morgan proved to be an appallingly domineering employer whom Fry soon grew to loathe.

They eventually fell out over a picture Morgan wanted for his private collection and Fry wanted for the museum. In 1910, aged 44 and in jobless limbo, Fry arranged with the directors of the Grafton Gallery in London to mastermind an exhibition of pictures by contemporary French painters. He had discovered Cézanne and had used the term Post-Impressionism to describe his method of painting. He assembled a show entitled 'Manet and the Post-Impressionists' that opened at the Gallery on 5th November containing work by Cézanne, Matisse, Van Gogh, Gauguin, Seurat, Picasso, and Derain.

Clive Bell helped him to gather in the paintings and Roger asked a fellow-Apostle, Desmond MacCarthy, to become the show's secretary. MacCarthy was, like Clive, a member of the gatherings Vanessa held to discuss the fine arts, the Friday Club. He was an all-round man of letters who currently made a living as a dramatic critic for *The Speaker*. He had reviewed the plays by Galsworthy, Ibsen and Shaw produced at the Court Theatre (later Royal Court) in Sloane Square during the epoch-making Vedrenne-Barker period of management from 1904 to 1907. In 1906 he had married Mary (Molly) Warre, daughter of the Vice-Provost of Eton. Vanessa and Virginia attended their wedding in Eton College Chapel and Desmond came to one of the earliest Gordon Square Thursday evenings.

David Cecil, Desmond's son-in-law, was at pains, in a posthumous portrait of him, to deny that Desmond was ever a member of Bloomsbury: 'Desmond is sometimes spoken of as belonging to it [the Bloomsbury Circle]. This was not so. As he himself said, "Bloomsbury has never been a spiritual home to me." Its characteristic attitude to the world was alien to him; its exclusiveness, its intellectual pride, the inability of its members to feel at ease with anyone but each other.'[44]

Well, if Desmond did not belong to the circle, Molly, his wife, certainly did. She was a friend of Virginia and Vanessa, and frequently attended their gatherings. David Cecil's denial of his father-in-law's membership shows how the Cecils felt about Bloomsbury. Nelly Cecil was a kind of middle-woman between Bloomsbury and Hatfield, the magnificent Jacobean mansion in Hertfordshire, home of the Cecil family since the 17th century, where much Tory party policy has been mooted. Kitty Maxse, Nelly's friend and confidante, was affronted by Virginia's new cool manner and deplored her new friends. 'The Stephens think a damned sight too much of themselves & that's the truth,' Nelly told Kitty.[45]

Uproar greeted Roger Fry's Post-Impressionist exhibition when it opened. It separated the old guard, who thought the paintings on show a grotesque insult to the art they cherished, from the tiny minority who saw with Fry that this was the way forward. The uproar was analogous to the storm created by the first performances of Ibsen in London 15 years earlier. Shock-horror was the reaction of most members of the public and of the leading art critics. *The Times* man thundered that 'this art is in itself a flagrant example of reaction. It professes to simplify, and to gain simplicity it throws away all that the long-developed skill past artists had perpetuated. It begins all over again—and stops where a child would stop...Really primitive art is attractive because it is unconscious; but this is deliberate —it is the rejection of all that civilisation has done, the good with the bad.'

Fry wrote in 1913 to his fellow-Apostle, the Cambridge don

Goldsworthy Lowes Dickinson: 'I'm continuing my aesthetic theories and I have been attacking poetry to understand painting. I want to find out what the function of content is, and am developing a theory which you will hate very much, viz. that it is merely directive of form and that all the essential aesthetic quality has to do with pure form.'[46] This theory was developed further by Clive Bell to become the now notorious doctrine of 'significant form', that it was the form not the content of a work of art that aroused the aesthetic emotion. But if that were true of a painting by Cezanne, for example, could it also be true of a novel? Surely in a novel the content was at least as important as the form? Virginia was writing a novel in which the content veers from external description of the shipboard life of the main characters to the random thoughts, the inner consciousness, of the heroine as she lies on her fatal sickbed. Virginia was finding her own way ahead out of the constrictions imposed by descriptive realism, but she did not yet have the confidence to abandon it completely.

She was leading a single life full of engagements. Any inhibitions she may have had about breaking new ground socially seem to have disappeared. In 1909 she made a friend in Society in whose drawing room she would meet many of her own kind. 'We [Vanessa and Virginia] have just got to know a wonderful Lady Ottoline Morrell, who has the head of a Medusa; but she is very simple and innocent in spite of it, and worships the arts,' she told Madge Vaughan.[47] 'Ott' and her husband Philip Morrell, the Liberal politician, lived in London at Bedford Square in the Bloomsbury area where at this period she held her salon. She was a sister of the Duke of Portland, and had a large private income, which she lavished on the company of artists and writers. Virginia came to be genuinely fond of her and to admire her courage in pursuing an eccentric way of life that made her the object of satire and ridicule. Clive Bell and Vanessa had first met her in the studio of the painter Augustus John. She was currently involved in a liaison with the artist Henry Lamb, who was much enamoured of her.

Duncan Grant meanwhile had taken a flat at 21 Fitzroy Street within easy range of Virginia and Adrian and Clive and

Vanessa. His latest conquest was the economist John Maynard Keynes, who supplanted Lytton Strachey as his lover, to the latter's near suicidal anguish. Maynard had gone from King's, Cambridge, to the India Office and was currently working on a dissertation on the Indian economy in a competition for a prize Fellowship back at King's. In his first term as an undergraduate at Cambridge in 1902, Lytton Strachey and Leonard Woolf had vetted him for membership of the Apostles and he had been elected an Apostle with unusual rapidity, in February 1903. In 1909, having won the Fellowship, he returned to Cambridge and began work on his first major study in economics, on Probability, while lecturing and teaching.

Virginia's circle of male friends, most of them gay or bisexual, was widening all the time, as was her circle of female friends. Her former Greek teacher, Janet Case, now became her friend. Case lived at Hampstead with her sister Emphie and was in touch with Margaret Llewelyn Davies, the General Secretary of the Women's Cooperative Guild, an organisation with branches throughout England devoted to advancing the rights and education of women, especially those of the working class. Virginia was inspired by these campaigning women to take an active part in their work for the suffragist cause. She spent some time in an office of the Women's Suffrage Movement addressing envelopes. It was experience she would use as background in her second novel *Night and Day* and in the characterisation of Mary Datchet, the single woman. For the moment she was still agonisingly, painstakingly, at work on her first, *The Voyage Out* (not yet given that title).

The narrative was comparatively straightforward in outline. Rachel Vinrace, the young heroine, whose mother is dead, goes on a sea voyage to South America with her father, a ship-owner, and her aunt and uncle. She stays at their villa in a village surrounded by jungle and distant mountains, and where, somewhat oddly, there is a hotel full of English visitors. One of the young men staying at the hotel forms a relationship with the heroine and proposes marriage. After much deliberation she accepts him and they announce their engagement. Soon after this she contracts a deadly tropical fever. Her state of mind as she lies on her sickbed and becomes delirious is movingly described. She never recovers and the novel concludes with her death.

In writing and re-writing the novel, with its long account of the heroine on her deathbed gradually sinking into delirium, Virginia brought to bear all the terrible memories she had as a witness to the deaths of her mother, her stepsister and her brother. It was an act of imaginative catharsis. In the timing of her heroine's death, after she had accepted a proposal of marriage but before the marriage had occurred, she gave expression to her own ambivalent feelings about the married state. Virginia was 'under pressure' from her women friends to marry; it was pressure she was stubbornly resisting. 'If either you [Violet Dickinson] or Kitty [Maxse] ever speak of my marriage again I shall write you such a lecture upon the carnal sins as will make you fall into each others arms; but you shall never come near me any more. Ever since Thoby died women have hinted at this, till I could almost turn against my own sex!'[48]

The ship in Virginia's novel stops at Lisbon at the mouth of the Tagus. The Dalloways come on board, characters inspired by Leo and Kitty Maxse. Virginia turns Leo into the politician he never became, a backbench busybody on a private mission to Europe studying social conditions. The novel's settings— shipboard life, the villa, the hotel and the jungle interior—are all realised with great verisimilitude. Each character is linked to a favourite author. This applies even to minor ones such as the ship's steward who is a Shakespeare-lover and ominously quotes 'Full fathom five thy father lies' (from *The Tempest*) as a violent storm impends. Clarissa Dalloway never travels without Pascal but reads Austen's *Persuasion* in bed. (She shares Sir Walter Elliot's delight in a perusal of that directory of hereditary knighthoods, *The Baronetage*.) The heroine quotes *Comus*— Milton's masque celebrating chastity—before she dies. Woolf scholars have thoroughly examined the significance of many further literary parallels in which the various drafts of the book abound.

Virginia lived as much through literature as she did through people. It was second nature to her to characterise the people in her novels through their favourite reading. Richard Dalloway wanders into the heroine's room after the storm: "'How jolly to meet again,' said Richard. "It seems an age. *Cowper's Letters?* ...Bach...*Wuthering Heights?* Is this where you meditate on the world, and then come out and pose poor politicians with questions?'"

He asks her if she has ever read Burke.

"'Burke?' she repeated. "Who was Burke?"

"No? Well, then, I shall make a point of sending you a copy. *The Speech on the French Revolution—The American Rebellion?* Which shall it be, I wonder?'"

Shortly after this we have one of the very few accounts of lust in action in Virginia's fiction: "'You have beauty,' he said. The ship lurched. Rachel fell slightly forward. Richard took her in his arms and kissed her. Holding her tight, he kissed her passionately, so that she felt the hardness of his body and the roughness of his cheek printed upon hers. She fell back in her chair, with tremendous beats of the heart, each of which sent black waves across her eyes. He clasped his forehead in his hands.

"You tempt me," he said. The tone his voice was terrifying.'[49]

Richard Dalloway has merged with Clive Bell. Virginia is dramatising her first erotic contact with a man after the traumatic assaults upon her person by her stepbrothers. It was both willed and fearful, leaving a residue of guilt.

The mental strain of writing the novel had begun to tell on Virginia. Its composition was interrupted by nervous collapse. She returned to Dr Savage for a consultation and he recommended she should take a rest-cure at a nursing home in Twickenham run by a Miss Jean Thomas. Virginia went there at the end of June 1910. She found Miss Thomas, who specialised in treating female mental patients, charming and grew to like her in spite of her devout Christian faith. When Virginia was well enough she went on a walking tour with her to Cornwall and by the end of the year she was able to resume work for the Women's Suffrage Movement

With no family Christmas in which to participate, Virginia and Adrian stayed for a week starting on Christmas Eve at the Pelham Arms in Lewes where Miss Thomas joined them. Virginia had discovered East Sussex, the part of England where she would spend much of the rest of her life. She arrived at the village of Firle beneath the Downs near Lewes and liked it so much she began to look for somewhere there to live. She found a villa she was able to rent and she renamed it Little Talland House. Here, with two servants to look after her, she had guests to stay (she invited Violet) and was free from

Rupert Brooke: poet and Neo-Pagan

potential suitors. When she returned to London she received a proposal that she politely refused from Walter Lamb, brother of the painter Henry and lecturer in Classics at Newnham, one of the two colleges for women at Cambridge, and later Secretary of the Royal Academy.

Virginia's love of Sussex did not prevent her making excursions to other parts of England. While she was at Oxford, she visited Marjorie Strachey, Lytton's younger sister who was an undergraduate at Somerville College, with whom she met Katherine Cox, a stockbroker's daughter who was a student at Newnham. She immediately liked this young woman, whom she thought a prettier, fresher version of Mary Sheepshanks, and was curious to observe someone of her own gender enjoying the university experience of which she had been deprived. She invited Ka (as she was known) to stay at Firle. They discussed Rupert Brooke and the Cambridge set that had formed around him. Brooke had met Ka Cox through the Cambridge Fabian society, of which Ka was the secretary. He was currently a postgraduate student living at the Old Vicarage at Grantchester, where Virginia went to visit him for a few days in August 1911.

Brooke's schoolmaster father had died recently and he had discovered a photograph in his desk of the Brookes and the Stephens in Cornwall, of himself aged six and Virginia aged eleven. Since then Brooke had passed through Rugby and King's College, where Walter Headlam had been his classics supervisor. Lytton's younger brother, James Strachey, had fallen in love with him, getting him elected to the Apostles with Maynard as his co-sponsor. Brooke had also made a close friend of Jacques Raverat, a student at Emmanuel College, the son of a French businessman who sent him to Bedales School in England. The future painter Raverat would become a close friend of Virginia's and a great admirer of her work.

Meetings between male students at Cambridge and their female opposite numbers at Newnham and Girton were always strictly chaperoned, but this had not stopped Brooke acquiring a large female following. Apart from Ka, there were Ray and Karin Costelloe, also at Newnham; the four Olivier sisters, Brynhild, Marjorie, Daphne and Noel, daughters of Sir Sydney Olivier, Governor General of Jamaica and one of the earliest Fabian Society members; and, living in Cambridge with their parents, the granddaughters of Charles Darwin, Gwen (who would marry Raverat) and Frances, whose father was Sir George Darwin, the mathematician and geophysicist. Virginia and Vanessa referred to Brooke's set as the Neo-Pagans on account of their passion for the open-air life, walking long distances, swimming in the nude and camping.

In the hope of gaining a fellowship Brooke was deeply engrossed in the Elizabethan and Jacobean period, its Puritans and its dramatists, especially John Webster, writing dissertations as well as poetry. His encounter with Virginia was not amorous for either of them but it did have its intimate moments, as Brooke's biographer revealed: 'One warm night there was a clear sky and a moon and they walked out to the shadowy waters of Byron's Pool. "Let's go swimming quite naked," Brooke said and they did.'[50] By day Virginia worked at her novel and Brooke at a poem, 'Town and Country'. At the line 'Cloudlike we lean and stare as...', he was stumped. 'Virginia!' he shouted. 'What's the brightest thing in nature?' 'Sunlight on a leaf,' she said. 'Thanks,' he replied and continued '...stare as bright leaves stare.'

Later that August Brooke persuaded Virginia to go camping with him and his friends in Devon. Her friends came, too, on a historic fortnight when the Neo-Pagans and the Bloomsberries joined forces. The camp site was at Clifford Bridge five miles from Drewsteignton in a meadow beside the mouth of the Teign on the edge of Dartmoor. The Olivier sisters and Ka were of the party on the one side; Duncan Grant, Maynard Keynes, his brother Geoffrey and James Strachey on the other. Lytton Strachey stayed nearby at Becky House, Manaton, on Dartmoor, a working-man's house with rooms to let. Nothing catastrophic occurred during the two weeks but Virginia noted that the men did not bother to shave and at the end, when they broke camp, many limbs were sore, many tempers frayed. The two groups never met as such again, though there were those who belonged to both like David (Bunny) Garnett, the son of Gerald Duckworth's literary adviser Edward Garnett and his wife Constance, the translator of Tolstoy and Dostoevsky.

While their friends were under canvas, first G E Moore and then Leonard Woolf, back in England on a year's leave, visited Lytton in his cottage. At the age of 31 and after seven years' absence, Woolf was a seasoned colonial administrator. After the reunion with his family, his next move had been to go back to Cambridge and resume Apostolic existence. Now he found two Apostles in a sunlit Devonshire garden wearing panama hats and both at work on books for the Home University Library: Strachey was writing *Landmarks in French Literature*, his first book, Moore was working on one on *Ethics*.

Of this encounter Leonard wrote: 'Talking to him [Moore] one lived under the shadow of the eternal, though silent, question: "What exactly do you mean by that?" It is a menacing question, particularly when you know that muddle and not knowing "exactly

76

what you mean by *that*" will cause to Moore almost physical pain which he will show involuntarily in his eyes.'[51]

He became reacquainted with Virginia during a visit he made to Clive Bell and Vanessa in Gordon Square. When Virginia returned to Firle she invited him (and Marjorie Strachey) to stay with her:

'August 31, 1911
Dear Mr Woolf,
(It would be much nicer to use Christian names).
I am very glad you can come. Saturday week, the 9th, suits me very well, or any time the week after. I shall be here, I expect, until the 18th. This is not a cottage, but a hideous suburban villa.—I have to prepare people for the shock.
Yours sincerely,
Virginia Stephen
I will explain the trains, if you will say which time suits you.'[52]

The two soon became on Christian name terms, though neither of them was a Christian. During this visit, Leonard became entranced by Virginia's beauty and her genius. He attempted to analyse both in *Beginning Again*, the volume of his memoirs covering the period 1911–1918. 'When she was well, unworried, happy, amused, and excited,' he writes, 'her face lit up with an intense almost ethereal beauty. She was also extremely beautiful when, unexcited and unworried, she sat reading or thinking. But the expression, even the shape of her face changed with extraordinary rapidity as the winds of mental strain, illness or worry passed over its surface. It was still beautiful, but her anxiety and pain made the beauty itself painful.'[53] As for her genius it marked her out in a most distinctive way. 'Virginia,' he continued 'had a great enjoyment of ordinary things, of eating, walking, desultory talking, shopping, playing bowls, reading. She liked and got on well with all kinds of everyday people, as soon as they got to know her well and she them. (She had a curious shyness with strangers which often made them uncomfortably shy.) In this day to day, everyday life and intercourse with other people she talked thought and acted, to a great extent, no doubt, as other ordinary people, though it is a curious fact that there was about her something, some intangible aura, which made her very often seem strange to the 'ordinary' person...

I think this element was closely connected with the streak in her which I call genius. For in conversation she might, at any moment, leave the ground as I used to call it. She was an unusually amusing talker in the usual way of talk and talkers, her mind being very quick and intelligent, witty and humorous, appropriately serious or frivolous as the occasion or subject demanded. But at any moment, in general conversation with five or six people or when we were alone together, she might suddenly "leave the ground" and give some fantastic, entrancing, amusing, dreamlike, almost lyrical description of an event, a place, or a person. It always made me think of the breaking and gushing out of the springs in autumn after the first rains. The ordinary mental processes stopped, and in their place the waters of creativeness and imagination welled up and, almost undirected, carried her and her listeners into another world.'[54]

We do not have a comparable analysis of Leonard's character from Virginia nor of the impression he made on her when his serious courting of her began. Her regular Diary-keeping came to a stop in 1909 and was not resumed until 1915, three years into their marriage. But from her letters to Violet and her other woman friends we may infer that his being a Jew was against him but being a 'penniless' (her word) Jew was in his favour; even more so was the fact he had been a Trinity College, Cambridge, contemporary and close friend of her late brother Thoby. Further points in his favour were his integrity, his love of literature and music, and his intellect, a match for her own. Whether she felt anything comparable to the physical attraction he clearly felt for her seems doubtful.

Back in London Virginia and Adrian were forced to move from Fitzroy Square when their lease ran out. They moved to a larger house in Brunswick Square, still in Bloomsbury, by Coram Fields. They decided to run it as a Bloomsbury commune, all the occupants having a floor of their own: Adrian the second, Virginia the third, Maynard Keynes and Duncan Grant the ground floor. Leonard was offered two rooms on the fourth. Sophie Farrell, their cook from HPG, was in charge of the culinary arrangements.

Virginia's letter to Leonard with the offer of rooms contained an enclosure about these arrangements:

'Breakfast 9 a.m.

Lunch 1.

Tea 4.30 p.m.

Dinner 8 p.m.

Trays will be placed in the hall punctually at these hours. Inmates are requested to carry up their own trays; and to put the dirty plates on them and carry them down again as soon as the meal is finished...

The proprietors reserve the right of ceasing to supply service at any time...'[55]

Leonard had no problem with these rules and moved in on 4th December. He, too, was at work on a novel, *The Village in the Jungle*, based upon his Ceylon experience. Both spent the mornings writing. The remainder of the day and night was devoted to pleasure. At the behest of Saxon Sydney-Turner they saw the whole of Wagner's *Ring* cycle at the opera house in Covent Garden. More to Leonard's taste were the performances of the Diaghilev ballet company, offering nightly spectacles of choreographic perfection to ecstatic British audiences.

When tired of London they repaired to Firle. Walking one bright day across the Downs, and along the Ouse valley, they noticed a romantic-looking house at Asham, on the road between Lewes and Seaford, with a large field in front of it.

They learned it had been built in Victorian times by the owner of the adjoining farm and that Asham (or Asheham) House, as it was called, was now empty. Virginia took a five-year lease on it from the original owner's granddaughter, gave up the Firle villa and moved in. In February she gave a weekend house-warming party, inviting Vanessa, Clive, Adrian, Roger Fry, Duncan Grant and Leonard as her guests. It was a happy occasion but the excitement and the strain of writing had begun to take their toll once more, and soon she was forced to return to Miss Thomas's for a rest-cure.

Meanwhile, yet one more Cambridge man had fallen in love with Virginia, Sydney Waterlow, who had gone from Trinity to the Foreign Office but who was now aiming to be a man of letters and hoping to infiltrate Bloomsbury. He was a friend of E M Forster and a nephew of the writer Elizabeth von Armin, author of the bestselling autobiographical novel, *Elizabeth and Her German Garden* (1898). His proposal was rejected. Leonard, now deeply in love with her, was a more formidable, more persistent suitor. If she accepted his proposal, he would resign from the service and try to make his living in some other way; but if she rejected him, what then? Back to Ceylon and a Governor Generalship in 20 years' time? That was never his ambition even though it was (he was told) within his capacity. Should he perhaps continue to serve on the island in some humbler capacity in a remote outpost?

Time was running out for him. His leave was due to end soon. He could ask for an extension but not if he was then going to hand in his resignation. By the beginning of May things had reached crisis point. Virginia was in two minds as to whether or not she should marry him.

'Dearest Leonard,

...The obvious advantages of marriage stand in my way. I say to myself. Anyhow, you'll be quite happy with him; and he will give you companionship, children, and a busy life—then I say By God, I will not look upon marriage as a profession. The only people who know of it, all think it suitable; and that makes me scrutinise my own motives all the more. Then, of course, I feel angry sometimes at the strength of your desire. Possibly, your being a Jew comes in also at this point. You seem so foreign. And then I am fearfully unstable. I pass from hot to cold in an instant, without any reason; except that I believe sheer physical effort and exhaustion influence me. All I can say is that in spite of these feelings which go chasing each other all day long when I am with you, there is some feeling which is permanent, and growing. You want to know of course whether it will ever make me marry you. How can I say? I think it will because there seems no reason why it shouldn't…'[56]

Many a man of 31 would have hesitated at this point, however much in love. Was there not too much stacked against such a marriage? But not Leonard. He was resolute and he was heartened by a letter he had received from Vanessa in whom Virginia had confided: 'You're the only person I know whom I can imagine as her husband,' Vanessa told him.[57] He resigned from the service on 7th May and resisted attempts by the Ceylon Government to get him to reconsider. He was rewarded by Virginia's acceptance of him as her husband on 29th May.

Virginia to Janet Case (June 1912):

'I want to tell you that I'm going to marry Leonard Woolf—he is a penniless Jew. He was a friend of Thoby's,—and I'm so happy…'[58]

Up to now, Virginia had been instinctively anti-Semitic and some of her friends—Clive Bell, Jacques Raverat, Rupert Brooke (Hilaire Belloc, whose writings were rife with anti-Semitism, was one of his heroes)—aggressively so. She went to tea with her future in-laws in Putney, an ordeal that she bore bravely. She was marrying Leonard, not his family; something he understood. Even so, it was cruel of him not to invite his mother to be present at the wedding ceremony that took place at the St Pancras Register Office on Saturday 10th August 1912 . She never forgave him for that. Clive was there with Vanessa, who interrupted the proceedings by saying to the Registrar she wanted to change her son's name to Quentin. 'One thing at a time, madam,' he replied. There was a lunch afterwards at which George and Gerald Duckworth came to toast their stepsister and her husband.

Life with Leonard

. . .interior decorations for bedrooms, nurseries etc, furniture, textiles, hand dyed dress materials, trays, fans and other objects. . . *Roger Fry's list of items for sale at the opening of the Omega Workshops in 1913*

Life with Leonard

They had six weeks of honeymooning, in Somerset, France, Spain and Italy. Pet names replaced Christian ones. The little Goat of HPG became a mandrill, Leonard, her mongoose. The marriage was a profound fulfilment for both parties save in the area often regarded as being of supreme importance to a marriage, the sexual. Virginia seems to have been unable to banish the memory of George's incestuous gropings as she lay on her marriage bed. Sex gave her no joy, but she revelled in the intellectual companionship, the understanding, the sensitivity of her adoring husband and the pleasures of exploring territory where neither of them had been before.

Virginia to Ottoline Morrell 17th August 1912: '...we are both as happy as we can be—at least I am—I suppose one oughtn't to say that of ones husband—but I think we do get an enormous amount of pleasure out of being together.'[59]

She felt that being married to Leonard had not altered her essential self except that she now had someone permanently at her side upon whom to vent her frustrations, as she explained three weeks later in a letter from Saragossa to Ka Cox: 'Why do you think people make such a fuss about marriage and copulation? Why do some of our friends change upon losing chastity? Possibly my great age [30] makes it less of a catastrophe; but certainly I find the climax immensely exaggerated. Except for sustained good humour (Leonard shan't see this) due to the fact that every twinge of anger is at once visited upon my husband, I might still be Miss S.'[60]

Should they try to have children? Virginia told Vanessa: 'I

Leonard Woolf at the offices of the Hogarth Press
Previous pages: The Omega Workshops interior

greatly envy you your brats.'[61] She would, she sometimes felt, have liked some of her own, and Leonard, surely, was made to be a father. They decided to put off a decision for the present. Meanwhile, Leonard had completed his novel *The Village in the Jungle*, set in the Ceylon he loved and had given up for good. Its characters were local tribesmen and women whose existence is one of bare subsistence working the soil but who suffer from violent passions of love and revenge. He had sent it to Edward Arnold, grandson of Thomas Arnold, the famous headmaster of Rugby, who had published E M Forster's *Howards End* in 1910.

Leonard's main employment for the present was as secretary to Roger Fry's second Post-Impressionist exhibition, a follow-up to the notorious first, with 36 paintings by Cézanne this time, and including work by contemporary British artists selected by Clive Bell. Among those he chose were paintings by Roger himself, Wyndham Lewis, Spencer Gore, Henry Lamb, Stanley Spencer, sculptures by Eric Gill, six paintings by Duncan Grant and four by Vanessa.

She had by now acquired a small reputation as an artist through works she had shown at exhibitions held by the Friday Club and at the New English Art Club. One of Vanessa's earliest paintings 'Iceland Poppies', a still life, shown there in 1909, had attracted the attention of Walter Sickert, the leading artist among a group of painters who had their studios in Fitzroy Street, not far away from the Bells in Gordon Square. He was friendly with them but had not realised that Vanessa, with whom he was wont to discuss his complicated love life, was an artist. 'I can't get over your wife being an interesting painter,' he told Clive and to Vanessa he said enthusiastically '*Continuez.*' (Carry on!)[62] Sickert's friendship with them survived his reservations about Roger Fry's 1910 Exhibition, in particular his contempt for the work of Matisse.

His exhortation to Vanessa was gratifying but unnecessary, as she was strongly motivated, working long hours in her studio in Gordon Square. Her still life 'Apples: 46 Gordon Square' (1909–10) showing three apples on a blue and white Chinese dish with a glimpse of the Square through a window, reveals how much bolder Vanessa had become in her composition since the earlier still life. However, it was Duncan's rapidly maturing art rather than hers that drew critical comment in the press, a fate that continued throughout their lives. Vanessa never resented this as she regarded his gift as superior. He had, as we have seen, been an inmate of the Brunswick Square household run by Virginia before she and Leonard were married. Duncan and Frederick Etchells had decorated the room occupied by Maynard Keynes. Frederick was a friend of Roger's, an architect and designer who had spent time in France where he had sought out Picasso and Braque. He and Duncan had covered the whole of Maynard's room with a mural depicting a London street in the pointillist manner (paint applied in a myriad of dots). Duncan's own large murals, 'Dancers' and 'Football', containing athletic human figures in rhythmic patterns, made in 1911 as part of a design project for the Borough Polytechnic, London, had brought his work to the attention of the public. Duncan had also painted portraits of Adrian Stephen

Duncan Grant at Garsington

and one of Virginia in an Edwardian hat and shawl, his only portrait of her. It was painted rapidly in one sitting when she was visiting Vanessa.[63] Throughout her life Virginia strongly disliked being painted or photographed though, fortunately, she was not, as we shall see, always able to avoid it.

Critics reviewing the British contribution to the Second Post-Impressionist exhibition singled Duncan out. Here his gift for portraiture was again to be seen, in 'Seated Woman', a painting of a large female in a long dress, with eyes downcast and hands in her lap, for which the model was Ka Cox, of whom he made several other portraits, and 'Pamela', a portrait he had made of one of Roger's daughters. The critics thought Duncan's future was as an English Impressionist.

Roger Fry was concerned to point out in the catalogue that the artists exhibited 'do not seek to imitate form, but to create form, not to imitate life but to find an equivalent for life.' Although, after the initial shock two years before, some of the more perceptive critics had begun to see that Cézanne's influence was there to stay, this idea had not yet got across to the general public. Leonard sat at the table in the main room of the gallery, listening to and himself the object of as much insulting comment as Desmond MacCarthy had endured.

Roger had contributed a chapter to the book *Socialism and the Great State*, edited by H G Wells and published in 1912, where he opined that in an ideal world 'the painter's means of livelihood would probably be some craft in which his artistic powers would be constantly occupied, though at a lower tension and in a humbler way.' The artist needed to earn enough money to pay the bills without corrupting his talent. Roger decided to set up a workshop that would employ genuine artists to design and decorate household artefacts for sale at prices affordable by members of the general public. Thus the Omega Workshops opened for business on 14th May 1913 at 33 Fitzroy Square. Apart from its mainstays, Duncan and Vanessa, among the artists who became associated with it during its four years of active life were Henri Gaudier-Brzeska, E McKnight Kauffer, Paul Nash, David Bomberg, William Roberts, Mark Gertler, Frederick Etchells and Edward Wadsworth. All the work was presented anonymously.

The staff was recruited from students at the Slade, whom Virginia called 'crop heads' on account of their bobbed hairstyles. One of them, Barbara Hiles, dark and attractive, we shall meet as the Woolfs' assistant when they begin their home-based publishing. The Wagnerian bachelor, Apostle and civil servant, Saxon Sydney-Turner, fell hopelessly in love with her and consulted Virginia for sessions of counselling about his passion. Another was Dorothy Brett, the sister of Lord Esher, and a third Dora Carrington. They had all been students at the Slade at the same time as Mark Gertler, the London-born son of East European Jewish immigrants, who had fallen in love with Carrington (as she became known). She, overcoming much reluctance, eventually became his mistress. Carrington showed some of her work to Roger Fry who advised her not to try to become a painter, a rare failure of discernment on his part.

Duncan designed an invitation card for the Omega's opening in December 1913. In Roger's elegant lettering, potential customers were 'invited to an exhibition of decorative art... examples of interior decorations for bedrooms, nurseries etc, furniture, textiles, hand dyed dress materials trays fans and other objects suitable for Christmas presents.' The venture caught on among the fashionable and the famous. Duncan's tray, inlaid with a drawing of a woman riding an elephant, was much in demand. Bernard Shaw bought one. Vanessa made patterns for fabrics; Roger designed and painted wooden chairs.

With the example of the Omega Workshops and the beneficial effect it had had on Vanessa's morale before him, Leonard began to wonder whether he and Virginia might not do something similarly practical. If they learnt to print, they could publish work from home that commercial publishers would eschew: such as limited editions of poetry, essays and short stories. Typesetting and the technique of printing would be a perfect occupation for Virginia to channel her surplus nervous energy into when she was not writing.

He and Virginia returned to Asheham House with two dogs and two servants, while for their London base they secured rooms at Clifford's Inn near St Paul's Cathedral. Virginia came to love living in the city as much as in the country. There was always so much to observe in its ancient streets and she was in easy range of the London Library in St James's Square (the subscription library founded in the Victorian period where her father had succeeded Tennyson as its president) and Days circulating library in Mount Street, Mayfair, that she used for recent fiction. Here is her account of her life on Wednesday 13ᵗʰ January 1915:

'I caused some slight argument (with L.) this morning by trying to cook my breakfast in bed. I believe, however, that the good sense of the proceeding will make it prevail; that is, if I can dispose of the eggshells. L. went off to the New Statesman office this morning with his article. I lunched here, & then went to Days, to get more books. Days at 4 in the afternoon is the haunt of fashionable ladies, who want to be told what to read. A more despicable set of creatures I never saw. They come in furred like seals & scented like civets, condescend to pull a few novels about on the counter, & then demand languidly whether there is *anything* amusing? The Days' assistants are the humblest & most servile of men—They tow these aged Countesses & pert young millionairesses about behind them, always deferential & profuse of "Ladyships". The West End of London fills me with aversion; I look into motor cars & see the fat grandees inside, like portly jewels in satin cases. The afternoons now have an elongated pallid look, as if it were neither winter nor spring. I came back to tea. L. arrived—having seen Gordon Sqre & Maynard (who says German finance is crumbling) & Saxon, who is recovering from Influenza. He (Leonard) had a headache, so, instead of going to the Co-op meeting, we are staying at home.'⁶⁴

Apart from reading novels she had been busy writing one. Leonard handed the final draft of *The Voyage Out* to Duckworth and Co on 9ᵗʰ March 1912. Edward Garnett, Gerald's colleague, the foremost literary adviser of the time, read it, recognised Virginia's genius and recommended publication.

When Virginia was in an upbeat mood she delighted in her married life and her devoted husband. She had, she thought, at last become liberated from all trace of the Victorian taboos of her childhood and the kind of people who stood for its conventional attitudes. She told Violet Dickinson that she found it hard now to believe in the very existence of people like Kitty Maxse, Nelly Cecil and Katie Cromer. Virginia's rejection of Kitty was such that when she encountered her at the funeral in 1916 at Hampstead of the Rev John Llewelyn Davies, that grand old man of the Church and father of such admirable offspring as the suffragist Margaret Llewelyn Davies, she cut her. It was a callous way on Virginia's part of proclaiming her maturity.

The women who formed part of Virginia's present world were those with a commitment to the cause of social justice like Margaret Llewelyn Davies and Virginia's cousin 'Marny' Vaughan who ran a charity in Hoxton in the East End of London. After Leonard had finished with the Post-Impressionists, Marny Vaughan persuaded him to investigate some cases there of people in dire need. The human misery he discovered came as a revelation to him. It turned him from being a liberal with a small l into a socialist. Marny's charity was a small effort towards the alleviation of a vast problem, one that Leonard addressed again when he then worked with Margaret Llewelyn Davies for her Women's Cooperative Movement and travelled to the north of England to study the lives of its women members.

Unhappily his enthusiasm for this work was marred by fresh anxiety about Virginia. After a year of marriage he began to realise how deeply rooted her mental instability was. They went back to Savage but Leonard, dissatisfied with his diagnosis, consulted other doctors who specialised in nervous disorder. They were on the whole against Virginia attempting to conceive a child. By late July she was in such a bad state she returned once again as a patient to Miss Thomas's nursing home at Twickenham. What was most distressing for Leonard was that in this condition she turned on him.

He had such love for her, and insight into her illness, that he was able to withstand even her abuse of him personally without breaking down. Vanessa had been right in her view that only Leonard could have coped with Virginia as a husband. He became reconciled to a sexless marriage (a noble sacrifice for someone who had a powerful sexual drive) in which his role would be that of nurse and therapist as well as marital partner. At the same time he threw himself into his work as a political journalist and social investigator; and now he was a novelist, too. As it happened, his novel appeared before Virginia's because the doctors he consulted thought it would be unwise for Virginia's novel to be published until she was restored to health and could face the exposure it would bring and the animadversions of reviewers.

The Village in the Jungle was published in 1913. The first edition sold out and was followed by two reprintings. The book made a literary reputation for Leonard but he earned only a pittance from it. While he was finding better paid literary work in journalism, they lived off Virginia's capital, which amounted to stocks and shares valued at £9,000, yielding an annual income of just under £400. Their basic expenditure was about £700 per annum, with heavy medical fees on top of that. Both of them needed to work hard writing for the periodical press to make up the shortfall. They never seem to have considered reducing it by having only one place of residence or fewer servants. It was a precarious existence they led, though by our standards a cosseted one.

By the time *The Voyage Out* was published in March 1915 war had broken out. To begin with it made surprisingly little difference to the Woolfs' way of life. The threat of conscription loomed but was not enforced by act of Parliament until 1915. Before that young men seen walking the streets in civilian clothes were shamed into joining up by being given a white feather and they were assailed by posters showing Lord Kitchener pointing at them saying 'Your Country Needs You!' His appeal fell on deaf ears among the Bloomsbury regulars. Philip Morrell, husband of Ottoline, was alone in the House of Commons in making a stand against the war and, after it had begun, opposing the introduction of conscription through the formation of the Union of Democratic Control. The lovely Tudor and Elizabethan manor house at Garsington in Oxfordshire, which the Morrells had bid for successfully in 1913 in order to be able to entertain their friends, became a rallying-ground for the Union of Democratic Control and the pacifist movement as well as the location of a permanent house party, where one lot of eminent visitors succeeded another.

Ottoline's lover Bertrand Russell was another who spoke

out publicly against the war. That cost him his fellowship at Trinity and earned him a spell in gaol. Others, like Maynard Keynes, who was recalled to the Treasury from Cambridge, served the war effort indirectly—likewise Saxon Sydney-Turner in his government job, and Sydney Waterlow at the Foreign Office. But there was no one of old Bloomsbury (if we do not count Desmond MacCarthy) who served in the armed forces during the entire war. Compare the experience of that earlier exclusive set known as the Souls to which Herbert Asquith and Henry James belonged. Most of those who married lost sons on active service during the war.

Lytton Strachey, medically unfit for service, was researching and writing a book of essays about the Victorians at his cottage in the country. Clive Bell was ostensibly working as a farmhand on the Morrells' home farm while writing his book *Art*. Leonard was also medically unfit because of his nervous tremor. Desmond MacCarthy joined the Red Cross where he was part of an ambulance unit in France and afterwards served in naval intelligence. Roger Fry with his Quaker background was a confirmed pacifist and anyway he became 50 during the war, well above the upper age limit for conscription. He spent it keeping Omega going with difficulty, facing intemperately hostile action from disgruntled artists he had employed like Wyndham Lewis, and in his personal life losing the love of Vanessa. She had become deeply enamoured of Duncan Grant and he, though not ceasing to have serial affairs with men, was enormously fond of her. They became partners while she remained in name married to, and on amicable terms with, Clive, whose current mistress was Mary Hutchinson, the wife of St John Hutchinson, whose portrait Vanessa painted. Their urgent problem, while these various liaisons took their course, was how to prevent Duncan Grant and his current lover David (Bunny) Garnett, son of Edward and his wife Constance, the translator of Dostoevsky and Chekhov, from having to join up.

Virginia wrote to Nelly Cecil (she came to believe in her existence again in an hour of need) hoping that she might be able to put in a good word for Duncan with her brother-in-law, Lord Salisbury, who presided over the tribunal that determined exemption from call-up. Nelly regretted she was unable to help; in the end Duncan and Bunny found farm work that kept them out of the army in the part of Sussex where Leonard and Virginia lived. The farm where they worked was next to a house that was up for sale. Virginia strongly urged her sister to take it: 'It is about a mile from Firle, on that little path which leads under the downs. It has a charming garden, with a pond, and fruit trees, and vegetables, all now rather run wild, but you could make it lovely. The house is very nice with large rooms, and one room with big windows fit for a studio.'[65] This was the Charleston farmhouse that Vanessa did indeed take, where she remained with Duncan Grant for much of the rest of her life and where she brought up her children. It soon became an outpost of Bloomsbury where Clive Bell, Roger Fry and Maynard Keynes often stayed.

In January 1915, with *The Voyage Out* at last announced for publication, Leonard and Virginia were themselves considering moving yet again. They wanted somewhere more spacious in Richmond where they could install that printing press of which they dreamed. They found Hogarth House in Paradise Road, Richmond, and planned to move there in March. However, the imminent publication of her novel unsettled Virginia so much that by the beginning of that month she was as violently insane as she had ever been and once again had to be placed in a nursing home under restraint while Leonard undertook the move. She was still there when her novel was published.

By April she was back home—her new home in Richmond—in the care of nurses and gradually throughout the summer she improved. By November she was leading a normal life, writing again and reading the widespread reviews of her work. Many of them were, like her own reviews, anonymous. Her particular stamping-ground, *The Times Literary Supplement*, in a friendly notice declared that 'never was a book more feminine, more recklessly feminine', adding: 'The story of the late development of a young woman who has been too long sheltered from life is nearly always sentimental or brutal, but it is here candidly told.' *The Observer* said, 'among ordinary novels it is a wild swan among good grey geese.' *The Morning*

Post found it 'a bewildering kind of book. We get confused among a mass of people, and worried by the talk that goes on whirling around us.'[66]

More perceptive criticism came in two signed reviews, from E M Forster in the *Daily News* and Gerald Gould in the *New Statesman,* the Fabian weekly periodical started by Sidney and Beatrice Webb, to which Leonard was now a regular contributor. Forster had high praise for the book's ultimate impact on the 'curious male' reader who if wise will not try to worry out female attitudes to marriage from its pages but 'will lift his eyes to where there is neither marrying nor giving in marriage, to the mountains and forests and sea that circumscribe the characters, and to the final darkness that blots them out. After all, he will not have learnt how women live, any more than he has learnt from Shakespeare how men perform that process; he will only have lived more intensely himself, that is to say he will have encountered literature.'

Virginia must have been over the moon when she read that— but wait! 'Mrs Woolf's success is more remarkable since there is one serious defect in her equipment; her chief characters are not vivid. There is nothing false in them, but when she ceases to touch them they cease, they do not stroll out of their sentences, and even develop a tendency to merge shadowlike.'[67]

This hurt because it had some truth in it but was too sweeping. The heroine, her father, her uncle and aunt are fully realised people; the young men, her betrothed and his friend, who has much of Lytton in him, less so. Many of the surrounding characters have deftly caricatured individuality.

Gould felt Virginia's novel depicted 'a quite extraordinary world. The people are unreal, not in the sense that such people don't exist—they do—but in the sense that they give one all the impression of unreality when one meets them in life. They are sophisticated and introspective, they are learned and witty, and they are abundantly interested in themselves. Mrs Woolf's account of them is very long and very clever—so long that even the cleverness cannot always hold the attention.'[68]

A new novelist, 'Mrs Woolf' aged 33, had made an impact on the literary world of London.

Marks on the wall

—We like the wood cuts immensely. It was very good of you to bring them yourself—We have printed them off, and they make the book *[The Mark on the Wall]* much more interesting than it would have been without. The ones I like best are the servant girl and the plates, and the Snail.

Virginia to Dora Carrington, July 1917

Marks on the wall

Virginia to Vanessa: 'Our press arrived on Tuesday [April 1917]. We unpacked it with enormous excitement, finally with Nelly's [their cook's] help, carried it into the drawing room, set it on its stand—and discovered it was smashed in half! It is a great weight, and they never screwed it down; but the shop has probably got a spare part. Anyhow the arrangement of the type is such a business that we shant be able to start printing directly. One has great blocks of type, which have to be divided into their separate letters, and fonts, and then put into the right partitions. The work of ages, especially when you mix the h's with the ns, as I did yesterday.'[69]

Their first publication in July, at 1/6d (15p) per copy, had inscribed on its title page: 'Two Stories/ written and printed/ by/ Virginia Woolf and L.S. Woolf/ Hogarth Press/ Richmond/ 1917'. It was a paperbound booklet of 32 pages in an edition of 150 copies. By the end of July 125 copies had been purchased. Leonard's story was entitled 'Three Jews' and Virginia's 'The Mark on the Wall'. 'I must say,' wrote Leonard in 1964, 'looking at a copy of this curious publication today, that the printing is rather creditable for two persons who had taught themselves for a month in a dining-room.'[70]

No review copies were distributed but Virginia did not lack feedback from her Bloomsbury friends. One of the warmest letters came from that Garsington farm hand, Clive Bell, particularly gratifying, she told him, because he was 'the first person who ever thought I'd write well.'[71] Lytton Strachey was no less enthusiastic: 'The liquidity of the style

Katherine Mansfield: close friend and rival author 1920
Previous pages: Dora Carrington in the garden at Garsington 1920

fills me with envy: really some of the sentences!—How on earth does she make the English language float and float? And then the wonderful way in which the modern point of view is suggested. Tiens!'[72]

Here for the first time in Virginia's work is the prose of free association. One would have to go back to Laurence Sterne to find writing that made its point so waywardly, so inconsequentially. Her piece was more of a rumination than a story, a thought-chain prompted by a mark on the wall. Approximately 5,000 words in length, it contains the seeds of much of Virginia's later work and style.

It begins with an attempt to fix the time when the narrator first saw a mark on the wall. She remembers the fire, the yellow light on the book she was reading and the three chrysanthemums in the glass bowl on the mantelpiece. This initial scene, the 'reality' from which all that follows is a departure, might be a painting by Vanessa: 'Virginia in armchair, reading, in the drawing room at Hogarth House'.

Her eye then turns to the burning coals of the fire and she is involuntarily whisked back to childhood. There was a fire in the grate of the drawing room at Hyde Park Gate; flames lapping around the black coal became a 'cavalcade of red knights riding up the side of the black rock.' (The novels of Scott read out to her by her father contain cavalcades of crusader knights.) She is glad to be released from this childish fixation by the mark on the wall that captivates her present thoughts.

Was it made by a nail on which to hang a picture frame? It would have had to be a small picture, a miniature perhaps 'of a lady with white powdered curls, powder-dusted cheeks, and lips like red carnations' (at Versailles, mistress of one of Virginia's aristocratic ancestors?). Did the last occupants hang such a picture? To judge from the one occasion the writer met them, when she first viewed Hogarth House, they were interesting people. The husband told her that in his opinion art should have ideas behind it. She was about to take him up on this (a topic dear to Virginia, Roger, Clive) when they 'were torn asunder' and she never saw him again.

Tearings-asunder, beginnings with no endings, moments left hanging for the mind to ponder (what in movies is known as a jump cut) were to become a crucial feature of her fiction. As she developed, the jump cut became the alternative to linear narrative, cause and effect worked to a conclusion. Other instances of tearing-asunder, she cites, are moments in other peoples' houses observed from the window of a moving train. Life is like being 'blown through the Tube [still a novel means of transport] at fifty miles an hour' or like a brown paper parcel pitched down the chute in the post office [parcels posted at Richmond Post Office containing copies of Hogarth publications sent to subscribers]. One is a mere passive object until one stops to reflect.

Then, reflecting, the narrator continues: what of the after life? There will be nothing when one is under ground 'but spaces of light and dark, intersected by thick stalks, and rather higher-up perhaps, rose-shaped blots of an indistinct colour—dim pinks and blues—which will, as time goes on, become more definite, become—I don't know what...' And so back to the mark. Perhaps it is just a tiny black leaf left over from summer, sticking to a wall that she 'not being a very vigilant housekeeper' should have dusted away? She notices the accumulated dust on the mantelpiece; from which she jump cuts to Troy and the dust that covers it: 'only fragments of pots' remain as testimony of its existence 'utterly refusing annihilation...' Her mind moves freely in time from present, to history, and to pre-history. She has her own way of refusing annihilation: 'I want to think quietly, calmly, spaciously, never to be interrupted, never to have to rise from my chair, to slip easily from one thing to another, without any sense of hostility, or obstacle. I want to sink deeper and deeper, away from the surface, with its hard separate facts. To steady myself, let me catch hold of the first idea that passes...'

This first idea is of Shakespeare. She fantasises a picture of Shakespeare at work: the literary imagination, its power to combine disparate experience into a meaningful whole. Dissatisfied with this she reverts to her own situation, the impression she reckons she makes on other people, how one tries to reflect credit on oneself.

She remarked that the seed of a flower she had seen growing on the site of an old house in Kingsway must have been sown in the reign of Charles I. 'All the time I'm dressing up the figure of myself in my own mind, lovingly, stealthily.' Our obsession with our self-image is something that 'the novelists in future will realise more and more the importance of...leaving the description of reality more and more out of their stories, taking a knowledge of it for granted, as the Greeks did and Shakespeare perhaps...' After this quasi-manifesto she returns to those 'descriptions of reality' that as a child at HPG Virginia took for reality itself: 'Sunday in London, Sunday afternoon walks, Sunday luncheons, and also ways of speaking of the dead.' What takes the place of these realities now? Here the future author of *The Waves*, an experiment in fictional meditation, gives way to the future author of *Three Guineas*, a topical polemic. Present reality consists of 'Men perhaps, should you be a woman; the masculine point of view which governs our lives, which sets the standard, which establishes Whitaker's Table of Precedency, [decreeing that on a state occasion the Archbishop of Canterbury takes precedence over the Lord Chancellor and so on] which has become, I suppose, since the war half a phantom to many men and women, which soon, one may hope, will be laughed into the dustbin where the phantoms go, the mahogany sideboards, and the Landseer prints, Gods, and Devils, Hell and so forth, leaving us all with an intoxicating sense of illegitimate freedom—if freedom exists...'

No wonder Lytton Strachey, who was putting the finishing touches to *Eminent Victorians*, his quartet of essays that would confine imperial precedence to the dustbin, admired this writing. Virginia was too pure an artist to end on this shrill note of invective. She returned once more to the mark. It seems to protrude slightly and in a certain light to cast a shadow 'a smooth tumulus [she is getting warmer] like those barrows on the South Downs which are, they say, either tombs or camps.' She employs a photographic distortion, blowing-up a small form to reveal its resemblance to a larger one.

The narrator's musings are brought to an end by the intrusion of present reality; someone (Leonard) is standing over her and saying:

'"I'm going out to buy a newspaper."

"Yes?"

"Though it's no good buying newspapers...Nothing ever happens. Curse this war; God damn this war!...All the same, I don't see why we should have a snail on our wall."

Ah, the mark on the wall! It was a snail.'

Dora Carrington (who insisted on being known solely by her surname) decorated the booklet with woodcuts, for which she was paid fifteen shillings. She had become infatuated by Lytton Strachey, in spite of knowing he was wholeheartedly homosexual. Carrington's passion for Strachey was not unlike Vanessa's for Duncan Grant. Now she was looking for a place in the country where she and Lytton could live together, an arrangement of which Bloomsbury disapproved, though it would be funded by Bloomsbury friends such as Maynard Keynes. She found Mill House at Tidmarsh in Berkshire, into which the odd couple moved at the end of the year. For the present Carrington sacrificed not only her freedom but also the full-time pursuit of her career as an artist in looking after the increasingly frail Lytton day and night.

This cursed war had begun by now to impinge on Virginia. Air raids, a perilous novelty, disrupted life in London. Richmond was vulnerable. There were direct hits. The Woolfs repaired to the cellar with the servants until the bugles sounded the all clear. Essential food such as butter and meat was scarce and so was fuel. Virginia met Marny Vaughan, who told her in a harangue how she had tramped the streets in search of coal but had found none for sale anywhere. Then Marny ran into Kitty Maxse to whom she confessed her plight. That same afternoon Kitty arrived at Marny's house in a taxi with two sacks of coal. Kitty was a frequent hospital visitor, raising the morale of those men who had come back mutilated from the Front, and inviting some of the walking wounded to her house in the Cromwell Road (where she had moved) to take tea while she played the piano to them.

The war had even begun to make itself felt in Sussex, where German prisoners could be seen at work in the fields, and at Garsington to where one walking wounded officer, the poet Siegfried Sassoon, had been invited. Ottoline had fallen in love with him, but to little avail. He was homosexual (though he married late in life and fathered a son). Disillusioned with the way the war was being handled by the High Command, and with encouragement from the Garsington regulars, he had denounced the generals in a letter published in a newspaper. He was reconciled to being court martialled for this offence but thanks to Edward Marsh, Winston Churchill's secretary and a patron of contemporary poets, who was approached by Ottoline, and after a complicated chain of events involving, too, the intervention of another army poet, Robert Graves, Sassoon was 'given a medical board'. Certified as suffering from neurasthenia, he was sent to Craiglockhart Hospital, a rehabilitation centre, near Edinburgh where he met Wilfred Owen, a fellow-patient, also writing anti-war poems.

The Woolfs had not yet been to Garsington and had not met one of its more recent acquisitions, the New Zealand-born short-story writer Katherine Mansfield, a pretty young woman with a sleek crown of jet-black hair cut in a fringe and a love of wearing fragrant scent, the partner of the earnest young writer John Middleton Murry. He was then employed at the war office in intelligence, vetting and translating German documents. Katherine, whose family surname was Beauchamp, was a cousin of Elizabeth von Arnim. Elizabeth's sister had married a city merchant named Waterlow whose son Sydney, the would-be member of Bloomsbury, was turned down as a husband by Virginia. In 1914 he and Desmond MacCarthy published an English version, *Nobody Dies*, of the novel *Mort de quelqu'un* by the French writer Jules Romains. In a dedicatory letter to Roger Fry of the translation, Desmond wrote: 'because you believe that something analogous to Post-Impressionism is possible and desirable in literature, because in M. Jules Romains' work there is a flavour of it, we dedicate this translation to you.'

The novel recounts the death of an engine driver, an obscure Parisian, whose passing brings many disparate individuals together through his funeral and its aftermath. It gave expression to the notion of 'unanimism' (group or collective consciousness). Romains was the author of *La Vie Unanime* (*The Collective Life*, 1909) and leader of the unanimist school of French writers. Waterlow was a Cambridge friend of E M Forster through whom Forster became the tutor in Germany to the Baroness von Arnim's children before he became a writer. In his review of *The Voyage Out* Forster made a comparison with *Nobody Dies* and detected a similar sense of group consciousness in Virginia's novel. It was a shrewd insight. This unanimist element was to become more marked as Virginia's fiction developed.

But to return to the other writer in the Beauchamp family, Katherine Mansfield—she was six years younger than Virginia. She had met Lytton at Garsington and told him how much she admired *The Voyage Out*. When they eventually met, Virginia, nauseated by the scent Mansfield wore, told Vanessa that she 'seems to me an unpleasant but forcible and utterly unscrupulous character.'[73] On further acquaintance, the hostility changed to mutual empathy, especially when Virginia learned the details of Katherine's extraordinary life. 'She seems to have gone every sort of hog since she was 17...'[74] Virginia commented. The 'hogs' consisted of an education at Queen's College, Harley Street, where she acquired a lifelong female companion, Ida Baker; an early marriage that soon fell apart; a Polish lover who infected her with gonorrhoea; writing unpaid for *The New Age*, an influential minority literary periodical whose editor, the Yorkshireman A R Orage, was first to discern her gift but then turned against her when she began to publish elsewhere, notably in *Rhythm*, an arts periodical started by Murry when he was still a student at Oxford.

Her 'hogs' with Murry consisted of various cheap lodgings and apartments in London and Cornwall, interrupted by sojourns in Italy and France in search of a warmer, drier climate on account of the TB she had also contracted. The final 'hog' would consist of their marriage in May 1918 when her divorce from her first husband became absolute. Along with all these 'hogs' she sustained a consistently high level of work.

Her chosen form of the short story suited her fits and starts way of life. She had the power of bringing acutely observed character to life in a few sentences through an exquisite ear for dialogue, but the massive haul of a novel seemed beyond her capacity. She had completed a long short story entitled 'Prelude', an account of her family's move in New Zealand during her childhood that she had been unable to place; the Woolfs were happy to agree to publish it.

Katherine arrived at Asheham for a weekend in August 1917 with most of the typescript. As she and Virginia walked across the South Downs in a high wind, Virginia could not help feeling there was an aura of what she called 'the underground' about Katherine. Virginia implied by that, a term she had coined, the shady Grub Street world of writers who churned out potboilers, met in teashops, and were perpetually in debt, but this was redeemed by a romantic streak in her. It emerged, she told Ottoline, when 'she describes your garden, the rose leaves drying in the sun, the pool, and long conversations between people wandering up and down in the moonlight.'[75] The next piece of fiction that Virginia wrote was a sketch of people wandering up and down past a flowerbed having long conversations, the setting being 'Kew Gardens' (the work's title). The Woolfs often went to the Gardens, which were in walking distance of their Richmond house.

It seems highly likely, from the evidence of a letter from Katherine to Ottoline, that the two women writers discussed the possibility of such a story, mooted by Katherine. Yet it was Virginia who actually wrote it (the moral being that if you have a good idea when you are with another writer, keep it under your hat). Katherine seems to have borne no resentment of the snatch (if such it was) and admired Virginia's story: 'Yes, your Flower Bed is *very* good. There's a still quivering changing light over it all and a sense of those couples dissolving in the bright air which fascinates me...'[76]

Katherine's story 'Prelude' ran to 26 pages and the Woolfs felt they needed to hire an assistant to help them to set it. The first one, Alix Sargant-Florence, a Newnham graduate who had also been a student at the Slade for a year and a friend of

Carrington's, resigned after one day's work but then became a research assistant for Leonard who was busy compiling reports published in the *New Statesman* on the effects of the war on industry and the influence on industry of the Cooperative Movement. Alix was replaced by Barbara Hiles, the former Slade crophead from the Omega Workshop, who became for a while a mainstay of the Hogarth Press. From her great age of 35 Virginia regarded Barbara and Alix as the younger generation, 'hypnotised' by Bloomsbury. She enjoyed observing the progress of their love affairs. Alix benefited from a change of sexual orientation in James Strachey, whom she married in 1920. Barbara, torn between the adoration of the Bloomsbury veteran Saxon Sydney-Turner and Nick Bagenal, an officer in the Irish guards, chose Nick as her husband in 1918; soon afterwards he was severely wounded in Flanders but survived to return and recover.

Gordon Square under Maynard Keynes's tenancy continued to be where Bloomsbury veterans congregated, as were the Omega's premises, but a more recent venue popular with the younger people was provided by the 1917 Club, founded by Leonard and others at the end of that year with premises in Gerrard Street, Soho. Its membership of men and women included left-wing politicians like Ramsay Macdonald and intellectuals alongside Virginia, Clive Bell, Lytton Strachey, Barbara Hiles (later Bagenal) and Alix Sargant-Florence (later Strachey).

There was now much talk of the need for reconstruction after the war ended. Leonard joined the board of the journal *War and Peace* where the new post-war international order was discussed. Virginia was a frequent visitor to the 1917 Club. She recorded the people she met there in her Diary, a continuous running commentary on her life with lengthy entries for most days. If she had written nothing else, this vast work, kept up every year until she died with some gaps, and published in full posthumously, would secure her a place among the major 20th–century writers. Her insights into her own state of mind and the vivid, witty, acerbic pen-portraits of other people are a constant delight though some readers have been put off by the flashes of malice in it.

Here is sample from 3rd January 1918: '...we went to the 17 Club Dinner [held after the first general meeting]; a great deal of eating by some 200 people at long tables [actually 120 according to Leonard]. Waiters thudding swing doors imitated guns so successfully that various officials came round & warned one of a raid. Jos. [Josiah Wedgwood of the Staffordshire pottery family, Liberal MP for Newcastle-under-Lyme and father of seven children by his wife Ethel whom he was in the process of divorcing] made a speech. I noticed poor Marjorie [Strachey, Lytton's sister much in love with Jos. whom she hoped to marry but never did] listening with eyes on her lap. She came up from Darlington, & was dressed, poor creature, in muslin picked out with red roses & cut low; though everyone else was more or less in working clothes, & fur capes. I was caught in the net of Sylvia Whitham [born Milman, granddaughter of Henry Milman, dean of St Paul's, part of Virginia's Hyde Park Gate girlhood, and now married to John Mills Whitham, author of a novel *Wolfgang*, published the year before], who cross-examined me about her husbands novels; & in despair of revealing my true opinion I pretended never to have read *Wolfgang*—Most suitably, of all our friends shes the one to have a bomb dropped next door, & to receive it without surprise. And she's taking to literature, & begins translating Flaubert—a remarkable instance of a person without gift of any kind, always pushing along in the wake of more advanced people.'[77]

Virginia's energy was phenomenal. Apart from the Diary, there were often five or six letters penned during the day, hundreds of them over the years to Vanessa. The tedious topic of Virginia's domestic staff who were always about to leave but usually relented at the last moment occupies many thousands of words. That was her private writing. Her professional writing consisted of reviews for *The Times Literary Supplement*, which now began to spread over 2,000 or 3,000 words, appraisals of the major authors of English literature occasioned by a new book of which her appraisal was in part a review. When not at her desk, she made regular journeys to Hampstead to see Katherine Mansfield, who had become a close and sadly ill friend, and to Janet Case and Margaret Llewelyn Davies, still working tirelessly for the Women's Cooperative Guild. A branch of it met at Hogarth House with Virginia chairing the meetings. But above all else, with fresh confidence acquired from the reception of *The Voyage Out,* Virginia was at work on a new novel. Her madness was happily a thing of the past, but she suffered sometimes from severe headaches that forced her to spend days in bed.

Katherine's story should have been the Woolfs' second publication but in fact it was their third. It was preceded by a book of poems for private circulation by Leonard's brother Cecil who had been killed in action in 1917; his youngest brother Philip had been wounded by the same shell. The labour of setting Mansfield's *Prelude* was finally completed in July 1917 and 300 copies were printed, price 3/6d. 'We have sent off our first copies this evening, after spending the afternoon in glueing & covering,' Virginia told her Diary on 10th July. 'They surprised us when done by their professional look—the stiff blue cover pleases us particularly. I must read the book through after dinner, partly to find possible faults, but also to make up my mind how much I like it as literature.'[78] Its literary merit was recognised but sales were slow.

In the meantime, Mansfield and Murry's relations with Garsington had been soured through the reception of another new work, Sassoon's *Counter-Attack* containing his anti-war poems. Murry had, to the fury of Ottoline, reviewed it unfavourably (and anonymously) in the *Nation*. Virginia was dragged into the row in July when she and Leonard spent their first weekend at Garsington and Virginia was accused of agreeing with Murry, but that little fracas did not spoil the weekend. 'Happily the weather was fine, the food good, & we flowed about happily enough, & without serious boredom, which is more than one can ask of a week-end. In fact, for some reason I was rather well content. My bed was like layer upon layer of the most springy turf; & then the garden is almost melodramatically perfect, with its grey oblong pool, & pink farm buildings, its soft whitish grey stone & enormous smooth dense green yew hedges.'[79]

Then Virginia read Katherine's story 'Bliss' in the *English Review* of August and she threw the periodical down in disgust: 'She's done for!…the whole conception is poor, cheap, not the vision, however imperfect, of an interesting mind. She writes badly too.'[80] This nonsensical snap judgment was inspired by professional jealousy. Katherine had stolen a march on Virginia by appearing in this prestigious magazine, originally edited by Ford Madox Ford and now by Austin Harrison (son of Leslie Stephen's friend Frederic Harrison). She was paid six guineas for her story (much more than the minute royalty from *Prelude*). Virginia's reaction to 'Bliss' did not put an end to their friendship however; it flourished in the midst of their literary rivalry. They had so much in common, not least their magical power over words. Virginia continued to make regular visits to Katherine in Hampstead for as long as she was well enough to see people. The Woolfs arranged to publish an essay by Murry, 'The Critic in Judgment', on their press.

They were back in Hogarth House when on 11th November 1918 the armistice was signed. 'Twenty-five minutes ago the guns went off, announcing peace. A siren hooted on the river. They are hooting still. A few people ran to look out of windows. The rooks wheeled round and round, & were for a moment, the symbolic look of creatures performing some ceremony, partly of thanksgiving, partly of valediction over the grave.'[81]

Among the celebrations was a party given by the rich patron of the arts Montague Shearman at his house near the Strand. Sir Osbert Sitwell, a captain in the Grenadier Guards, arrived at it in the company of the dancer Massine and the great impresario and choreographer Diaghilev, whose ballet company was performing in London. They drove there in a taxi impeded by the massed cheering crowds. Here is how Sitwell recalled the occasion:

'Eventually we reached the Adelphi. The spacious Adam room, covered with decoration as fine as a cobweb, was hung inappropriately with a few large pictures of the Paris school—by Matisse, for example—and by several of the Bloomsbury Group, its satellite and English Correspondent. There were a number of paintings, for instance, by Mark Gertler—at that moment an artist much patronised by the *cognoscenti*: (heavy designs of Mile-End-Road figures, very stiff but oily, of trees fleshy in their aspect, under the solid shade of which trod ape-like beings, or still-lives, apples and pears of an incomparable rosy rotundity falling sideways off cardboard cloths—yet these possessed some kind of quality).'[82]

This bandying of the term 'Bloomsbury Group', including people who were not strictly speaking part of it, was already in current use. Gertler was never a member in spite of his long involvement with Carrington. He had, though, contributed work such as woodcuts to decorate artefacts sold by Omega. Roger Fry's conception of Omega was that it should be a much broader church artistically than that represented by the Bloomsbury artists (himself, Duncan and Vanessa). Earlier that year Gertler had been to dinner with the Woolfs in the company of his friend, S S Koteliansky, always known as Kot. Both were Jewish and of Eastern European background though Gertler was born in London. Kot, who made a living by translating Russian literature, was also a close friend of Katherine Mansfield and Middleton Murry. Virginia had warmed to both of them. Osbert Sitwell's account of the Armistice parties continues: '...All equally, soldiers, Bloomsbury beauties, and conscientious objectors—all except Diaghilew [*sic*]—danced. I remember the tall, flagging figure of my friend Lytton Strachey, with his rather narrow, angular beard, long inquisitive nose...jigging about with amiable debility. He was, I think, unused to dancing...'[83]

The Woolfs were not present on that occasion, but Virginia met Osbert and his brother Sacheverell for the first time soon afterwards in October. They invited her to a party at the house in Chelsea they shared with their sister Edith, the poet. Leonard had a dinner engagement he did not wish to break that evening and arranged to meet Virginia afterwards in Sloane Square so that they could return home together.

Attending such a fashionable gathering without his support was an ordeal that Virginia felt she triumphantly overcame:

'That very morning a review by me of Edith Sitwell's poems had appeared in the Times. It's strange how whole groups of people suddenly swim complete into one's life. This group to which Gertler & Mary H. [Hutchinson, current mistress of Clive Bell] are attached was unknown to me a year ago. I surveyed them with considerable, almost disquieting calm. What is there to be excited about, or to quarrel over, in a party like this, I asked myself; & found myself saying the most maternal things to Gertler, who was wearing evening dress... for the first time. We stood & compared our sensations. Edith Sitwell is a very tall young woman, wearing a permanently startled expression, & curiously finished off with a high green silk headdress, concealing her hair, so that it is not known whether she has any. Otherwise I was familiar with everyone, I think. Nina Hamnet [the artist], Mary H., Jack H. [Mary's husband, J T] Sheppard [a Cambridge friend and fellow-Apostle of Lytton's. He worked at the war office during the war and lived at Gordon Square. A scholar of ancient Greek and a don, he became Provost of King's College, Cambridge in 1933.] Norton [Henry, another Cambridge don and Apostle, a mathematician and early member of Bloomsbury] & so forth. I found myself discoursing to Sheppard about Sophocles. Never before have I seen him even momentarily serious.

"I think of nothing but Greek plays, he said, & people—And I'm not sure that I don't always see people as if they were in Greek plays." I liked him better than before; still I think he found it awkward to stand discussing Sophocles seriously; & so we parted. My complete mastery of evening parties is shown by the indifference with which I am deserted, [i.e. she did not mind being deserted; perhaps she was not quite so indifferent as she makes out] & the composure with which I decide upon my next choice. I was a good deal impressed by this; & how calmly too, I looked at my watch, & saw it was time to leave, & went out alone, & drove to Sloane Square, not excited, not depressed, but contemplative & introspective.'[84]

The early post-war period was a time of definition for the

Bloomsberries. Several of them arrived at landmarks in their careers and, as we have seen, they had become famous—or was it infamous?—as a group. In December Leonard sealed his reputation as a foreign affairs specialist by becoming editor of the *International Review* and publishing a book, *After the War*. Maynard Keynes, in despair at the terms imposed on the defeated enemy, walked out of the Paris Peace Conference, resigned from government service, and wrote his seminal work, *The Economic Consequences of the Peace*, while staying at Charleston, before returning to Cambridge as a don. Lytton Strachey acquired universal notoriety after the publication of *Eminent Victorians*, whose booming sales necessitated several reprints (to Virginia's envy). Clive Bell published a book of criticism, reprinted journalism candidly called *Pot-Boilers*, in which he described Virginia (on the strength of one published novel) as being as great a novelist as Hardy and Conrad. Desmond MacCarthy published a similar book of reprints, *Remnants*.

T S Eliot, then working in the foreign department of Lloyds Bank and editing its *Review*, had published *Prufrock and Other Observations*, his first book of poems, with *The Egoist*, a literary magazine edited by Ezra Pound, in an edition of 500 copies in 1917. The Woolfs admired the work and, when they heard from Roger that Eliot lacked a regular publisher, wrote to him and arranged to bring out a book of his poems. Harriet Shaw Weaver, the American patroness behind *The Egoist*, sent them the typescript of James Joyce's *Ulysses*. It had been turned down by every publisher in London, who all feared prosecution. The Woolfs turned it down, too, for this reason and on account of its length. For a similar reason, fear of an obscenity charge, no publisher would bring out D H Lawrence's novel *Women in Love*, the sequel to his *The Rainbow*, in which he satirised Ottoline Morrell, having fully availed himself of her hospitality and financial support. Ottoline's hand was continually being bitten by those she had fed. Katherine Mansfield and Middleton Murry had become intimate friends of D H Lawrence and Frieda. Murry admired Lawrence as a man and a writer to the point of idolatry, but by now relations between the Lawrences and the Murrys were even more fraught and complex than those between the Woolfs and the Murrys.

Murry himself, on relinquishing his job at the War Office, where he had been highly successful, had had an enormous stroke of good fortune. He was appointed editor of the weekly *Athenaeum* (a journal rooted in Victorian Higher Journalism, funded now by Arnold Rowntree) with the brief of rejuvenating it in terms of contemporary post-war literature and art. Murry seemed to Virginia several inches taller after this had been announced. She was mildly flattered when he said he hoped she would write for him.

Once it was off the ground, Aldous Huxley (having given up being a master at Eton) became Murry's assistant. He, too, had a Garsington novel up his sleeve, *Crome Yellow*. James Strachey, who had been sacked from the *Spectator* on account of his pacifism, became the drama critic. Lytton was a frequent contributor and so was T S Eliot, Virginia an occasional one. The outlook was global: Murry had been *The Times Literary Supplement*'s expert on modern French literature and was among the first in Britain to recognise the genius of Proust. There were Literary Letters from various countries, the ones from Italy being written by Norman Douglas and Ezra Pound. It was a stunning galaxy of contributors. Who became the periodical's reviewer of new fiction? Yes, Katherine.

Murry's critical essay, Eliot's *Poems* and Virginia's *Kew Gardens* were all published as booklets on 12th May 1919 by the Hogarth Press. From Virginia's point of view this seemed a minor event compared with the fate of *Night and Day*, her completed new novel. Leonard had read it before anyone else, as would be the form with all her books from now on, and was enthusiastic, while finding her philosophy 'very melancholy' (like his own).[85] And the week before the story appeared she had received a letter from Gerald Duckworth saying that he had read the novel with 'the greatest interest' and would be delighted to publish it. That was very gratifying; her pleased reaction was quelled to some extent when she recalled who her publisher actually was: 'The first impression of an outsider, especially one who proposes to back his opinion with money, means something; though I can't think of stout smooth Gerald smoking a cigar over my pages without a smile.'[86]

There was bad news from Sussex. Their landlord at Asheham House had told them their lease would not be renewed; he needed the house for a farmer. They spent the Whitsun weekend of June house-hunting in Sussex while taking a lien on two cottages at Zennor in Cornwall where D H and Frieda Lawrence had lived during the war. Then Virginia saw the Round House, a converted windmill near Lewes, and was enchanted by it. The price was within their budget. She made an offer that was accepted. They left Sussex in the knowledge that after Asheham was no more they still would have a roof over their heads beside their beloved South Downs.

When they returned to Richmond, Surrey and Hogarth House, they were astounded to see the hall table stacked with envelopes from booksellers containing orders for copies of *Kew Gardens*. The avalanche had been set in train by a review in *The Times Literary Supplement*. The editor Bruce Richmond had rewarded his hard-working regular contributor with a notice. A new short story published by itself would not normally have been given a notice; it would have had to wait until it appeared as part of a collection. Virginia thought that the reviewer was Logan Pearsall Smith, the American man of letters based in London and a friend of Roger Fry's, but she was wrong; it was an in-house review by Richmond's assistant Harold Child. He appeared to have been well briefed because in emphasising the remarkable visual effects of light and shade, he took the line that what mattered was not the content but the form; or as he put it, 'the colour, the rhythm, the "atmosphere", the "observation" (as we call it, when for all we know or care, it is pure creation), the suggestiveness of Mrs Woolf's prose.' This was praise from the leading journal of criticism, focused on the essence of her gift as a writer, with appreciative mention, too, of the Omega-style woodcuts that Vanessa had contributed to the publication. All this for a book only ten pages long. The review not only identified Virginia as a writer at the forefront of the modern movement in English literature; it also established the Hogarth Press as a publisher of original work.

Monk's House

—Dearest, We are now more or less settled. Of course my necklace broke the first thing, but I think necklaces always do go on getting into a new house (Monk's House, Rodmell).

Virginia to Vanessa, 7th September, 1919.

Monk's House

On the way to the Round House at Lewes Virginia and Leonard noticed a poster announcing the sale at auction of Monk's House in the village of Rodmell, and they proceeded at once to inspect this empty property, 'an unpretending house, long & low, a house of many doors; on one side fronting the street of Rodmell, & wood boarded on that side…'[87] It lacked the spaciousness of their house at Asheham (sometimes spelt like their house without an 'e') but had the potential to suit their work and social requirements, even though there was no WC and the kitchen reeked of damp. What attracted Leonard, who had not shared Virginia's enthusiasm for the Round House when he saw it, was the three-quarters of an acre of land that went with it. The former owner, who had lived there from 1877 until his death in that year, had grown fruit and vegetables in abundance; there were outhouses and a granary, an expanse of lawn, and beyond it water meadows. The bidding started at £300. They acquired it for £700 and luckily recouped Virginia's expenditure on the Lewes house.

They moved on 1st September 1919. It seemed cramped and there was flooding to cope with but Virginia told Lytton: '…there are charms in this place, though very humble and unromantic compared with Asheham. I like the morning sun in one's window…'[88] She would spend the rest of her life in this house when not on holiday or in London. For all their love of Sussex, the Woolfs did not wish completely to forego easy access to institutions like the London Library, the 1917 Club, and to Bloomsbury where most of their circle still had rooms.

T S Eliot, whose The Waste Land *the Woolfs published, photographed here in 1919*
Previous pages: Monk's House, Rodmell, Sussex

Gerald published *Night and Day* on 30th October 1919. The novel was altogether different in style from 'The Mark on the Wall', now going into a new edition, and *Kew Gardens*, also much in demand. A weighty work of nearly 500 pages, it represents a return by Virginia to linear narrative with a coherent plot and carefully drawn characters with settings indicative of their incomes. The drama of courtship is played out in drawing rooms, offices, on holiday excursions. The heroine from a well-to-do family comes to seek the 'illegitimate freedom' that more and more women were beginning to demand.

The desired freedom went much deeper than the right to vote, now granted by act of Parliament to women aged 30 and over. Enfranchisement did not mean much to Virginia even though she had a husband active in Labour and international politics, a future parliamentary candidate through whom she met people like those architects of the Fabian Society policy with ambitious plans for reforming Britain, Sidney and Beatrice Webb and G D H and Margaret Cole. The freedom that her heroine Katherine Hilbery seeks is one that comes to her through a gradual process of self-realisation, as after much soul-searching she rejects the married life she was expected by her parents to lead. She breaks off her engagement to a man of her own affluent set; and she forms an alliance with one who lacks wealth, connections, and prospects, discerning the strength of his ambition, his dedication to trying to improve the lot of his fellow men and his deep love for her.

Virginia said, in a letter to her sister, to whom the novel is dedicated, that she was the model for the heroine but this is not nearly so obvious as with some of Virginia's other models drawn from life and refashioned in her fiction. To be sure, we can find a parallel between Vanessa's alliance with Duncan Grant who was by no means rich, indeed often penniless (by whom she was now pregnant with a daughter to be called Angelica), in preference to her husband Clive Bell with his hunting, shooting, horse-riding English country house background, and, in the novel, Katherine's abandonment of Rodney, the masterful man of letters with a private source of income, to throw in her lot with Ralph. But if Vanessa's amorous progress underlies the plot, so does Virginia's repudiation of a conventional Kensingtonian existence. In the character of her heroine's mother Virginia gently mocks the lady she called Aunt Anny (Lady Ritchie, Thackeray's daughter, who venerated her father's memory excessively); in Mary Datchet, the feminist, robbed of her beloved by the heroine and accepting a life of work for good causes, there are borrowings from the world of Mary Sheepshanks and Margaret Llewelyn Davies; while the rejected Rodney, neatly paired off with a partner at the close, derives his erudite egocentricity from Walter Headlam.

Once again Bruce Richmond at *The Times Literary Supplement* requested Harold Child to review Virginia, and again he was lavish in his praise: '…the story as a whole and every separate incident of it show an apprehension of values which is rarely found even in days like these when fiction is commonly supposed to be troubled with too much thinking'.[89] As Virginia had feared, Murry had sent the novel to Katherine Mansfield. Her review for *The Athenaeum* was headed ironically, 'A Ship Comes into Harbour.' She began by likening a regular novel-reviewer to someone who lingers at the docks, watching the ships setting out and returning. Such a seasoned observer was confronted now by 'the strange sight of *Night and Day* sailing into port serene and resolute on a deliberate wind. The strangeness lies in her aloofness, her air of quiet perfection, her lack of any sign that she has made a perilous voyage—the absence of any scars. There she lies among the strange shipping—a tribute to civilisation for our admiration and wonder.

'It is impossible to refrain from comparing *Night and Day* with the novels of Miss Austen. There are moments, indeed, when one is almost tempted to cry it Miss Austen up-to-date.'[90] Jane Austen was the last writer to whom in her current mood Virginia wished to be compared. To add insult to injury, Katherine echoed Forster's main criticism of the earlier book: the minor characters lacked reality. There is no one like a friend and rival author better placed to stab one in the back.

Another adverse reaction came from H W Massingham, editor of the *Nation*. He contributed a weekly Diary column in which on 29 November he made *Night and Day* the burden of his song, reiterating the Jane Austen comparison, noting the author's preoccupation with tea-drinking and taxis, and describing the principal quartet of lovers as 'impassioned snails'. But though never reconciled to negative criticism of her work and outraged at Katherine's performance, Virginia had begun to accept such barbs as one of the hazards of writing novels. The splash made by this least typical novel of Virginia's established her as a novelist to follow; her fame spread across the Atlantic. George Doran, a leading New York publisher, sent offers for *Night and Day* and *The Voyage Out*.

Margaret Llewelyn Davies confessed to Virginia she did not enjoy the novel in spite of the feminist element; perhaps she lamented the absence of the kind of working-class women she tried to help better their lot. Margaret also told Virginia that Kitty Maxse had read *Night and Day* and found it dull and the characters bloodless compared with those in the novels of her friend Elizabeth von Arnim, but at the same time Kitty had fondly inquired after the two sisters from whom she was now estranged. Virginia suggested to Vanessa that she might invite her to dinner. Kitty was much more a part of Vanessa's past than her own; and there was another barrier to renewed contact: Leonard and Leo Maxse were diametrically opposed in their stance as political commentators.

The Woolfs' social life was expanding all the time. T S Eliot, 'that strange young man,' came to dinner at Hogarth House. 'His sentences take such an enormous time to spread themselves out that we didn't get very far; but we did reach Ezra Pound and Wyndham Lewis, and how they were great geniuses, and so is Mr James Joyce—which I'm more prepared to agree to, but why has Eliot stuck in this mud?' she inquired of Roger Fry.[91] E M Forster, an acquaintance since his attendance at Friday Club meetings before the war, came to Asheham for one of the last weekends there. He confessed he preferred *The Voyage Out* to *Night and Day*. At a grand luncheon at the Cecils, Virginia met Prince Antoine Bibesco, a friend of Marcel Proust and a former counsellor at the Rumanian Legation in London. He had married Elizabeth Asquith, the former prime minister's daughter, a budding fiction-writer. Virginia found him 'handsome, amiable, a man rather too much of the smooth opulent world to be of particular interest.'[92] Another sign of their social advance came from Roger's friend Logan Pearsall Smith. This naturalised British subject and man of letters, from wealthy American Quaker stock, had many influential friends. The Webbs and George Bernard Shaw frequented the Logan Pearsall Smith family house in Sussex. His sister Alys was Bertrand Russell's first wife and his sister Mary married the art expert Bernard Berenson. He informed Virginia that Sybil Colefax, an avid collector of the famous, wished to receive her. There was hardly a fashionable London hostess who did not.

Before *Hamlet* and *King Lear* Shakespeare wrote two long narrative poems, *Venus and Adonis* and *The Rape of Lucrece*, and made his name as a poet with them. They were exercises in a kind of verse-form with which Elizabethan readers were familiar. He needed to prove to himself, and to them, that he could do the expected thing not just competently but outstandingly before giving his imagination its head. It was the same with Virginia's two earliest published novels. Having written them against a background of all manner of ailments and reviewing assignments, and having observed the reception of them by the literary world, she was now in a position to write what she really wanted to write, to try to impose her vision on that most accommodating of forms, prose fiction. Her short stories pointed the way. There were several more after 'Kew Gardens' where she employs violent time-shifts and rapidly changing orientations, blow-ups and juxtapositions, where the observed material is split up into discrete fragments leaving the reader to put them together as a coherent narrative. In one, 'An Unwritten Novel', Virginia is sitting opposite a woman in a Southern Railway train. The woman cracks a hard-boiled egg and the shell settles in her lap like the pieces in a jigsaw puzzle. The shattered fragments might stand as an emblem of the story itself and the future novels it anticipates.

The story was one of eight of Virginia's published in 1921 by the Hogarth Press as *Monday or Tuesday*. The title story and one other, 'Blue and Green', are no more than a page in length. We can observe Virginia trying here to capture the

Fake Abyssinians: the notorious Dreadnought hoax in which Virginia participated

impact of the sister arts of painting and music, to do with words what Vanessa and Duncan were doing with pigment. 'String Quartet', where she transmutes the effect of listening to chamber music into verbal images, was inspired by a recital organised by the Booths, the shipowner's family, at their house in Airlie Gardens, Kensington, and the audience is sketched into the picture. In it were Virginia's editor Bruce Richmond and his wife Elena (born Rathbone) who, as a beautiful young woman, had been a frequenter of Hyde Park Gate. Her story (what happens when time takes its toll and fair from fair declines) fascinated Virginia though she never wrote it. When Elena came to see her later, she was reminded of her own youth and told her of George's gropings. Elena confessed she had never liked George. Virginia thought that Elena nourished a secret, unrequited passion for Stephen Massingberd, the widowed husband of Kitty Maxse's sister, Margaret.

One longer story, 'A Society', sounded the feminist note. A group of women decide, like those in the Aristophanes comedy *Lysistrata*, to refuse to procreate. Their ban on sex lasts until they have found out what men really do in their professional lives. One disguises herself as an Abyssinian Prince to investigate a battleship. Virginia here recalls the scandalous occasion in 1910 when thus disguised she, Adrian and Duncan Grant participated in an elaborate practical joke at the expense of the Royal Navy. At the instigation of Horace Cole, a Cambridge friend of Adrian's and a celebrated deviser of such pranks, they purported to be the foreign dignitaries accompanying the Emperor of Abyssinia on a visit to England. They sent a fake telegram supposedly from the Foreign Office to the Commander-in-Chief of the Home Fleet saying that the royal party would be arriving at Weymouth where HMS *Dreadnought* (its latest top-secret armoured vessel) was lying at anchor and they wished to inspect it.

The hoax succeeded only too well. They were welcomed aboard with full honours. No one penetrated either Adrian's or Virginia's disguise, not even their cousin William Fisher who was the ship's flag commander. The Dreadnought Hoax has gone down in history as one of the most audacious examples of the Edwardian Englishman's passion for practical joking. In Virginia's story young women also use disguise to penetrate the Law Courts, the Royal Academy and Oxbridge.

Such sharp, satirical, whimsy would emerge fully in her non-fiction books. Virginia's indignation had been aroused by an article Desmond MacCarthy had written as 'Affable Hawk', his pen name in the *New Statesman*, of which he became the literary editor in 1920, condoning the opinion of Arnold Bennett (whose book *Our Women* was a peg for the article) that women are inferior to men in intellectual power and that no amount of education would ever lessen the difference.

'How, then, does Affable Hawk,' demanded Virginia, 'account for the fact which stares me...in the face, that the 17th century produced more remarkable women than the 16th, the 18th than the 17th, and the 19th than all three put together?' She gave a list of examples to prove her point and followed her letter up with an even longer one asking the question, 'Can he [Desmond] point to a single one of the great geniuses of history who has sprung from a people stinted of education?'[93] At which the Hawk, proving his affability, flew away from the argument to the safety of his nest, saying: 'If the freedom and education of women is impeded by the expression of my views, I shall argue no more.' Virginia had become a polemicist as well as a novelist.

Questions of character

I'm seeing Lydia [Lopokova who married Maynard Keynes] and will ask her about the
Ballet. She is rather touchy now about her dancing and apt to say she must retire...

Virginia to Ethel Smyth, August 1932

"They waited; a clock ticked; Bond Street hummed, dulled, distant; the woman went away holding gloves." Mrs Dalloway's Party

Questions of character

Virginia Woolf's next novel *Jacob's Room* was written without the long gestation of the earlier ones. She began in April 1920, finished it in November of the following year, and it was published by the Hogarth Press in the autumn of 1922, Gerald having relinquished his option on it. It was Virginia's first attempt to create a lasting image of her brother Thoby. From now on she begins to draw heavily on her past in her fiction.

The title refers to the room of the protagonist Jacob in a literal sense, his room in his lodgings in London, but it can also be taken to mean the space he occupies in the minds of a great many other people. We jump cut from one episode and one character to another with sometimes bewildering abruptness. The book is a third the length of *Night and Day* but covers vastly more ground and represents a revolutionary advance in technique.

Like Thoby, Jacob is an undergraduate at Trinity, Cambridge, before living in London and becoming immersed in the worlds of society women, Slade cropheads and prostitutes. These minor characters are shuffled on and off-stage by Virginia with the speed of a quick-change artist. Jacob loses his virginity, breaks several hearts and rides enthusiastically to hounds even though he cannot afford the correct habit. His own heart remains intact until in Greece he meets Sandra Wentworth Williams and her husband, a replica of the Dalloways in the earlier novel. Jacob and Sandra climb up the Acropolis by moonlight in a scene charged with burgeoning mutual love

A view up Bond Street 1925
Previous pages: Maynard Keynes and Lydia Lopokova at Gordon Square, 1940

held back on a taut straining leash. Sandra's unfulfilled passion for Jacob, and his for her, mirrors, I suspect, the relationship between Kitty Maxse and Thoby. The imminence of war is hinted; then in a brief last chapter we are made to infer that Jacob has been killed in action. His mother and his best friend, the two people his death will hurt most, meet in his room to sort out his belongings as the novel ends.

'The technique of the narrative is astonishing—how you manage to leave out everything that's dreary, and yet retain enough string for your pearls I can hardly understand', wrote Lytton Strachey in one of many laudatory letters Virginia received.[94] The reviewers were less kind to it. In America Maxwell Bodenheim in the *Nation* (a different journal from the English one) dubbed it 'a rambling, redundant affair'[95] and in March a more sustained broadside came from the old guard in England: an article by Arnold Bennett in *Cassell's Weekly* with the title, 'Is the Novel Decaying?' He stated his premise clearly: 'The foundation of good fiction is character creating and nothing else'. Virginia's novel, 'which has made a great stir in a small world…is packed and bursting with originality, and it is exquisitely written. But the characters do not vitally survive in the mind because the author has been obsessed by details of originality and cleverness. I regard this book as characteristic of the new novelists who have recently gained the attention of the alert and the curious.'[96]

The words ring hollowly now but Virginia felt they needed answering. She responded with an article 'Mr Bennett and Mrs Brown' that appeared first in the *New York Evening Post* in November 1923 in which Virginia hit back at Bennett as a novelist. Why (she asked) were the people in Bennett's novels so lifeless compared to those of the great Victorians and so flat compared to the people we meet and come to know in real life? In her answer she cited again the example of the lady in the railway carriage and her own attempts to bring her character to life by insight, or guessing, based on a brief rapport with her, in contrast to the Bennett method of an accumulation of facts relevant to her place in society. Bennett's attack and Virginia's response begot further articles on the subject of the creation of character in fiction from other novelists and men of letters. The whole affair became one of those 'Whither the Novel?' debates that break out from time to time for the entertainment of the reading public.

Virginia returned to the controversy in a paper she read to the Cambridge University Heretics Society printed under the title 'Character in Fiction'. She divided novelists into two camps: the old guard, the Edwardians—namely Bennett, Wells and Galsworthy—and the Georgians (whom we now call moderns or modernists)—herself, E M Forster, D H Lawrence, James Joyce, Lytton Strachey and T S Eliot. (Katherine Mansfield was conspicuous by her absence from Virginia's list.) The two last-named were not novelists but no matter, they shared her basic assumption that 'on or about December 1910 human character changed.'[97] This was a cleverly provocative way of saying that at the time of the accession of George V a new era had dawned in art and literature.

John Middleton Murry's brief, brilliant editorship of the *Athenaeum* had ended. The periodical merged with the *Nation* in 1921 and two years later Maynard Keynes became chairman of the combined journal. Hubert Henderson, a Cambridge economist colleague of Keynes's, replaced H W Massingham as editor. The weekly became a platform for Keynes's views on monetary matters and those of other members of the Bloomsbury set on literature and art. Keynes still occupied 46 Gordon Square, where, alongside the pre-war veterans, younger people one might call a second generation of Bloomsbury, foregathered: young men like Raymond Mortimer, George (Dadie) Rylands, Angus Davidson, David Cecil, Ralph Partridge, F L Lucas and Frank Ramsay.

Keynes, after sounding Eliot, who turned the job down, proposed that Leonard should become the literary editor of the merged journal. Leonard had (to Virginia's delight) failed to get elected to Parliament when he had stood as a candidate for the Combined Universities seat, competing against H A L Fisher. In those days universities were represented in the House of Commons by MPs elected by their graduates. Instead Leonard accepted the literary editorship, rightly fearing the killing routine of producing weekly pages of reviews, but heartily glad of the regular salary that went with it. For all the critical attention they were receiving, Virginia's novels only earned a pittance. It was her reviews and articles, of which she was continuing to write a great many, that yielded a much more substantial reward and would do so for several years to come. Being such a voracious consumer of literature she thoroughly enjoyed writing about the work of others past and present. She was cogitating a book to be called simply *Reading* that would contain her vision of a huge historical spread of writers.

The Press continued to flourish. Leonard and Virginia collaborated with Kot to translate the short stories of Ivan Bunin, Countess Tolstoy's memoirs and works by Tolstoy himself. They thus contributed to the current explosion of Russian literature, of which Dostoevsky's work was the focus, becoming available in English translation, thanks to the efforts of Constance Garnett and others. The Woolfs published more poetry by women poets and by Robert Graves, but their biggest catch was their American friend, Tom Eliot, who came to dinner one Sunday with his new poem, 'The Waste Land'. Virginia wrote, 'He sang it & chanted it rhythmed it. It has great beauty & force of phrase: symmetry; & tensity. What connects it together, I'm not so sure.'[98] They published it in September 1923. He meanwhile had left the bank and become editor of *The Criterion*.

Their latest assistant for the Press had come via Lytton Strachey and Carrington. He was an ex-army officer named Reginald (Ralph) Partridge who lived with the other two at Tidmarsh in what even by Bloomsbury standards was the most extraordinary triangle. Ralph was in love with Carrington, she was in love with Lytton and Lytton was in love with Ralph. Lytton realised that he could only keep Ralph by permitting him to marry Carrington, and she realised she could only insure her continued proximity to Lytton by marrying Ralph. And so—to cut short a long and very messy story in which Virginia became embroiled as Carrington's confessor—Carrington married Ralph, a union soon under stress from infidelities on both sides. Meanwhile Strachey scored another triumph with the appearance in 1921 of his biography of *Queen Victoria*. It was dedicated to Virginia. She insisted he put her name in full, not just the initials, and, when the book appeared, she wrote him an appreciative letter praising especially his gift for enlivening the narrative with pen-portraits of the minor figures.

Virginia, though envious of his success, continued to see Strachey at Tidmarsh and in London. He introduced his young friend Gerald Brenan who was off to Spain, north of Granada, to live and write. Brenan struck a chord of sympathy in Virginia. She and Leonard stayed with him when they went on holiday to Spain, a visit he never forgot. Virginia also saw Lytton once a month at the recently formed Memoir Club. It was here, as we have seen, that Virginia came out with her account of Hyde Park Gate and George's sexual gropings. The club had a small exclusive membership, consisting of Virginia and Leonard, Molly and Desmond MacCarthy, Saxon Sydney-Turner, Maynard Keynes, Lytton Strachey, Duncan Grant, Clive and Vanessa Bell, Morgan Forster, Roger Fry, Bunny Garnett and Sydney Waterlow.

While never accepted as a fully-fledged Bloomsberry, Waterlow crops up frequently in Virginia's letters and Diary. She has even more withering things to say about him than about other close friends but continued to see him and even to stay with him and his wife. As soon as she had finished *Jacob's Room* Virginia was meditating her own next contribution as a novelist in addition to the book on reading. From her sickbed (headaches, influenza, dental worries and other ailments continuously plagued her) she conceived the backbreaking schedule of writing the two books simultaneously. While thinking about more fictional experiment, she had to admit to herself that there was something in Bennett's strictures. She had attempted to create the character of Jacob as much through his absence as through his presence, even as in certain works of Cézanne a part of the canvas is left blank. When you stand back you do not see the blanks. That had been a valuable experiment but this time she intended to put her main character, a woman, centre stage and leave nothing blank. She would show the impression her heroine made on other people, to be sure, but her main purpose would be to show the impressions other people made upon her. For such a project the woman in the foreground would need to be one surrounded not merely by her own family, relations, and a few close friends, but by a much wider circle representative of the leading figures of British society (politicians, diplomats, Harley Street doctors, colonial administrators, writers and their womenfolk). She would need to be a social centre, a party-giver, in addition to being a wife and mother. She would live in London, at Westminster, within sight of the Abbey and the Houses of Parliament, in earshot of Big Ben, at the hub of the British Empire.

Among Virginia's acquaintances past and present, Kitty Maxse seemed the most likely model for such a role. She had had supporting parts in Virginia's novels so far. Now she would play the lead. Virginia had a preliminary try at this casting in a short story, 'Mrs Dalloway in Bond Street', part one of an intended series of linked stories concerning Clarissa Dalloway. In this story Clarissa has aged since she came on board in *The Voyage Out*. Her golden hair has turned white (as had Kitty's when Virginia last saw her); she is 50 but she has lost none of her joy in the fact of being alive. She sallies forth from her house in Westminster, listening to the great clock striking 11: 'The leaden circles dissolved in the air.' She makes her way jauntily on foot to Bond Street to purchase a fresh pair of white gloves, the garments Kitty was never to be seen without. Virginia succeeds in a few pages in alternating the current of Clarissa's thoughts about other people with the counter-current of other people's thoughts about her.

Hardly had Virginia got this all down on paper and was planning the next episode when she heard the news that Kitty had fallen over the banisters in her house in Cromwell Road and, severely injured, had died soon after. It was almost certainly suicide, but why? She was only 52 and in good health; she was still the life and soul of any party she attended or gave. She had innumerable distinguished friends in every walk of life, who all adored her. She still played beautifully on the piano. She had been delighted by a performance she had recently attended of *The Beggar's Opera* at Hammersmith.

The cause of Kitty's suicide (if that is what it was) is a greater mystery than that of Virginia's 18 years later. Virginia wrote in her Diary on 8th October 1922:

'...the day has been spoilt for me—so strangely—by Kitty Maxse's death; & now I think of her lying in her grave at Gunby [in Lincolnshire where Kitty's sister Margaret was buried], & Leo going home & all the rest. I read it in the paper. I haven't seen her since, I guess, 1908—save at old Davies' funeral, & then I cut her, which now troubles me—unreasonably I suppose. I could not have kept up with her; she never tried to see me. Yet, yet—these old friends dying without any notice on our part always—it begins to happen often—saddens me: makes me feel guilty. I wish I'd met her in the street. My mind has gone back all day to her; in the queer way it does. First thinking out how she died, suddenly at 33 Cromwell Road; she was always afraid of operations. Then visualising her—her white hair—pink cheeks—how she sat upright—her voice—with its characteristic tones—her green blue floor—which she painted with her own hands: her earrings, her gaiety yet melancholy; her smartness: her tears, which stayed on her cheek. Not that I felt at my ease with her. But she was very charming—very humorous.'[99]

Virginia did not attend Kitty's memorial service in London nor did she write to her surviving sister, Susan. This was not so much callousness or insensitivity, I believe, as the desire to keep intact and pure in her imagination a figure she intended to celebrate in her work. Virginia had sketched out a second Mrs Dalloway episode, 'The Prime Minister', that survives in manuscript. It shows the progress of his car in Bond Street momentarily drawing together the passers-by in their curiosity about its hidden occupant. The piece also foreshadows the character of Septimus Warren Smith, the shell-shock victim, but it was set aside. The story had by now branched into a novel, she told T S Eliot, for whose *New Criterion* it had been intended. The novel would culminate in a party, similar to those Kitty gave. Virginia also wrote some sketches, later discarded too, containing the silent thoughts of some of Mrs Dalloway's guests. They were rescued from the manuscript and published in 1973, as *Mrs Dalloway's Party: A Short Story Sequence*; charming miniatures, they reveal Virginia's abundance of creativity once she had started on a work.

Mrs Dalloway, as the novel became, had the working title of *The Hours* and it, too, opens with Clarissa setting forth from her house in Westminster on a walk (the actual route of which is somewhat puzzling) to Bond Street. The hours of a single day in June are made to contain an inward and outward view not just of

her, but that of the male figure corresponding to the other side, the dark, mad side of Virginia's being. Clarissa's life-enhancing gift for bringing people together is contrasted with Septimus's sense of isolation and dislocation, like that of the inmates of the psychiatric hospital where Siegfried Sassoon was sent.

Virginia shows her heroine's girlish past impacting upon her present fashionable existence as society hostess and mother through the device of introducing her rejected suitor. He arrives back in England on the day of her party, and his unexpected presence at it—the man who has 'failed'—by the standards of the other guests basking in worldly glory—illuminates the shallowness of their values.

Beside the contrast between success and failure is that between sanity and insanity, Clarissa and Septimus, the returned soldier who is haunted by the memory of his comrade shot dead in front of him on the battlefield. The section depicting Septimus's sense of divine mission, of being the Saviour of mankind, as he wanders with his wife across Regent's Park is among Virginia's most remarkable pieces of writing.

136

Septimus and the Londoners who form the minor figures in this novel are linked to Mrs Dalloway by Virginia's sense of group-consciousness. She uses the unanimist device of showing how a disparate group of individuals reacts in its separate ways to the same events, here the appearance of a limousine in Bond Street followed by an aeroplane engaged in sky-writing. At the beginning, as in the earlier sketch, Mrs Dalloway's shopping (for flowers for her party this time, not gloves) is interrupted by the sound of a car backfiring. The car belongs to some very important personage concealed inside it. A group of passers-by forms, speculating as to the identity of the car's occupant. Mrs Dalloway guesses correctly: it is the Queen and, leaving Mrs D behind with her party flowers, we follow the car on its stately progress to Buckingham Palace:

'A breeze flaunting ever so warmly down the Mall through the thin trees, past the bronze heroes, lifted some flag flying in the British breast of Mr Bowley [a figure we never meet again] and he raised his hat as the car turned into the Mall and held it high as the car approached; and let the poor mothers of Pimlico press close to him, and stood very upright. The car came on.'[100]

But then an aeroplane appears overhead and everyone's attention switches from the car to it.

The device enables Virginia to draw a number of minor characters into the web of the novel whose presence serves a similar purpose to the chorus in a Greek tragedy: people not directly involved in the main action whose detached remarks throw those of the principals into sharper relief.

Septimus and his Italian wife Lucrezia, who had seen the car in Bond Street, arrive in Regent's Park by the time the skywriting aeroplane appears (they must have covered the distance with remarkable speed). Lucrezia, obeying the instructions of their doctor, who insists there is nothing the matter with Septimus that rest and fresh air will not cure, and that he should be made to take an interest in things outside himself, tells him to look up at the sky.

'So, thought Septimus, looking up, they are signalling to me. Not indeed in actual words; that is, he could not read the language yet; but it was plain enough, this beauty, this

137

exquisite beauty, and tears filled his eyes as he looked at the smoke words languishing and melting in the sky and bestowing upon him in their inexhaustible charity and laughing goodness one shape after another of unimaginable beauty and signalling their intention to provide him, for nothing, for ever, for looking merely, with beauty, more beauty! Tears ran down his cheeks.'[101]

Then she points to boys playing cricket. 'Look' she repeated: 'Look the unseen bade him, the voice which now communicated with him who was the greatest of mankind, Septimus, lately taken from life to death, the Lord who had come to renew society, who lay like a coverlet, a snow blanket smitten only by the sun, for ever unwasted, suffering for ever, the scapegoat, the eternal sufferer, but he did not want it, he moaned, putting from him with a wave of his hand that eternal suffering, that eternal loneliness.'[102]

In the savagely drawn characters of Dr Holmes and Sir William Harcourt, the consultant, Virginia concentrated her resentment at the treatment she had received from Savage and others. Harcourt tells Lucrezia her husband is seriously ill and must be taken away for observation in the nursing home he runs for his patients. Septimus's decision to jump from the window of his house, rather than face any more treatment from Harcourt, seems to recall, in Virginia's mind, the fatal fall of Kitty, and as we read the novel today, to foreshadow her own suicide a decade and a half after it appeared. Harcourt becomes the messenger of death at Clarissa's party, shattering the mood of contentment and wholeness emanating from the hostess, when he refers to the demise that day of one of his patients.

Septimus dies in sight of his Italian wife, for whose character Virginia borrowed some touches from a new recruit to Bloomsbury, the Russian dancer, Lydia Lopokova, prima ballerina of the Diaghilev company. Rezia (Lucrezia) has her bewildered foreignness, simplicity and charm. Lydia was recognised as being a superb dancer, often partnered by Léonide Massine, unlike Rezia who, when she married Septimus, was a milliner's assistant, trimming hats in Milan. In Sally Seton, the madcap friend of Clarissa's youth,

138

Virginia drew on memories of Madge Vaughan, the friend of her own youth. Miss Kilman, the aptly named governess, who has such power over Clarissa's daughter, is a repulsive hate-figure from the depths of Virginia's imagination.

The novel provoked much discussion of its method among reviewers with an especially perceptive article from Richard Hughes whose début as a novelist with *A High Wind in Jamaica* was still a few years away. 'Mrs Woolf touches all the time the verge of the problem of reality: not directly, like Pirandello, but by implication,' he wrote in the New York edition of the *Saturday Review of Literature*. Luigi Pirandello, the Italian philosopher-playwright, whose work was at this time attracting much attention when performed in Paris, shows imagined reality in conflict with historical reality in plays such as *Six Characters in Search of An Author*. Woolf, Hughes explained, bases her novel on the single reality of the London she so vividly depicts but, 'In contrast to the solidity of her visible world there rises throughout the book in a delicate crescendo *fear*...Clarissa Dalloway herself, the slightly more speculative Peter [her former suitor], the Blakeian "lunatic" Septimus Warren Smith, each with their own more or less formulated hypothesis of the meaning of life—together are an unanswerable illustration of that bottomlessness on which all spiritual values are based. That is what I mean by fear.'[103] One negative reaction came, oddly, from Lytton Strachey, who thought the book was flawed by Virginia's ambivalent attitude to Clarissa. Perhaps he sensed who her original was.

Virginia had been reminded recently of Madge Vaughan when she wrote a short review of *Out of the Past,* Madge's memoir of her father, the Renaissance historian John Addington Symonds, for Leonard in his capacity as literary editor of the *Nation*; and she had come to know Lydia Lopokova through seeing her at Bloomsbury gatherings in Gordon Square. To the great astonishment of Virginia and his other friends, especially Duncan Grant, Maynard Keynes had fallen in love with her. At first they could not believe it and then when they did, they deeply resented it. Lydia was not, in spite of her prowess as a dancer, Bloomsbury material. Writing to Jacques Raverat in

September 1924 Virginia said: 'She [Lydia] came to tea on Sunday…and really I had the hardest time in the world. Her contribution is one shriek, two dances; then silence, like a submissive child, with her hands crossed. At 30 this is pathetic. Soon she will be plaintive. And they say you can only talk to Maynard now in words of one syllable. This he will tire of.'[104] Maynard had the force of character to override their dismay: in July 1924 Lydia's divorce from her first husband came through and in August 1925 she and Maynard became man and wife. By then Virginia's view of her had completely changed, an example of the way her judgments about people close to her were continually revised. In May Virginia met her at a dinner party in Chelsea and wrote in her Diary: 'Little Lydia I liked: how does her mind work? Like a lark soaring; a sort of glorified instinct inspires her: I suppose a very nice nature, & direction at Maynard's hands'.[105]

The death of Katherine Mansfield in January 1923 left a gap in Virginia's life. Katherine, whose TB has worsened, had, hoping for a miraculous cure, become an inmate of the Institute for the Harmonious Development of Man at Fontainebleau near Paris, run by the Armenian-born guru, George Gurdjieff. She died from a haemorrhage brought on by a coughing fit while Murry was visiting her there. Though Virginia had resented her as a rival and a reviewer, she had admired her as a woman leading her own defiant life, and she was saddened by her loss. Now in the absence of Katherine, Virginia turned against John Middleton Murry, as did Leonard, who confessed he had never liked him and thought he had been a bad influence on Katherine. Relations had already become soured when Murry had attacked Leonard and S S Koteliansky's translation of Chekhov's notebooks in an article in the *Athenaeum*.

Living in Richmond, Surrey, had become a source of discontent for Virginia. Her social life had expanded so much that she and Leonard were rarely free of engagements and as they did not have a car, they had difficulty in reaching many of their friends. Even so Leonard was reluctant to give up his garden at Richmond. In the end she persuaded him it was time for them to live once again near the centre in London and in

March 1924 they moved back to the Bloomsbury area—to 15 Tavistock Square, of which they took a ten-year lease.

They occupied the upper floors of the building and a firm of solicitors the two below. Along with all their personal belongings, books, pictures and writing materials, all the paraphernalia of the Hogarth Press went with them, to be installed in the basement of their new house. Beyond the basement, instead of a garden there was a huge room with a skylight, once a billiard-room. This, known as the Studio, became Virginia's workroom. For the production of full-length books the Press used commercial printers. The Woolfs had received offers from general publishing companies to take the Press over, leaving them in editorial control, but so far these had been resisted. But more and more they needed assistants. The job as assistant to the Woolfs as publishers had its rewards but it was not an easy or well paid one. Leonard sometimes forgot he was not still dealing with the underlings in his government office in Ceylon. Ralph Partridge departed, to be followed by Marjorie Joad, the girlfriend of the philosopher Cyril Joad, a young woman whose harsh voice grated on Virginia's nerves but she soon became fond of her. She was succeeded by George (Dadie) Rylands, who stayed only a short time before he returned to Cambridge to take up a fellowship at King's. After him Angus Davidson took over.

What had started out as *Reading* became *The Common Reader* and was published by the Hogarth Press on 23rd April 1925, three weeks before the publication of *Mrs Dalloway*. It began not at the start of our literature with *Beowulf* and the Anglo-Saxons—they were a closed book to Virginia—but with Chaucer, whom she combines with the Paston Letters, the private correspondence of an English family living in Norfolk in the 15th century, letters rich in historical detail. She fancies its head sitting reading the poet who had died some 20 years earlier.

The volume and its companion, *The Common Reader Second Series* in 1935, are a sustained attempt to explore that 'strange intoxication' Virginia received from books of English, French and Russian (via Kot and Mrs Garnett) literature. There was no genre that lay outside her range, an omnivorousness she inherited from her father. Poetry, drama, fiction and memoirs were all devoured with equal relish. Her suite 'Lives of the Obscure' reveals her power of captivating us with witty vignettes of historical figures whom we have never heard of before. As for the truly great (Sophocles, Chaucer, Montaigne, Chekhov), Virginia has fresh observations on their work through the recreation of the conditions surrounding its composition and reassembling their characters through their writings. She is less concerned with text than with texture, with significant selection rather than comprehensiveness. She is content, for instance, to generalise on Chaucer's greatness with no mention of either *Troilus and Criseyde* or the *Knight's Tale*. She entitles her exploration of the Athenian dramatists 'On Not Knowing Greek'—an ironic touch because, as we have seen, Virginia did know Greek. What she means is that we know so much less about them than we do about the Pastons and she moves from this premise of our ignorance to discuss the Greek dramatists in terms of their impersonality.

Her essays cover several hundred years more, coming up through the 18th century, where she is very much at home with Addison, Defoe, Scott (she never lost the love for his novels, which her father's readings had given her) and Jane Austen. Then into the 19th with the Brontë sisters, George Eliot, Walter Pater, and one of the more obscure for whom she has much sympathy, George Gissing.

Then we reach Virginia's own period. Joseph Conrad had just died and she reflects upon his genius. In an essay on Modern Fiction (originally, like many, a main article for *The Times Literary Supplement*) she returns to the work of Bennett, Wells, Galsworthy and makes that statement, quoted above in the Introduction where I tried to unravel it, so relevant to her own work: 'Life is not a series of gig lamps symmetrically arranged; life is a luminous halo, a semi-transparent envelope surrounding us from the beginning of consciousness to the end. Is it not the task of the novelist to convey this varying, this unknown and uncircumscribed spirit, whatever aberration or complexity it may display, with as little mixture of the alien and external as possible?'[106]

A thoughtful review of the book appeared in *The Calendar of Modern Letters* by the critic Edgell Rickword. *The Calendar* was a periodical that he and two friends had founded in March 1925, in an attempt to raise the standard of literary journalism in Britain and to relate contemporary literature to the needs of society as a whole. Rickword tempered his approval of the essays with some general observations about the kind of criticism to be found in Virginia's book. He thought that the concept of a Common Reader, derived from the addressee of Virginia's essays, Dr Johnson, was a misleading one, given the small discriminating class of readers to which modern literature appealed. He felt they were directed to the uncommon readers who formed this minority:

'If the common reader could really be identified with the author of these essays we should not have been able to make them an excuse for a tirade. Unfortunately the sensitiveness which is common to them is a quality with which we rarely meet in contemporary criticism. Perhaps we may hope it is a property of the inarticulate, who silent and unnamed, form the real modern audience. Whether or not Mrs Woolf's title be an appeal from the self-styled *illuminati* to the anonymous throng, at any rate she may claim the attribute which is the most valuable in Johnson's definition of the common reader, one whose sense is "uncorrupted by literary prejudices".'[107]

Virginia's *Common Reader* volumes appeared just before the great expansion of English as a university discipline. Living as we do now after that expansion has occurred, Rickword's 'anonymous throng' has become swollen by readers (many of them also writers) who possess degrees in English literature. The critical faculty of such readers and their capacity for experience of literature was developed within the academy when they were university students. Virginia's essays bear witness to an earlier period when the reader she is addressing was expected to be prepared to read Chaucer or Sidney or Donne in depth, not for the purpose of acquiring an honours degree, but purely for personal enrichment. While we are in contact with her lively essays we become such a reader, whether common or uncommon, a most refreshing experience.

Lesbos

—Vita's real claim to consideration, is, if I may be so coarse, her legs. Oh they are exquisite—running like slender pillars up into her trunk, which is that of a breathless curiassier (yet she has two children) but all about her is virginal, savage, patrician...

Virginia to Jacques Raverat, December 1924

Lesbos

Virginia's marriage was a happy one. It could not have been happier she told Leonard in her suicide letters to him and we have no cause to doubt her word. It was a white marriage (one without sex), a triumph of love, respect, admiration, compatibility, companionship and the Victorian work ethic in which both partners had been reared: a Bloomsbury mixture of stoicism and hedonism.

Not all Virginia's attitudes were admirable by our criteria. In spite of being married to a Jew, the anti-Semitism she grew up with never weakened. This is usually played right down by her biographers. It would be painful to quote all the offensive remarks about Jews in her novels, letters and diaries. Let two suffice. When she and Adrian went to Spain in 1905 she writes to Violet Dickinson: 'There are a great many Portuguese Jews on board, and other repulsive objects, but we keep clear of them.'[108] In *The Years*, a novel published 32 years later, after she had been married to Leonard for a quarter of a century, in 'Present Day', the concluding section, there is a disgusting description of a Jew in the bathroom opposite the room where two of the main characters are talking and quoting poetry:

"'The Jew,' she murmured.

"The Jew?" he said. They listened. He could hear quite distinctly now. Somebody was turning on taps; somebody was having a bath in the room opposite.

"The Jew having a bath," she said.

"The Jew having a bath?" he repeated.

Duncan Grant's portrait of Virginia
Previous pages: Vita Sackville-West and her sons Nigel and Benedict at Long Barn 1923

"And tomorrow there'll be a line of grease round the bath," she said.

"Damn the Jew!" he exclaimed. The thought of a line of grease from the strange man's body on the bath next door disgusted him.

"Go on—" said Sara: "Society is all but rude," she repeated the last lines, "to this delicious solitude."

"No," he said.

They listened to the water running. The man was coughing and clearing his throat as he sponged."[109]

The stereotype of the physically repulsive Jew is a standard figure in Victorian and Edwardian fiction (though not, incidentally, in Bennett, Wells or Galsworthy) but one hardly expects to find it in Virginia Woolf. One might perhaps say in mitigation that anti-Semitism was taken for granted in those days in her circle and often combined with friendships with individual Jews. Clive Bell (who had at least one Jewish mistress), Rupert Brooke, Lytton Strachey, T S Eliot, Jacques Raverat, Harold Nicolson, to name but a few of the more eminent, were anti-Semitic their entire lives.

After World War One Virginia's circle remained centred on Bloomsbury but widened greatly as her reputation as a writer increased. Among many new friends were Ethel Sands, the American-born painter who lived in England, a former pupil of Sickert, and her friend Nan Hudson, also a painter; and Hugh Walpole (an odd but lasting friendship with a novelist of the old guard). Virginia continued to frequent Garsington (from where the garden at Bourton in *Mrs Dalloway* derives). She discovered to her embarrassment and amusement that Ottoline Morrell's husband Philip (who had affairs on the side) had fallen in love with her, a passion not returned. She accepted invitations from society hostesses like Margot Asquith, the wife of the Liberal Prime minister, and continued to do so from Lady Colefax while making fun of them both in a paper she read in December 1936 to the Memoir Club entitled 'Am I A Snob?' In a hilarious performance she concluded with a show of mock-guilt that she was. By contrast there was nothing satirical in her admission to being a 'highbrow' in a letter she wrote but never sent to the editor of the *New Statesman*. She defines such a person as 'a man or woman of thoroughbred intelligence who rides his mind at a gallop across a country in pursuit of an idea. That is why I have always been so proud to be called highbrow. That is why, if I could be more of a highbrow I would. I honour and respect highbrows. Some of my relations have been highbrows and some, but by no means all, of my friends.'[110] Here we have Virginia's real snobbery breaking out—an intellectual snobbery deriving from her ancestry and those continually inter-marrying families of thoroughbred intelligence (Stephens, Darwins, Wedgwoods, Stracheys) whose members had surrounded her in her youth. In her eyes they were comparable to the aristocracy of the turf, bloodstock bred to outpace their rivals in any race for which they were entered. Against them were the hacks of what she dubbed the 'underworld', who were, she knew, more in tune than her with ordinary men and women. Even at the height of her fame and glory an inbuilt sense of failure would overwhelm her that no amount of reassurance could quell.

As the 1920s progressed there was one member of the English aristocracy destined to play a part in Virginia's life, second only to that of Leonard. At the end of 1922, at a gathering at Clive Bell's, Virginia met Victoria Sackville-West (always known as Vita), the wife of Harold Nicolson, a member of the diplomatic service. The Nicolsons and the Woolfs were married couples with much in common: a love of gardens and gardening and an enormous range of literary appreciation. Both men were exponents of the Higher Journalism for which Harold eventually abandoned the Foreign Office, making it his main career. He wrote several biographies and also became an MP for a time. Both women had been writing non-stop since childhood with several published books to their credit and many more waiting inside them to get out. But in spite of the knowledge of French literature they had in common—Harold's admiration for Sainte-Beuve was a match for Leonard's and Lytton's for Voltaire—the first meetings in Bloomsbury were awkward. It took all of Clive's bonhomous charm to make the conversation flow. The Nicolsons failed to enchant. For all their reading and prolific published output they did not quite pass the Apostolic test of distinction.

In 1922 Vita published *Knole and the Sackvilles,* a study of her family and the magnificent Tudor mansion in Kent, near Sevenoaks, where she was born. Her father became the third Lord Sackville in 1908 and they inhabited Knole in style. Her mother, his cousin, also named Victoria Sackville-West, was an illegitimate daughter of the second Lord Sackville by a Spanish dancer known as Pepita. Vita wrote a book about her maternal grandmother who, they said, had gypsy blood in her. A solitary cloud hung over Vita's privileged life. Though she was her father's only child, she would never inherit Knole, the house and grounds she had grown to identify with and love so much and where she still had a room of her own. The property was entailed in perpetuity to the male Sackvilles. She and Harold lived nearby at a renovated cottage known as Long Barn where they had planned and planted a fine garden and they had, too, a London house in Ebury Street; but Vita never cared much for London. She had begun to write a long poem to be called *The Land* tracing the agricultural year in Kent.

Although she was ten years younger than Virginia, Vita was more experienced in a number of ways, especially, to put it crudely, carnally. She had married Harold in October 1913 in the chapel at Knole and had had two surviving sons by him, Ben born in 1914 and Nigel in 1917. For five years or so she been contented in her marriage and her writing, her garden and her dogs, but then she met again a friend from her childhood, Violet Keppel, the daughter of Alice Keppel, the longtime mistress of Edward VII. Vita, Violet Keppel and another friend, Rosamund Grosvenor, had had schoolgirl crushes on each other. Now in adulthood Violet, who was engaged to Denys Trefusis, a major in the Horse Guards, conceived an obsessive passion for Vita. She inducted her into the joys of lesbianism and found her enthusiastically responsive. The result was a tempestuous affair that lasted from 1918 to 1921. Afterwards, to purge herself, Vita wrote an autobiographical account of it from start to finish and, like Miss Prism in *The Importance of Being Earnest,* she locked it up in a Gladstone bag she hid away.

Whether or not she intended it for posthumous publication is unclear. It was discovered after Vita's death by her younger son Nigel who ripped it open with a razor, and published it in 1973 as the centrepiece of his book *Portrait of a Marriage* to a storm of controversy. It reveals how two highborn young women were prepared to sacrifice everything—marriage, family, reputation—in order to satisfy their passion for each other and live together in complete freedom.

The climax came in February 1920 when the two women's husbands (Violet had agreed to marry Denys Trefusis provided the marriage was not consummated) travelled to Amiens, where their wives were preparing to leave them for good, and through a combination of threats and cajoling succeeded in reclaiming them, conducting them separately to Paris and back to the marital yoke. That episode was, however, not the end of the affair; it took a whole year more to run its course. In the end Violet went to live at Auteuil, where she kept a salon, frequented by Jean Cocteau and other writers, rarely seeing her husband. She became the lover of the Princesse de Polignac, the former Winaretta Singer, heiress to the American sewing-machine fortune. And Vita returned to Long Barn, to Harold and her sons Ben and Nigel, to her elkhounds and her garden.

The Nicolsons' marriage was restructured to accommodate what she and Harold called Vita's 'dual nature'. They loved each other deeply while leading separate sex-lives with other partners. The arrangement worked brilliantly—for them. Stretching her duality almost to breaking point, Vita then acquired a male lover in Geoffrey Scott who had assisted Bernard Berenson, the scholar of Italian Renaissance art, at I Tatti, his villa at Settignano near Florence. Clive had taken Vanessa and Virginia to lunch there to meet Berenson and his wife when they were in Italy in 1909. The art expert made surprisingly little impression on Virginia. She was more interested in his American wife, Logan Pearsall Smith's sister, who had left her first husband Frank Costelloe, an Irish barrister, by whom she had two daughters, Ray and Karin, for Berenson. Ray Costelloe married Lytton Strachey's brother Oliver, and Karin married Virginia's brother Adrian.

Scott was a versatile man who had been the lover of Mary Berenson (19 years his senior), a liaison that ended when Scott married a wife of his own. He had written a classic work on architecture and helped to redesign I Tatti and its gardens. He was about to publish *The Portrait of Zélide*, a Strachey-like biography of Madame de Charrière, an 18th-century Dutch beauty and novelist, courted by James Boswell among others. She turned him down and married a Swiss nonentity and then fell in love with the writer Benjamin Constant with whom she had a passionate friendship. It became an iconic book for Vita and her circle. The presence of Scott in her life (or, when he was absent, his daily letters) did not preclude Vita's erotic friendships with women. Lady Gerald (Dorothy) Wellesley was her main girlfriend at this period. Harold was away abroad working for the newly formed League of Nations. He had attended the Paris Peace Conference after the war and would soon be posted to the Persian Embassy while Vita remained in Kent to enjoy her female amours. He fulfilled his not very ardent homosexual longings with male partners. The literary journalist and Bloomsbury member, Raymond Mortimer (Tray they called him), went out to Teheran and became his lover.

On the morning before her party Clarissa Dalloway ruminates about her friendship with Sally Seton (modelled on Madge Vaughan). 'Had not that, after all, been love?' As the memory deepens she recalls 'the most exquisite moment of her whole life passing a stone urn with flowers in it. Sally stopped; picked a flower; kissed her on the lips.'[111] Virginia's friendships before her marriage with Madge, Marny and Emma Vaughan and Violet Dickinson were of a similar nature, consummated in her imagination through an endless flow of whimsical correspondence. Now in her friendship with Vita she had a brush—or was it more than a brush, no one seems quite sure —with homosexual experience.

On 17th December 1925, six months after both *Mrs Dalloway* and *The Common Reader* had been published (a great year for her in her professional life but a poor one for her state of health), Virginia stayed at Long Barn. Leonard did not join them until 19th December. It was just at the time when Vita's affair with Scott was reaching its climax. Virginia stepped in and supplanted him in Vita's affections for which he never forgave her. She responded by disliking *The Portrait of Zélide*.

If Virginia was briefly one of Vita's many female conquests (or was it vice versa?), she remained thereafter her devoted friend. In an aloof, eloquent, unphysical way, Virginia remained in love with Vita as with Leonard, drawing great personal and artistic satisfaction from the relationship. She revelled in Vita's arrogant ascendancy and would later respond to it in the way she knew best: by writing a book about it.

While this was going on in England, a former one-time neo-Pagan, the artist Jacques Raverat lay bed-ridden in his house in Vence, near Cannes, dying of multiple sclerosis, nursed by his wife, also an artist, the former Gwen Darwin. Virginia had always admired him and now she wrote him many letters in which she discussed both the details of her present life and confided in him thoughts about her work usually restricted to her Diary. Here is what she wrote to him about Vita: '...her real claim to consideration, is, if I may be so coarse, her legs. Oh they are exquisite— running like slender pillars up into her trunk, which is that of a breathless cuirassier (yet she has 2 children) but all about her is virginal, savage, patrician; & why she writes, which she does with complete competency, and a pen of brass, is a puzzle to me. If I were she, I should merely stride, with 11 Elk hounds, behind me, through my ancestral woods. She descends from (the Dukes of) Dorset, Buckingham, Sir Philip Sidney, and the whole of English history, which she keeps, stretched in coffins, one after another, from 1300 to the present day, under her dining room floor. But you, poor Frog [a tease; Raverat was a highly anglicised 'frog'], care nothing for all this.'[112]

Despite the 'pen of brass,' Virginia asked Vita if she would write a book she and Leonard could publish. Vita replied with a long story *Seducers in Ecuador* (76 printed pages) written while she was away in Persia, where she joined Harold for a time. The hero of it takes a cruise to Egypt and becomes involved with the fantasies of his fellow-passengers. It is as if Vita was taking a hint from Pirandello and exploring the truth of fantasy.

Before Jacques Raverat died in February 1925, Virginia sent him an early proof copy of *Mrs Dalloway*. His wife read it to him during his last days when he was in great pain and wished to die. He told Virginia that the arrival of her novel almost made him want to live longer. Unfortunately the letter he dictated giving his detailed reactions that gave Virginia so much pleasure has been lost. In the following months of that year, *Mrs Dalloway* was widely read in London's literary circles. In the past the period immediately after publication of one of her novels had been an anxious one for Virginia while she awaited reactions of friends and enemies alike; but not this time. As she wrote in her Diary: 'I am scarcely a shade nervous about Mrs. D. Why is this? Really I am a little bored, for the first time, at thinking how much I shall have to talk about it this summer. The truth is that writing is the profound pleasure & being read the superficial. I'm now all on the strain with desire to stop journalism & get on to *To the Lighthouse*. This is going to be fairly short: to have father's character done complete in it; & mother's; & St Ives; & childhood; & all the usual things I try to put in—life death & c.'[113]

To the Lighthouse may have started in her mind as being fairly short but by the time she had completed it, it had become a full-length novel. On 5th May 1927 the Hogarth Press published it, as it now did all Virginia's books including the

154

two earliest ones, in which Gerald as the original publisher relinquished his rights. In America, where her reputation was growing all the time, Harcourt Brace was her publisher. We have already examined *To the Lighthouse* for the insights it gives into Virginia's childhood. Now let us view it in relation to her work as a whole.

'Each of Mrs Woolf's novels has inspired a lively curiosity as to the next [declared the anonymous *Times Literary Supplement* reviewer on the day of publication]. One wondered what would follow *Mrs Dalloway*; and its successor, with certain points of likeness, is yet a different thing. It is still more different from most other stories. A case like Mrs Woolf's makes one feel the difficulty of getting a common measure to estimate fiction; for her work, so adventurous and intellectually imaginative, really invites a higher test than is applied to most novels.'[114]

The main points of likeness lie in the penetration of the inner consciousness of the characters to carry the narrative forward and the restriction of the narrative to a short period of time: a single day in *Mrs Dalloway*, two days separated by some ten years in the case of the later novel. The main events that occur during the intervening time, such as the death of Mrs Ramsay, are given to the reader in single sentences between square brackets during the Time Passes interlude. The structure represents an even more ambitious, difficult scheme than the earlier book. We meet the characters in close-up, so to speak, reacting to their experience of the present moment, but we also see them through the other end of the telescope in a perspective of their whole life-history.

Where *To the Lighthouse* differs not just from *Mrs Dalloway* but from Virginia's earlier novels, with the possible exception of *The Voyage Out*, is in the sense it gives of her own commitment to those characters. It is a novel about a family, an extended family, but brought to life in such a vivid, fully realised manner that the reader feels the novel must have been lived by the novelist before it was written. Although there is no character in *To the Lighthouse* with whom Virginia herself may be identified, it was, I think, her *Bildungsroman* (a novel tracing a person's formative experiences). She recreates her first world, its serenity shattered by her mother's death, in her maturity as a novelist. She settles her debt to the past.

Even her old antagonist Arnold Bennett was impressed, give or take a few quibbles. 'I have read a bunch of novels,' he told his *Evening Standard* readers on the 23rd June. 'I must say, despite my notorious grave reservations concerning Virginia Woolf, that the most original of the bunch is *To the Lighthouse*. It is the best book of hers that I know. Her character drawing has improved. Mrs Ramsay almost amounts to a complete person. Unfortunately she goes and dies, and her decease cuts the book in two. Also there are some pleasing records of interesting sensations outside the range of the ordinary novelist. The scheme of the story is rather wilful—designed seemingly, but perhaps not really, to exhibit virtuosity. A group of people plan to sail in a small boat to a lighthouse. At the end some of them reach the lighthouse in a small boat. That is the externality of the plot.

'The middle part, entitled "Time Passes", shows a novel device to give the reader the impression of the passing of time—a sort of cataloguing of intermediate events. In my opinion it does not succeed. It is a short cut, but a short cut that does not get you anywhere. To convey the idea of the passage of a considerable length of time is an extremely difficult business, and I doubt if it can be accomplished by means of a device, except the device of simply saying "Time Passes", and leaving the effort of imagination to the reader. Apart from this honest shirking of the difficulty, there is no alternative but to convey the impression very gradually, without any direct insistence —in the manner of life itself.

I have heard a great deal about the wonders of Mrs Woolf's style. She sometimes discovers a truly brilliant simile. She often chooses her adjectives and adverbs with beautiful felicity. But there is more in style than this. The form of her sentences is rather tryingly monotonous, and the distance between her nominatives and her verbs is steadily increasing. Still, *To the Lighthouse* has stuff in it strong enough to withstand quite a lot of adverse criticism.'[115]

During the process of its composition Vita had returned from

Persia. She visited Monk's House, Virginia visited Long Barn and both of them together visited Knole while the passionate attachment of the two women to each other grew ever stronger. The Woolfs acquired a car which made their travels a lot easier. On 1st May 1926 there was a General Strike in Britain that lasted for twelve days during which Leonard took the side of the workers. He and Virginia were involved in collecting signatures from leading writers in support of a compromise proposal but it was not successful. The strike ended in a face-saving defeat for the workers.

In October the poem on which Vita had been working for so long, *The Land*, was published and was given an enthusiastic welcome in the *Observer* by J C Squire, one of Virginia's 'underworld' hate-figures. 'I think the better of him for it,' she told Vita apropos of the review, 'though his manner is always that of a curate, a grocer, a churchwarden, someone sticky with jam and buns at a School treat, however, he admires you; and I'm jealous.'[116] She was soon to have more serious cause for jealousy where Vita was concerned.

Roy Campbell, the South African poet who had founded the satirical literary magazine *Voorslug* (Whiplash) with his friends William Plomer and Laurens Van der Post had come to live with his wife and two small children in Sevenoaks Weald, the village that contained Long Barn. His poem *The Flaming Terrapin* had made a stir when it had been published by Jonathan Cape in 1924. He had been a student in Oxford but failed to get into a college. He had then tramped around Europe, returning in 1921 to England where he met Mary Gorman, a beautiful, dark-haired young woman, whose father was, like his, a wealthy doctor. Roy and Mary were married in 1922.

Now the Campbells met the Nicolsons in the village post office, were invited to Long Barn and a friendship between the two families ripened. The cottage where Ben and Nigel lived was empty as they were at boarding school and the Nicolsons offered it rent-free to the Campbells. Vita's motivation was not wholly philanthropic. Mary Campbell had a 'dual nature' too. She fell in love with Vita and Vita with her. An affair ensued to compete in intensity with the one between Violet Keppel and Vita. When Virginia discovered what was going on she was both very angry and intensely jealous; but Virginia's rage was as nothing to Roy's when Mary confessed to him what had happened. He left Kent in a fury. His biographers say he went to London but I think it must have been Oxford where, seeking solace in a pub over pints of beer, as was his habit when things went wrong, he met C S Lewis (whom he had known earlier) and poured out his troubles. 'Fancy being cuckolded by a woman!' Lewis is alleged to have responded.

It was another friend of his named Lewis, the artist and writer Wyndham Lewis, in whom Campbell found a sympathetic ally at this crisis. Virginia, it will be remembered, had heard Wyndham Lewis's name mentioned, by T S Eliot when he came to tea in 1918, alongside that of Ezra Pound as a writer to watch. His novel *Tarr* had been serialised in Pound's journal *The Egoist* before publication. He was also a painter and draughtsman in an energetic robust manner that came to be known as Vorticist. He had exhibited a work in Roger Fry's Second Post-Impressionist Exhibition. He had, as we saw, quarrelled violently with Roger during the period of the Omega Workshops. (They came to an end in 1919.) He had seceded from them in 1913, taking with him Frederick Etchells, Edward Wadsworth, Gaudier-Brzeka, and William Roberts, all Vorticist sympathisers. The movement had a short-lived journal, *Blast*, co-edited by Lewis and Ezra Pound. Lewis joined the artillery after the war began and did active service in the front-line where he caught trench fever; in 1917 he was appointed an official war artist. After the war he had exhibitions at the Leicester Galleries, became friendly with the Sitwells, met Roy Campbell in 1920 and made a drawing of Virginia in 1921 in spite of his hostility to Bloomsbury and all it stood for. He detested the art criticism of Clive Bell, whom he virulently attacked in an article in the *Daily Herald* in 1922. 'Never did I read such an outburst of spite...' Virginia told Vanessa. He hated the Bloomsbury circle for their war record of pacifism (he mourned the deaths in action of his friend the thinker T E Hulme and fellow-artist Gaudier-Brzeka), for their aestheticism and for their private incomes —he himself was constantly hard-up. He edited a journal called *The Enemy* containing his drawings and articles among other contributions.

In 1924 he began to write *The Apes of God*, a critical onslaught on both the Bloomsbury veterans and the Sitwells. Among others, Lytton Strachey, Carrington, Clive and Vanessa were mercilessly caricatured in figures whose originals could easily be identified. Eliot published an extract from it in the *Criterion* and wrote a letter about it to Virginia intending to blunt the shock. She treated the whole episode as a joke and said: 'everyone—that is Lytton, Osbert Sitwell, Mary Hutchinson is claiming to be an Ape of God and identifying the rest of the pack.'[117] When the completed novel was published in full in 1930 it damaged Lewis by its excessive virulence rather more than its victims. However, it found in Roy Campbell an avid reader and it inspired him to write a similar satire but in verse and at not such vast length, *The Georgiad*, a poem in heroic couplets echoing Pope's *The Dunciad* with a vicious portrait of Vita in revenge for her seduction of his wife. Here are some lines from it:

One hoary sage, for dinner having dressed,
And hoping so to soothe her troubled breast,
Thus to the faded nymph his theme addressed:–
'Alas, poor Georgiana [Vita], what's amiss?
Like Sappho poised above the steep abyss
In what new flood of Stephen's would you drown,
Through what new gulph of bathos hurtle down?
So rapt is your expression that I guess
You have, as usual, nothing to express –
(Sappho, the Greek lyric poetess born in Lesbos in the seventh century BC, dominated a circle of women and girls, several of whom were her lovers. She is said to have thrown herself off a cliff and drowned after an unrequited passion.)

Vita's reaction to the poem when it was published in the autumn of 1931 was typical of the good breeding it satirised.

She said she never got herself involved in literary quarrels and she continued to think that Roy Campbell was a good poet. The general public were puzzled to know why he had turned so viciously on his former benefactors and friends. His marriage survived the poem's publication, but so did his wife's lesbian love affair. Virginia's repossession of Vita took the form of writing a biography of her in disguise, *Orlando*. It is a fantasy evoking Knole, the great house in Kent during its Elizabeth heyday. Virginia, who had been entertained there several times, was making Vita a present of the house that in reality she would never have; and by making the young male aristocratic hero turn into a woman half way through she was depicting Vita's sexual ambivalence.

To give added credence to the notion that it really was a biography, she included an Index and a Preface, acknowledging all the people to whom she had been indebted. Among them she named Daniel Defoe, Sir Thomas Browne, Laurence Sterne, Sir Walter Scott, Lord Macaulay, Emily Brontë, Thomas De Quincey and Walter Pater: an admirable short list of Virginia's literary ancestry. Among the living she thanked Bloomsbury friends like Desmond and Molly MacCarthy, Sydney Waterlow, Duncan Grant, Clive Bell—'that most inspiriting of critics'—Vanessa, of course, and her son Quentin (now 18 and described as 'an old and valued collaborator in fiction'), Maynard Keynes and Lydia Lopokova (for correcting her Russian knowledge), Lytton Strachey, E M Forster, Ottoline Morrell, Harold Nicolson, Sibyl Colefax, Dorothy Wellesley, Nelly Cecil (for old times' sake), Gerald (Lord) Berners, the composer, whom she had come to know and who helped her over Elizabethan music, Mrs Sidney Woolf, her mother-in-law, and Miss Nellie Boxall, her cook.

Virginia saw Vita as a living anachronism, the end product of a long line of Sackvilles going back to the Tudor period when 'dual nature' was not uncommon in poetry and drama, and even sometimes, it seems, in life. (In one of his sonnets Shakespeare addresses the 'master-mistress' of his passion and his heroines often adopt a male disguise.) Virginia strikes an aggressively androgynous note in her first sentence, giving us a view of her hero in his room at Knole at the age of 16: 'He —for there could be no doubt of his sex, though the fashion of the time did something to disguise it—was in the act of slicing at the head of a Moor which swung from the rafters.'[118]

Orlando is writing a tragedy in verse like a good Elizabethan. Vita wrote several before she was 16. He dashes off ten pages. Vita, like Virginia, was an astoundingly fluent writer. Orlando is stumped for words when trying to describe the shade of green in nature, looks out of the window at a laurel bush and is struck by the difference between description and reality. 'Green in nature is one thing, green in literature another.'[119] He escapes to the garden and flings himself on the ground at the foot of an oak tree. 'He loved, beneath all this summer transiency, to feel the earth's spine beneath him.'[120] He veers between his love of writing and reading poetry, and his love of country life in rural England. And so the Vita-Orlando parallels pile up, one after the other. The most audacious is when Orlando falls in love with Sasha, a Russian princess in a London snowbound during the Great Frost. He abandons his position at court and his betrothed in order to woo her with great passion. Virginia fantasises a version of the Violet Keppel episode, and echoes its ending with Sasha's ship pulling out of its mooring on the Thames, the tryst broken, leaving Orlando utterly forlorn.

The prose in which all this is brought to life is as visually rich and fluid as the 'Time Passes' interlude in *To the Lighthouse*, only here we experience the passing not of a mere decade but several centuries as Tudors become Stuarts and the 17th century turns into the 18th, the 18th into the era of Queen Victoria. Virginia's reading of Pepys, Macaulay and other chroniclers of English history when she was a girl seeped into her bones and she is able to convey the feel of each succeeding period authentically. Orlando changes his posture and his dress in harmony with the shifting periods, but he is no chameleon. His courage and upright nobility of spirit remain whatever costume he is wearing. For once Virginia pays close attention to her principal figure's attire. His most startling transition is one of gender. He goes into a trance and when he is awakened to the sound of trumpets 'we have no choice left but confess —he was a woman.'[121]

By putting her people in fancy dress Virginia was able to discuss the question of sexual ambiguity without any censorious reaction from the guardians of public morals in the Britain of the late 1920s. Radclyffe Hall, whose novel *The Well of Loneliness* (1928) had a lesbian heroine, had her book prosecuted for obscenity. The case was heard at Bow Street six days before *Orlando* appeared. Virginia would have testified on behalf of the author but literary evidence was ruled out. Virginia's novel worked both for those who possessed the key to it and equally well for those who took it at face value as pure fantasy. The former group, to which, thanks to the biographies, we all now belong, would have instantly recognised the references to family history in the gypsy episode, to the law-suits echoing those that Vita's parents suffered, the quotations from Vita's *Georgics* poem *The Land* about the farming seasons of Kent, and such puns as the one where Virginia writes: 'The hostess is our modern Sibyl. She is a witch who lays her guests under a spell', a sentence which must surely have given Lady Sibyl Colefax, hostess extraordinary, mixed pleasure, comparing her to an awesome prophetess of antiquity.[122] Only Vanessa perhaps would have picked up the nostalgic allusion when Orlando first puts on a dress that reaches to the ground and exclaims 'these skirts are plaguey things to have about one's heels. Yet the stuff (flowered paduasoy) is the loveliest in the world.'[123] 'Flowered paduasoy' was the stuff their bridesmaids' dresses for Stella's wedding were made of.

In terms of its theme *Orlando* was a work in advance of its time; in terms of its style it belongs to the cult of Beauty, to the aesthetic movement alongside the fiction of Pater, Oscar Wilde and the young W B Yeats, to the 1890s rather than the 1920s. Fascinating as those fuzzy photographs are, in an ideal world we would have an edition illustrated by Aubrey Beardsley.

Coming soon after *To the Lighthouse*, whose exploration of the characters' inner consciousness had given the reviewers something they could confidently expound, *Orlando* caught them off their guards. Was it a biography or a fantasy? A spoof or a masterpiece? It was endlessly discussed and in one article bracketed with Lytton Strachey's *Elizabeth and Essex*, also published in 1928, a year of Bloomsbury rampant.

Once again Arnold Bennett devoted his entire space to it in his book review column in the *Evening Standard*. His article inevitably boosted sales in key outlets of book consumption in London like Hatchards in Piccadilly, Harrods and the Times Book Club, a shop in Wigmore Street which, like Harrods, as well as selling books to its customers, would, as part of an expensive library service, guarantee to lend them any new book on publication and deliver it, if required, to their homes. 'You cannot keep your end up at a London dinner-party in these weeks unless you have read Mrs Woolf's *Orlando*.' That opening sentence of his was enough to send the customers of those shops rushing to the telephone to order the book to be sent without delay. No matter that most of the article was, unlike his response to *To the Lighthouse*, distinctly negative. ('I shall no doubt be told that I have missed the magic of the work. The magic is precisely what I indeed have missed.')

Before *Orlando* was published on 11th October 1928, Virginia went to Burgundy for a week's holiday with Vita. On her return to Tavistock Square, she wrote to Harold: 'I meant to write you a letter of thanks from Auxerre…I was going to thank you for having married Vita; and so produced this charming and indeed inimitable mixture—But I won't describe her. I've written quite enough about her and got it all wrong too… Anyhow we had a perfect week, and I never laughed so much in my life, or talked so much.'[124]

Women, waves & wings

—Look, Percival, while they fetch the taxi, at the prospect which you are soon to lose. The street is hard and burnished with the churning of innumerable wheels. The yellow canopy of our tremendous energy hangs like a burning cloth above our heads. *The Waves*

Women, wings & waves

Virginia's next published work, *A Room of One's Own*, grew out of two papers on Women and Fiction she read to societies of Newnham and Girton, the women's colleges in Cambridge. The account in the book that appeared in 1929 of her visits to the university is highly entertaining. She poses as an innocent abroad, reprimanded by 'a beadle' (shades of Oliver Twist) for walking on the grass plot that covers the centre of the court of a male college. He informs her that only fellows and scholars are permitted to tread on it. She then decides to visit the library but an officious custodian shuts the doors on her. 'Ladies,' she is told, 'are only admitted to the library if accompanied by a fellow or with a letter of introduction.' The college is not identified by name but we know it is Trinity (with all the family resonance it had for Virginia—her brothers Thoby and Adrian, Leonard and Lytton Strachey were all there) because what she particularly wished to see were the manuscripts of Milton's *Lycidas* and Thackeray's *Esmond*.

She continues with an account of a luncheon in Dadie Rylands' rooms at King's. Although never a gourmet, Virginia could describe food when she wished in such a way to make one's mouth water. She surpasses herself here as she recalls the 'soles...over which the college cook had spread a counterpane of the whitest cream...the partridges...with all their retinue of sauces and salads, the sharp and the sweet, each in its order, their potatoes thin as coins but not so hard'[125] and the accompanying wines.

Virginia photographed in 1930
Previous pages: Piccadilly Circus in the fog 1925

The occasion is contrasted in its conviviality with the stodgy food she received when she was given dinner before her talk at the woman's college. 'Soup...plain gravy soup...beef...sprouts curled and yellowed at the edge...prunes and custard...here the water-jug was liberally passed round.'[126] Virginia conveys the difference between the immense riches poured over the centuries into the colleges dedicated to the education of men and the meagre funds afforded to the foundations that exceptional women managed to bring into being, in the face of enormous odds and entrenched male hostility, to give young women the same educational opportunities as their brothers. (One such woman, the feminist campaigner and founder of Girton, Emily Davies, was her and Leonard's friend, and Margaret Llewelyn Davies's aunt.) Writing fiction, Virginia concluded, was as much a matter of education as of talent.

Vita, who accompanied Virginia to Girton for the second talk, was at this time speaking regularly on the wireless (as the radio was called) about books. She discussed Virginia's work on the air at the end of October just after it had been published, without declaring her interest. 'I hope all men will read this little book; it will do them good. I hope all women will read it; it will do them good, too,'[127] she wound up. Virginia described her friend's broadcast, which at once boosted sales, as 'flamboyant'.

Arnold Bennett, the archenemy (whose non-fiction book, *Our Women*, which sought to confine them to the home, had provoked Virginia's first feminist outburst a long time before) wrote a piece under the heading, 'Queen of the High-Brows'. He took up her main point that to write fiction you need a room of your own and an income of five hundred a year: 'I beg to state that I have myself written long and formidable novels in bedrooms whose doors certainly had no locks, and in the full dreadful knowledge that I had not five hundred a year of my own—nor fifty.'[128] Five hundred pounds a year was a comfortable income in those days—certainly enough for a writer without dependants not to have to supplement it by reviewing or any non-literary part-time work.

By February sales of *A Room of One's Own* had topped the 10,000 mark and Virginia received many letters from women saying how much the book meant to them. One from Ethel Smyth, the composer, led to her coming to tea at Tavistock Square on 20th February 1930. She and Virginia had much in common to chat about, not least Vita. Ethel was lesbian, too. She was fascinated by Virginia's Pattle ancestry and saw it coming through in her beauty—a beauty that stunned her.

She herself came from a county background and had fought a heroic battle with her military father to be able to go to Leipzig and study music.

In spite of her overbearing and preposterous, manner Virginia really liked her: 'I'm not sure that she is the egoist that people make out. She has never had anybody to admire her, & therefore might write good music to the end. Has to live in the country because of her passion for games. Plays golf, rides a bicycle; was thrown hunting two years ago. Then fell on her arm & was in despair because life would be over if she could not play games. "I am very strong" which she proved by talking till 7.30; then eating a biscuit & drinking a glass of vermouth & going off to eat a supper of maccaroni when she got to Woking at 9.'[129] The last of Virginia's great female friendships had begun. Ethel, who was 71, fell completely in love with Virginia who, a mere 48-year-old, admitted her into the charmed circle of those to whom she wrote wonderful letters full of gossip and meditation.

She was one of a dozen or more regular correspondents, among them her intimates like Vanessa and Clive; her two nephews, Vanessa's grown-up sons, Julian and Quentin; Vita and Ethel; and old chums like E M Forster, 'Bunny' Garnett and so on. Once you became a regular recipient of Virginia's letters you were one for life. And there were those people who wrote to her out of the blue with praise of her work like Theodora Bosanquet, Henry James's one-time amanuensis, who told her how much she admired *A Room With a View*, to whom she always replied in full.

What is fortunate for posterity is that almost everyone who received letters from her seems to have carefully preserved them, enabling them all to be collected and printed in the order in which they were written. After her death they were published in six volumes—*Leave the Letters Till We're Dead* is the title of the last volume, a quotation from Virginia to Ethel— overlapping with the five of the Diary. We can observe the different tone she adopts for each individual, giving as much of herself as she feels is his or her due and reacting to the events for which she knows he or she will want her impression.

In 1930 Julian Bell, aged 22, was up at King's College, Cambridge, where his contemporaries were William Empson and John Lehmann, all three of them writing poetry. Some of Bell's poems were printed in a Cambridge student publication, *The Venture*. Virginia demanded a copy of it. 'I am sitting over the fire with influenza and would like to read your works,' she writes to him in February 1930. 'Lord! How precocious you are—flourishing in all the public prints at your age, when I, at the same, modestly cowered anonymous in the review columns of the Times!'[130]

He had suggested Empson called on the Woolfs and she tells him: 'Mr Empson came to see us. A raucous youth, but I think rather impressive and red as a turkey, which I like.' While to his brother, the younger Quentin, an art student, in another letter written on the same day (signed 'Your poor dear old dotty Aunt V') she says of one of his female contemporaries he sent to see her: 'She is a nice girl—yes, I liked her. She stood fire from Roger [Fry] very well. He was at his most sweeping and searching, raking her with terrific questions and denunciations. There was Julian's Mr Empson too—a black and red sort of rook, very truculent, and refreshing.'[131] (Julian Bell published his first book of poems *Winter Movement* in 1930. Reviewers compared it to W H Auden's *Poems* of that year. William Empson, aged 24, published the seminal work of poetic criticism, *Seven Types of Ambiguity*.)

To her older friends Virginia's reactions were more ironic, though she was never wounding to anyone in a letter about their work. Vita's career as a broadcaster continued as did Harold's at the behest of their BBC talks producer, Hilda Matheson, who soon became one of Vita's most ardent lovers. She broadcast them separately talking about books and together in conversation on such general topics as marriage (!) and happiness. Virginia to Vita:

'I dont think I can stand, even the Nicolsons, on happiness for three quarters of an hour" I said at 8.15.

"Well, we can always shut them off " said Leonard. At 9 I leapt to my feet and cried out,

"By God, I call that first rate!" having listened to every word. This is (for a wonder) literally true. How on earth have you mastered the art of being subtle, profound, humorous, arch, coy, satirical, affectionate, intimate, profane, colloquial, solemn, sensible, poetical and a dear old shaggy sheep dog— on the wireless? We thought it a triumph: Harold's too.'[132]

But of all her correspondents at this period, it was to Ethel Virginia was most forthcoming, writing to her and seeing her frequently, and confiding in her the most intimate details of her private life. In this garrulous, elderly, egomaniac musician and golfer, Virginia had found an unlikely substitute for her long-lost mother.

Both *Orlando* and *A Room of One's Own* had been profitable diversions from work on Virginia's next novel, *The Waves*, which appeared in September 1931. It took an immense amount of hard work against a background of debilitating minor ailments and difficulties with domestic staff. Over many successively discarded drafts, its working title was, thanks to Vanessa, *The Moths*. In 1927 Vanessa had gone with her daughter Angelica to live for a time at Cassis, the port, east of Toulon, in the South of France. It was a favourite place for artists. Roger Fry had been there as far back as 1915, when he was in France for the Quaker Relief Mission run by his sister Margery. He made a painting of the harbour. He was back in 1925 painting a view of the town.

Duncan Grant, who was to take a house and find much inspiration there, was staying with his parents. Roger Fry and Clive Bell, whose long liaison with Mary Hutchinson had now collapsed, joined them; and so did Leonard and Virginia for a week in April, 1927. 'Vanessa and Duncan are painting the loveliest pictures of rolls of bread, oranges, wine bottles... every street corner has an elderly gentleman on a camp stool', Virginia told Vita.[133]

As Vanessa sat reading of an evening by the light of a lamp she was plagued by moths with beautiful markings, some of which were enormous. Remembering the 'sugaring' of moths they had so enthusiastically practised when they were children at St Ives, she felt obliged to try to trap them and pin them down. When she was back in England the image of moths swirling around a solitary human figure haunted Virginia after she had a letter from her sister describing them and she decided to write a story centred on this image.

She had been thinking a great deal about the rationale of novel writing and feeling the urge to make a fresh experiment. In 'The Mark on the Wall' she had prophesied that our obsession with our self-image is something that 'the novelists of the future will realise more and more the importance of.' The time had come to fulfil this prophecy. But first she needed to formulate it more fully. New York newspaper editors were continually tempting her with lucrative invitations to write pieces for them. She wrote one in August 1927 for the *Herald Tribune* headed 'The Narrow Bridge of Art' in which she declared that in future prose would attempt 'some of the duties which were once discharged by poetry.'[134] A new kind of novel will emerge. 'It will give, as poetry does, the outline rather than the detail. It will make little use of the marvellous fact-recording power, which is one of the attributes of fiction. It will tell us very little about the houses, incomes, occupations of its characters; it will have little kinship with the sociological novel or the novel of the environment. With these limitations it will express the feeling and ideas of the characters closely and vividly, but from a different angle. It will resemble poetry in this that it will give not only or mainly people's relations to each other and their activities together, as the novel has hitherto done, but will give the relation of the mind to general ideas and its soliloquy in solitude.'[135]

A year later she was cogitating such a novel but had not begun writing. 'The Moths hovers somewhere at the back of my brain.'[136] Another year passed and in September 1929 she began to get something down on paper: 'Yesterday morning I made another start on The Moths, but that wont [won't] be its title. & several problems cry out at once to be solved. Who thinks it? And am I outside the thinker?' In October the working title was beginning to be replaced: 'The Moths; but I think it is to be waves, is trudging along...'[137] A more potent image than Vanessa's moths surfaced from an earlier meditation when she had sunk into a depressed, isolated mood of self-examination: 'I wish to add some remarks to this, on the mystical side of this solitude; how it is not oneself but something in the universe that one's left with. It is this that is frightening & exciting in the midst of my profound gloom, depression, boredom, whatever it is: One sees a fin passing far out. What image can I reach to convey what I mean? Really there is none I think.'[138]

The genesis of *The Waves* may be studied in the two abandoned early manuscripts discovered among Virginia's papers and published with all her corrections and notes. In these documents we can watch her creative process at work, the constant trial and error, the great swathes of rejected material that paved the way for the finished product. The published novel contains six main characters, three male and three female, whose lives we follow from childhood to old age. They speak in soliloquies, addressing the reader directly. There is an ever-present danger that continual monologue becomes monotonous. It is avoided through the rich and distinctive imagery Virginia finds to communicate her six characters' emotions; a disciple of Elizabethan drama is trying here to resuscitate in prose the poetic energy of that golden age. Every sentence makes a visual impact. There is no direct dialogue

173

and confrontation between the characters is rarely shown.

At the outset during childish play Jinny (who stands for femininity) kisses Louis (who always remains an outsider). We observe the impact on Susan (who stands for the maternal instinct) but after this initial episode there is no consistent narrative line for the reader to cling to. We are obliged to discover most of what happened to these six people from the references that occur during their self-communings. We are given their locations—St Paul's, Piccadilly Circus underground, Hampton Court, Greenwich, Paris, Rome—as we follow them through place and time but we never observe them making crucial decisions. Thus we gather that Susan wished to marry Bernard, but failed and settled for a country squire instead; that Rhoda became Louis's mistress for a time and that afterwards she committed suicide. In an ordinary novel such happenings would be carefully planted climaxes at the end of a chapter. Here, unless you read attentively, you might miss them altogether; they are dropped in along the way as asides.

What we remember about Rhoda is the bowl she held as a girl with water in it on which floated white petals, her ships; about Louis his exotic vision of a chained elephant and women carrying pitchers down to the banks of the Nile; about Jinny her swirling gown, yellow scarf, her background of gilt chairs; about Susan, her dogs, bunches of keys, bags of currants; about Neville his room in its firelight and the apple tree he saw silhouetted after he became aware of death; about Bernard the pellets of bread he calls people. These constantly recurring images are revelatory of the ruling passions that govern the behaviour of each member of the sextet and give their lives their distinctive patterns, their identities (for want of a better word). Each section of the work covers a phase of their existence and is prefaced by a passage describing a seascape (Virginia was recalling St Ives and perhaps Manorbier where she had been on holiday as a child after the death of her father) from sunrise to nightfall. The time-scale of a single day is thus superimposed upon that of human life as a whole. The ceaseless beating of the waves upon the shore under different conditions of light mirrors the endless endeavour of human life.

It was a risky venture and, although *The Waves* is rightly to be seen as the jewel in Virginia's crown, a fictional work quite unlike any other, yielding fresh rewards and delights at each reading, not all the problems were solved. One cannot help asking, first of all, why these six children should have spent a summer together at some kind of residential home in an idyllic country setting and then remained so close for the rest of their lives. The answer must lie in the fact that they all have prototypes among the earliest inmates of Bloomsbury. This explains why Louis, the Australian (who for no given reason has been sent to England where he stays forever) should have such a crushing sense of apartness because he speaks with a 'colonial accent' (which at that age he would rapidly lose). He feels so apart that he cannot even enjoy playing or watching cricket when he arrives at his public school with the other two boys. The girls also go together to a girls' boarding school.

It is only when 'Australian' is decoded as 'Jewish' that the character of Louis comes properly to life as deriving from Leonard, with his classical learning and his outstanding ability in the world of administration and finance as well as in scholarship and intellectual pursuits. Angelica Garnett in her introduction to the definitive collected edition of *The Waves* confirms this and suggests that Susan, the wife and mother, is one aspect of Vanessa (Angelica's mother); that Jinny, the eternal female who never ceases to be attractive, is an amalgam of Virginia's mother Julia, Kitty Maxse and Virginia; that Rhoda is another aspect of Virginia, the shy, manic, withdrawn Virginia; that Bernard with his supreme self-confidence owes much to Clive Bell (though in his story-telling aspect he is Virginia yet again) and Neville, the most mysterious of them, has characteristics in common with Duncan Grant.

What they all have in common is a deep sense of loss on account of the early death in a horse-riding accident in India of Percival, a born leader and conqueror who first appears at the boys' public school and whose image dominates the mind of each member of the sextet afterwards. (Virginia knew her Wagner; could she have been thinking of *Parsifal* whose hero of that name stands surrounded by those dependent on him as their saviour?) His fatal accident is related soon after it happens in a letter to Neville who was in love with Percival and is shattered by his death. In real life Percival is Thoby for whom the book is a requiem. We see him solely through the eyes of the other characters. He is their common soul as in an unanimist novel; and is an absent presence at their reunion dinner party at a restaurant in Hampton Court, one of the finest sections of the book, enshrining the Moment, when everything seems to coalesce. The word had a special meaning for Virginia. (Compare James Joyce's use of the word 'epiphany' from Christian tradition—the occasion of Christ being presented to the Magi—to describe a similar experience, a sudden spiritual manifestation, in his early works, *Dubliners* and *Stephen Hero*.)

"'The flower," said Bernard, "the red carnation that stood in the vase on the table of the restaurant when we dined together with Percival, is become a six-sided flower; made of six lives."

"A mysterious illumination," said Louis, "visible against those yew trees."[139]

Virginia set her reviewers an exceptionally difficult task with this book. A wise, positive reaction came from Harold Nicolson: 'It is important that this book should be read twice over. The book is difficult. Yet it is superb.'[140] Not everyone agreed. Frank Swinnerton, a novelist of working-class life, writing in the *Evening News*, disliked the book but tried to be fair to it. He defined it as 'a series of rhapsodies, linked and contrasted, by which the spiritual life of half-a-dozen people, from childhood to maturity, is presented. I am not a great admirer of Mrs Woolf's work, and I find the present book as bloodless as its predecessors; but it would be idle to deny great distinction to the style, great beauty to many of the similes, and much subtlety and penetration to the author's intentions. If to these qualities life had been added, I should have been lost in admiration of Mrs Woolf's gifts.' Gerald Bullett, a poet as well as a novelist, said more or less the same thing but with a positive spin to it. 'The characters are not analysed, as in a laboratory: they are entered into, intuited. In each soliloquy in this pattern of soliloquies we ourselves are at the centre. We *are* Bernard, we *are* Susan, but with this difference: that we have borrowed, for a moment, the lamp of genius, and by its light may read the secrets of our private universe.'[141]

The ripples of the reviews of *The Waves* spread across the Atlantic, where opinion was sharply divided. In a thoughtful piece in the *New York Times Book Review* Louis Kronenberger articulated what many felt about Virginia's characters: 'They are not six people but six imagist poets, six facets of the imagist poet that Mrs Woolf is herself.'[142] Was it a novel or a poem? Was it a masterpiece or a monumental piece of self-indulgence? These questions were asked incessantly not just in Britain and America but in France and Italy, too. And they are still being asked three-quarters of a century after publication.

Pressing matters

—Ralph was in love with Carrington, she was in love with Lytton and Lytton was in love with Ralph

Pressing matters

If the deaths of loved ones were the story of Virginia's girlhood, they were also the story of the last decade of her life after she had reached the age of 50. First to go was Lytton. He had never been very strong physically. His poor health had reduced him to an armchair for much of the time and latterly he was bed-ridden. Mill House at Tidmarsh had been picturesque but infernally damp. He and Carrington moved in 1924 to a larger, drier, more solid house at Ham Spray overlooking the Newbury Downs. In December 1931 he took a turn for the worse and his doctors thought he might have typhoid. Greatly concerned, Virginia wrote letters to Ethel Smyth by every other post giving news of him (as she had to Violet Dickinson when Thoby was mortally ill). Ethel had taken over from Vita as Virginia's prime confidante though Virginia still felt 'dying embers' of her former closeness to Vita. Lytton seemed to be recovering but in the new year he became bad again and on 14th January the Woolfs drove to visit him. They found several Stracheys there but Lytton was too ill to see them, though he was made aware of their presence. He died on 21st January 1932. A postmortem revealed he had cancer of the intestines.

Virginia had lost an integral part of her life, a friend from youth until now, a colleague, a rival, a mentor, a liberator, one of the very few people whose judgment of her books mattered to her. She had felt that his later work on *Elizabeth and Essex* and *Queen Victoria* had not measured up to the high standard of his *Eminent Victorians* and his many superb essays on the major and minor figures of French and English literature.

Soul-mates: Lytton and Virginia in the garden at Garsington 1923
Previous pages: Lytton Strachey, Dora Carrington and Ralph Partridge at Ham Spray 1928

However, she had considered his most recent book, *Portraits in Miniature and Other Essays*, when it was published in May 1931, had shown him at his best. 'The compressed yet glowing account which requires logic, reason, learning, taste, wit order & infinite skill—this suits him far better, I think than the larger scale, needing boldness, originality, sweep.'[143] It was the man himself, his indomitable eccentricity, that she missed most of all—'I see him coming along the street, muffled up with his beard resting on his tie: how we should stop: his eyes glow'— and his spontaneous wit and intellectual penetration during one of those encounters. 'One knows now how irremediable…' she began to confide to her Diary the day after he died, then added, 'I cant think of any words for what I mean, & yet go on writing, numb, torpid as I am.'[144]

Carrington had vowed never to outlive Lytton. Her friends mounted a 24-hour vigil to prevent her putting her suicide threat into effect and this kept her alive, albeit inconsolably, for several weeks. Virginia and Leonard went to see her on a bright day in March. When she took Virginia into Lytton's sitting room she burst into tears and said that she owed everything to Lytton, that he had been like a father to her, that looking after Lytton was the only thing in life she had ever done at which she had not failed. 'I did not want to lie to her'—Virginia wrote in her Diary—'I could not pretend there was not truth in what she said. I said life seemed to me sometimes hopeless, useless, when I woke in the night & thought of Lytton's death. I held her hands. Her wrists seemed very small. She seemed helpless, deserted, like some small animal left.'[145]

The vigil was not thorough enough. Next morning at 8.30 the gardener heard an explosion coming from her bedroom and found she had shot herself. She was not dead but severely wounded. She insisted she had been shooting rabbits; three hours later she died, seven weeks after the demise of Lytton. The coroner recorded a verdict of accidental death.

During her lifetime Carrington was never thought of as part of Bloomsbury or one of its artists even though Duncan Grant protested after her death that he had always admired her work. Seen now her portraits of her father, Samuel Carrington, of E M Forster, Lytton Strachey, Lady Strachey and Gerald Brenan, her paintings of the Mill at Tidmarsh, mountains in Andalusia and other landscapes suggest she holds her own very well against the work in those genres of Vanessa and Roger, although her style is simpler, more direct, more radiant. After her break with Mark Gertler, so poignantly described in her Diaries and Letters (extracts from them were published, edited by David Garnett, in 1970), everything in her life was subordinated to Lytton. He certainly encouraged her to practise her art. Perhaps it assuaged the guilt he may have felt at her devotion, as she worked at her easel in tandem with the housework. She was always reluctant to exhibit and only had one or two works hung in mixed shows during her lifetime. She had no one to promote her and she did not have the desire to promote herself. The only reward she craved, apart from the satisfaction she got from painting, was praise from Lytton.

Prosperity, material as well as artistic, did not fundamentally alter the Woolfs' way of life but as their annual income rose steadily, thanks to the ever-growing sales of Virginia's work, they scrapped the Victorian system of sanitation in their Sussex house, and installed such basic amenities as running hot and cold water and a flushable lavatory. Meanwhile at the Hogarth Press in the basement at Tavistock Square two women typists and a male assistant were employed to cope with the increasing volume of sales and publications. They took on Richard Kennedy, a lad of 16, as a general dogsbody. He later in life wrote an entertaining account of his experience, *A Boy at the Hogarth Press* (1972), where we see Leonard, given to bursts of rage over the slightest error, his hands violently trembling and Virginia calmly rolling her cigarette and annoying Leonard by saying that the Press was like keeping a grocer's shop. 'I think she is rather cruel in spite of the kind dreamy way she looks at you,' Kennedy opined. Before he left he was promoted to being sales representative and he went on afternoon walks with Leonard around the Square, exercising the dog, Pinka, a cocker spaniel given to Virginia by Vita.

With so many other commitments, the Woolfs were finding the day-to-day administration of their 'grocer's

Leonard as publisher with John Lehmann at the Hogarth Press offices

shop' ever more burdensome. Leonard had been appointed co-editor of the *Political Quarterly* and was writing books on international affairs. They were always trying to think of ways of lightening their Hogarth Press load without losing editorial and financial control. In 1930 John Lehmann, whose youthful verses had appeared alongside his friend Julian Bell's in Cambridge university periodicals, had sent them the manuscript of a volume of his poems. Lehmann, and his sisters Rosamond, the novelist, and Beatrix, the actress, had a publishing background. Their grandmother came from the Chambers publishing family and their father had been a contributor to *Punch*. John, who had a private income, was destined for a career in the diplomatic or museum service. Leonard wrote to him, saying how much they liked his poems and that they were recommending

to Dorothy Wellesley that she should include them in the Hogarth Living Poets, a series she financed and edited. Leonard had been briefed about Lehmann by Dadie Rylands, who had been his contemporary at Cambridge. He added in his letter that Lehmann might like to come to see him with the view to his taking over some of the duties of running the Press.

This led to an agreement by which Lehmann, after eight months' apprenticeship, became the manager of the Press and within two years would have the option of becoming a partner. The advantage for the Woolfs was that Lehmann brought a capital sum with him as well as a sum of literary knowledge; for Lehmann it gave him as soon as he left Cambridge a job to step into in which he hoped to continue to develop his own poetic gifts and to publish his fellow-poets and, above all, where he would be in regular contact with Virginia, whom he greatly admired. He had heard from both Dadie Rylands and Julian Bell that the Woolfs were difficult employers of whom many previous incumbents had fallen foul, and he saw for himself the sordid, cluttered basement conditions under which he would have to work; but he did not let any of this dampen his enthusiasm.

At first all went well. Lehmann benefited from Leonard's counselling: 'he managed to inject my idealism with a necessary drop or two of cynicism without destroying it.'[146] They devised a series of Hogarth Letters, pamphlets on a variety of topics from Disarmament to French Painting to Anti-Semitism. Virginia wrote a Letter to a Young Poet (addressed to John himself) in which she gave her views on the work of his poetic generation. Lehmann was a friend of Stephen Spender, then aged 21, and through him was in touch with W H Auden and Louis MacNeice, all up at Oxford together, and Christopher Isherwood living in Berlin. The Press published Isherwood's second novel *The Memorial*, thanks to Lehmann. But in spite of Lehmann's fresh input into the Press's list, the partnership foundered through some bitter disagreements between him and the Woolfs. The worst came when Leonard and Virginia turned down Louis MacNeice's first volume of poems, which Lehmann had recommended. When his contract was up he left somewhat abruptly. Virginia and Leonard were incensed at the manner of his going. He went to Austria to write poetry and (he said) to study working-class conditions there at close range and (as he later confessed) to consort with young Austrian men. He then joined Isherwood in Berlin.

It was the canine element in the Woolfs' marriage that inspired *Flush,* Virginia's next book, a biography of the dog owned by Elizabeth Barrett when she eloped with her fellow-poet Robert Browning to Italy. After the draining effort of her last novel, Virginia needed to write a book light-heartedly, and this well-researched fantasy proved to be just the thing. In a mood of wry humour she gets inside not only the dog but also its mistress, a virtual prisoner in her father's house in Wimpole Street, and reveals her battle with the Whitechapel dog-stealers to retrieve her beloved animal from their clutches. The book appeared in October 1933 and sold well in spite of some adverse reviews.

That autumn Agnews art gallery held a retrospective exhibition of paintings by Walter Sickert, then in his 70s. He had been a member of Vanessa's Friday Club and on friendly terms with Bloomsbury ever since, though he disagreed with Roger Fry's and Clive Bell's Post-Impressionist views on art. (Duncan and Vanessa now had London studios at 8 Fitzroy Street, a street traditionally inhabited by Sickert and his circle of artists.) Virginia went to the exhibition, enjoyed it, and at Vanessa's suggestion wrote him a fan letter.

The elderly artist was delighted by her letter and suggested she should write something publicly about him. Stimulated to try some art-criticism, she wrote *Walter Sickert: A Conversation*, in the form of an after-dinner discussion among a group of friends about the artist's work in which she offers her own interpretations of the paintings. She wrote of one of the most famous he called *Ennui* (boredom): 'You remember the picture of the old publican, with his glass on the table before him and a cigar gone cold at his lips, looking out of his shrewd little pig's eyes at the intolerable wastes of desolation in front of him? A fat woman lounges, her arm on a cheap yellow chest of drawers, behind him. It is all over with them, one feels. The accumulated weariness of innumerable days has discharged its burden on them.'

Sickert said Virginia's was the only criticism worth having he had received in his whole life. The essay appeared from the Hogarth Press as a pamphlet in October 1934.

In September of that year another of the original members of Bloomsbury died: Roger Fry, of heart failure. He was 68. Virginia and Vanessa heard the news in Sussex and prepared to go to London for the funeral at the Golders Green Crematorium on Thursday 13th. Even though Vanessa's affair with him belonged to the distant past, he had remained among their closest friends, often seeing them in England and France, participating in discussions about art and literature; his and Leonard's favourite pastime was chess, to which both were addicted, and they had had many games together.

For many years Roger's mistress had been Helen Anrep, the

wife of the Russian-born mosaic artist, Boris Anrep, a virile, handsome man and himself a notoriously unfaithful husband. When he worked on the commission to design mosaics for the floor of the National Gallery in Trafalgar Square, he jokingly portrayed some of his Bloomsbury friends in them as Greek gods and goddesses.

Helen Anrep and Roger's sister Margery were the chief mourners at the funeral. His insane wife Helen did not die until 1937. As the coffin, draped in red brocade with two bunches of brightly coloured flowers, disappeared to the strains of Bach, Virginia thought of Roger as: 'Dignified & honest & large—"large sweet soul"—something ripe & musical about him—& then the fun & the fact that he had lived with such variety & generosity & curiosity.'[147] Hardly had he gone to rest when Margery and Helen began to hint that Virginia might like to consider writing his biography.

The life of 'old Bloomsbury' as they now thought of themselves continued with as much intensity of work and frivolity as before. Duncan and Vanessa's studio at 8 Fitzroy Street was sometimes used for their gatherings. In January 1935 there was an especially hilarious one when a play titled *Freshwater*, written by Virginia, was performed. She had written it some dozen years previously, a one-acter in which she made fun of the Victorian worthies who lived on the Isle of Wight, the society of her great-aunt Julia Margaret Cameron. It was an occasional Bloomsbury practice to round off a gathering with a performance of a short play. In this one Mr and Mrs Cameron are about to go to India but they cannot leave until the coffins they wish to take with them for their burials arrive. At the same time the actress Ellen Terry is posing to G F Watts (to whom aged 16 she was briefly married) for the sculpture 'Modesty at the feet of Mammon'.

Virginia's power of puncturing pomposity with absurdity was never seen to better effect. She had revised the play and the new script had Vanessa's daughter Angelica as Ellen Terry, Vanessa as Mrs Cameron, Leonard as Charles Cameron, Julian Bell as Tennyson and Duncan Grant as Watts. Clive Bell, who did not have a part except as a member of the audience, laughed so much, as did his brother Cory, that the performance was seriously disrupted.

Another death that impinged on Virginia's professional life during the decade had been that of Arnold Bennett in March 1931 of typhoid fever through drinking tap water at his flat in Paris. Despite his adverse reviews they had known each other socially and now that he was gone she was rather sad: 'A lovable genuine man; impeded, somehow a little awkward in life; well meaning; ponderous; kindly; coarse; knowing he was coarse; dimly floundering & feeling for something else. Glutted with success: wounded in his feelings: avid; thick-lipped: prosaic intolerably; rather dignified; set upon writing; yet always taken in; deluded by splendour & success; but naïve; an old bore; an egotist; much at the mercy of life for all his competence; a shop keepers view of literature; yet with the rudiments, covered over with fat & prosperity & the desire for hideous Empire furniture, of sensibility. Some real understanding power, as well as a gigantic absorbing power.'[148]

Virginia never became 'glutted with success' but as the 1930s—that 'low dishonest decade' Auden called it—saw the rise of Fascism in Italy and Nazism in Germany, Virginia's stature as a writer increased greatly, not just in England and America, where her work was discussed in academe in periodicals such as the *Yale Review,* the *Sewanee Review,* as well as being reviewed in the New York daily press, but also on the continent of Europe. A French critic wrote an article in 1931 in the *Revue Anglo-Americaine* pointing to the similarity between the notion of time in her novels and that of the contemporary French philosopher Henri Bergson: 'time as made up of heterogeneous elements, varying with each individual, changing ceaselessly.'[149] The Italian critic Salvatore Rosati thought that *Jacob's Room, Mrs Dalloway* and *To the Lighthouse* were 'three moments in the tendency towards an increasingly rigorous interiorisation' and he stressed the debt she owed to Laurence Sterne and his great wayward novel *Tristram Shandy* by abandoning linear development. The critic Maud Bodkin in her book *Archetypal Patterns in Poetry* (1934) relating the theories of the psychiatrist Carl Gustav Jung to literature suggested that the habit Virginia's main characters, like Mrs Dalloway, had of quoting lines of poetry during their monologues, showed them drawing upon the collective unconscious (a key Jungian concept) 'the recurring, amid the flux of an individual sensibility, of symbols of a group tradition.'[150]

That 'raucous youth', William Empson, whom she had met with her nephew Julian, wrote a penetrating article on her novels for Rickword's *Calendar* in a series called 'Scrutinies' (reprinted in book-form in 1931), applying the technique of 'practical criticism' (close analysis of the text), evolved by his Cambridge mentor I A Richards, to Virginia's prose. The result is fascinating. Here is one example. Empson quotes a passage from the 'Time Passes' section of *To the Lighthouse* that recalls Mrs Ramsay's shawl, which she had wrapped around a skull of a boar's head so that it would not frighten her small daughter. Now, after her death, it is all that remains of her in the empty house.

'Nothing it seemed could break that image, corrupt that innocence, or disturb the swaying mantle of silence which, week after week, in the empty room, wove into itself the falling cries of birds, ships hooting, the drone and hum of the fields, a dog's bark, a man's shout, and folded them round the house in silence.'[151]

Empson comments: 'Mrs Woolf can show very brilliantly how the details of her characters' surroundings are woven into their moods; this is an important part of a novel, and what I have just called her poetical use of language is the best way of doing it. But here the whole point of the situation is that *no* character is in the room; what is eerie about the sounds is that they are *not* being woven into anybody's mood; and the sentence seems to have the falsity that comes from always using a single method. As long as this sort of method is being used dramatically, to show how a character felt, it is excellent if only because it is true; people's minds do work like that; it may really be the only way to deal adequately with motivation. But when it is being used to show merely how Mrs Woolf is feeling about what she describes the result is not always formal enough to be interesting. One thing reminds her of a lot of others, and the story is held up while they are mentioned; but one feels that the reasons why she thought of these things at the moment of writing are not part of the book.'[152]

Two more practical critics, Dr F R Leavis and his wife Q D (Queenie) Leavis, in Cambridge borrowed Rickword's key-word 'Scrutinies' (with acknowledgment) and in 1932 with some colleagues started the critical journal *Scrutiny* aimed at exposing what they considered to be the 'literary racket' of London and the pretensions of fashionable mutually-publicising coteries like that of Virginia and her friends. It was a vicious onslaught that never let up until the journal ceased publication in 1953.

In the number for May 1932 M C (Muriel) Bradbrook in 'Notes on the Style of Mrs Woolf' wrote that in *The Waves* 'there are no solid characters, no clearly defined situations and no structure of feelings: merely sensation in the void. Without any connections of a vital sort between them, with no plot in the Aristotelian sense, the sensations are not interesting. Emotions are reduced to a description of their physical accompaniments: the attention is wholly peripheral.'[153] (As a student the writer had attended the talk at Girton that Virginia gave there, the paper that became *A Room of One's Own*. She told me that 'we found her very odd.' After that Dr Bradbrook ceased to be a scrutineer and became a scholar of Elizabethan drama, a much-loved supervisor of her women pupils studying English, and ultimately the Mistress of Girton College.)

Nearer home there were several critics determined to undermine Virginia's reputation, chief among them the persistent Enemy, Wyndham Lewis, who had followed the fictional *Apes of God* with a critical study, *Men Without Art*, in 1934. He singles out Virginia for special treatment, making comparisons between her self-indulgent novels, as he viewed them, and those of James Joyce. He lampooned her essay 'Mr Bennett and Mrs Brown' as mere salon (drawing-room) criticism. His more serious points were weakened by being smothered in gratuitous insult and a hillbilly style of expression copied from Ezra Pound.

She shrugged it all off, hurt but reconciled to such attacks as the price to be paid for fame; even so her critics must be held in

191

part responsible for her decision to return in her next novel to the straightforward realism she had derided. In particular she remembered her fellow-practitioner Arnold Bennett's strictures on the 'Time Passes' section of *To the Lighthouse* where he said that there was no way a novelist could give the sense of the passing of time except by doing it 'very gradually, without any direct insistence—in the manner of life itself.' In 1932 Virginia took the momentous decision to write a novel covering the period of her childhood to the present day in England, using the gradual approach recommended by Bennett. It started out as *The Pargiters* and, after five years of agonising work that almost drove her mad again and much cutting of the original text, it appeared in 1937 as *The Years*. The novel tells the story of one English family from 1880 until that time. Colonel Abel Pargiter lost two fingers during the Indian Mutiny, a detail Virginia emphasises as he grips the decanter of port at his house in London. He has a large family of daughters and sons and a wife dying in bed upstairs attended by a nurse. He also has a mistress whom he visits in the slum dwelling where she lives with her daughter. Part one centres upon the death of the colonel's wife and the different reactions to it of his daughters, the youngest of whom has narrowly escaped a sexual assault from a stranger. Scholars have not been slow to identify the Pargiters with the Stephens, the colonel with Leslie and the youngest daughter with Ginia (as she was).

While the novel thus lends itself to a game of hunt the trauma, it is better read as a straightforward family chronicle in which Virginia is saying to Bennett and Galsworthy: 'Anything you can do, I can do better than you'. As such it has pleasures to offer, not least period descriptions of London, where much of the book is set. Eleanor Pargiter, the spinster eldest daughter, is the character with whom Virginia most closely identifies. Among many other relationships seen as they fluctuate against a backdrop of historical events, which includes the deaths of the Irish politician Charles Stewart Parnell and King George V, carefully noted as historical markers, she gives much attention to Eleanor's view of her cousin, Kitty Malone, the striking daughter of the head of an Oxford college, whom she likens to

Antigone and with whom her brother Edward is in love.

Now that Kitty Maxse was dead Virginia did not need to use another name for her. She is resuscitated here in Virginia's imagination as she might have been had she married Charley Howard. As Lady Kitty she gives even grander parties than the real Kitty gave. In the end when both Eleanor and Kitty are stout elderly women with white hair they meet at an all-night party in London given by Eleanor's sister. They are doughty survivors into a serene old age; not, as they were in life, two childless women of exceptional gifts who in their 50s took their own lives.

Once shot of writing it, Virginia suffered her usual depressed sense that the novel on which she had spent so much time was worthless. Because of a tight Hogarth and American publishing schedule, it was set up in galley proof before Leonard had had a chance to read it. In Virginia's eyes he was the ultimate arbiter. If he approved, adverse reactions from others might wound but in the end they would not count. Leonard read and Virginia awaited his verdict in fear and trembling. She was in such a state of nerves that he knew that anything less than complete approval might topple her into another prolonged breakdown. The trouble was, he did not like it nearly as much as her more experimental novels; but dare he say so? He was an Apostle still and the brethren believed in truth at whatever cost. Unlike Virginia in a similar situation with Carrington, when a lie might just conceivably have saved her life, Leonard put Virginia's sanity above the truth. 'I think it is extraordinarily good', he said when he had reached the end.

The frozen state of the Woolfs' relations with Lehmann began to thaw as the war clouds gathered over Europe. He had spent his years on the continent getting to know writers opposed to fascism (such as the Italian Ignazio Silone, the Frenchmen Jean-Paul Sartre and André Chamson, the Czech Jiri Mucha, and the Greek poet George Seferis) and publishing them alongside their British contemporaries in collections titled *New Writing*. By 1938 several volumes had appeared that had made a powerful impact in the literary world but he lacked a publisher for the coming one and he approached the Woolfs.

They had not forgiven his swift unceremonious exit but they welcomed him back. By now reaching their late 50s, they really did wish to hive off the day-to-day responsibility of running the Press to a responsible partner while Lehmann was concerned to find a permanent home for *New Writing*. As they were trying to work out a fresh arrangement with him, all three were stunned by the news that Julian Bell, who had gone out to Spain to act as an ambulance-driver in the civil war, had been killed. It was a kind of reprise of the death of Thoby with an even greater impact on Vanessa, petrified in grief, never fully to recover from it. Virginia was remorseful that in her last contact with him she had been critical of an essay he had written about Roger Fry for a memorial volume they were planning. For her part she felt the resemblance between Thoby and Julian should not be pushed too far: '...nor do I think that Julian was like Thoby, except in the obvious way he was young & very fine to look at. I said that Thoby had a natural style, & Julian had not.'[154]

Leonard and Lehmann disagree in their memoirs as to whether at this point Leonard intended to sell the Press as a whole to Lehmann. In the end what happened was that Lehmann bought Virginia's shares to become managing director and joint-owner with Leonard. One of the first indications of the new agreement was the appearance in August 1938 of a new series of *New Writing* with the Hogarth logo (a wolf's head) on its first page. Collections drawing in part on the hardback volumes, (later called *Folios of New Writing* and *New Writing and Daylight*) appeared throughout World War Two in paperback as *Penguin New Writing*. Meanwhile, Lehmann's friendship with Virginia was to his delight resumed. While she admitted him and his fellow-poet Stephen Spender to her circle, she had her reservations about their work as poets and that of their group. She had first articulated them in her *Letter to A Young Poet* addressed, as we saw, to Lehmann in 1931. Virginia followed her playful show of humility (her opinions, she confessed, were those of a mere prose-writer who could not tell a dactyl from an iambic and therefore hardly worth having) by revealing her distaste for the lack of beauty, the

194

coarseness and the obsession with themselves in the work of the poets of Lehmann's generation, ending with the advice that they should refrain from publishing until they were 30, the age at which they would have had time to begin to mature as writers. This infuriated them.

Virginia returned to the attack in 'The Leaning Tower', read originally as a paper to the Rodmell Women's Institute during World War Two. Here she quotes from Louis MacNeice's *Autumn Journal*, a long personal poem about the events leading up to the appeasement of Hitler at Munich and now regarded as one of his masterpieces. She finds it 'feeble as poetry, but interesting as autobiography'. MacNeice, son of a distinguished Northern Ireland Protestant clergyman, had been educated at Marlborough College and Merton College, Oxford, where he took a first in Greats (Latin and Greek, philosophy and ancient history), met W H Auden and Stephen Spender, and became a university lecturer before in 1941 becoming a writer-producer at the BBC. MacNeice writes in the poem:

'...the so-called humane studies
May lead to cushy jobs
But leave the men who lead them spiritually bankrupt,
Intellectual snobs.'

This rouses Virginia's anger. These poets, she says, are making their families, their education, the cultural riches they have inherited, a scapegoat for their own malaise. 'They are profiting by a society which they abuse. They are flogging a dead or dying horse because a living horse, if flogged, would kick them off its back. It explains the destructiveness of their work; and also its emptiness. They can destroy bourgeois society, in part at least; but what have they to put in its place?'[155]

MacNeice among others gave answers to that question in Lehmann's *New Writing* of Autumn 1941. By then the once secure upright tower (the security given them by their inheritance as Virginia's metaphor went) had not merely begun to lean, it had toppled over altogether in the confusions and destructiveness of war; and Auden, the leading poet of the group (whom Virginia does not mention) had gone to live in America.

Donations

—This is Oxford Street. Here are hate, jealousy, hurry, and indifference frothed into a wild semblance of life. These are our companions. *The Waves*

Donations

To Virginia's surprise *The Years* was enthusiastically received by the public and the press and sold better than any of her previous books. After the difficulties of *The Waves*, the lead reviewers sounded grateful to be back on familiar territory. The *Evening Standard* critic Howard Spring, a journalist, who had taken the paper's weekly book-article over from Arnold Bennett and J B Priestley, and who later became a bestselling novelist himself, was fulsome in his praise. He likened the time-span to Noël Coward's play *Cavalcade* and declared: 'though Time itself is here the primary force, enigmatic and inscrutable, against which all these lives have their transient being, with what vitality Mrs Woolf invests the little lives themselves, their affairs and their habitations!'[156]

In its first versions Virginia had conceived *The Pargiters* as an 'essay-novel' in which the chapters of narrative would be interleaved with her reflections on the male dominance of society and public life, the culture that confined women to domesticity and child-bearing exemplified by the lives of the women in the novel. It would have been a further development of the themes of *A Room of One's Own* but when she tried to set it down she found the structure of such a massive work to be impossible. Now, having published the novel, she decided to make a separate book out of the essay parts on which she had spent much time in research. The result was *Three Guineas*, in which Virginia again took up the literary convention of an open letter addressed to a single individual to press home her views on what she saw as the continuing injustices to women

Ottoline Morrell: hostess of Garsington Manor in Oxfordshire
Previous pages: A traffic jam in Oxford Street, 1939

and to vent her anger at this state of affairs. The background was 'the gathering storm', the feeling that a war, which no one except Hitler wanted, was bound to happen. Virginia replies to a letter she had received from a gentleman asking her how she thinks war may be prevented and for a donation to enable him to proceed with his work running an organisation aimed at its prevention. She explains what her priorities are in the disposal of the three guineas she has set aside to donate to deserving causes.

In a preamble she points out what a unique occurrence it is that he should be writing to her at all, 'since when before has an educated man asked a woman how in her opinion war can be prevented?'[157] It is the word 'educated' that opens the flood-gate to Virginia's rhetoric throughout the remainder of the book. She assumes her correspondent to have begun his education at one of the great public schools and finished it at Oxford or Cambridge, and to have pursued a successful career at the bar before devoting his time and energy selflessly to try to preserve the peace of the world.

He and she have much in common: 'When we meet in the flesh we speak with the same accent; use knives and forks in the same way; expect maids to cook dinner and wash up after dinner.'[158] In spite of these revealing assumptions on Virginia's part (the Woolfs' creative, literary and publishing existences depended on their long-suffering servants) there is a great gulf fixed between her and her correspondent because Virginia has not had the same educational start in life. It is not just a question of book-learning but of the opportunities for networking at Oxford or Cambridge which her correspondent—like her brothers, her husband, her brother-in-law and her nephew —had enjoyed. It is this that weighs when Virginia considers on whom to bestow the first of her three guineas. Would not it be better sent to an organisation aimed at reversing the educational imbalance?

In the extensive notes to *Three Guineas* Virginia refers to speeches by contemporary politicians, statistics, newspaper articles, official reports, to substantiate her presentation of female deprivation over the centuries; but her main thrust in the body of the text comes from the Victorian England in which her own childhood was rooted. She quotes from a biography of Mary Kingsley (niece of the novelist Charles) who wrote: 'I don't know if I ever revealed to you the fact that being allowed to learn German was *all* the paid-for education I ever had'[159] Virginia then points to the existence of an item with its equivalent in many household ledgers, Arthur's Education Fund (in Thackeray's novel *Pendennis*), 'a voracious receptacle' siphoning off money for the education of the sons at the expense of the daughters. This was the situation in 1850 and it remained to that very day.

No work of Virginia's has aroused more controversy than *Three Guineas* and not all those who have found it misguided have been male. Mrs Queenie Leavis penned a blistering attack on it in *Scrutiny* for September 1938: 'What respectable ideas inform this book,' she said at the outset, 'belong to the ethos of John Stuart Mill. What experience there is of domineering and hostile men (for that purports to justify the undertaking) is second-hand and comes from hearsay.' Her destruction of the book hinged on what she saw as the wholly unrepresentative nature of the 'women of our class', 'the daughters of educated men', in whose name Virginia is addressing her correspondent. Virginia, she said, was not reliable with her facts and gave as an example her remark, 'Not a single educated man's daughter is thought capable of teaching the literature of her own language at either university [that is, Oxford and Cambridge].' Mrs Leavis pointed out that: 'There are at present (1938) six women regularly on the lecture-list for the English Tripos [the final honours examination].' The article is an interesting statement of the writer's views on the state of female education and liberation before the war, taking us some considerable way

from Virginia's book, with one or two wisecracks thrown in for good measure. Virginia writes: 'Daughters of educated men have always done their thinking from hand to mouth...They have thought while they stirred the pot, while they rocked the cradle.' Mrs Leavis countered: 'I myself...have generally had to produce contributions for this review with one hand while actually stirring the pot, or something of that kind, with the other, and if I have not done my thinking while rocking the cradle it was only because the daughters of even uneducated men ceased to rock infants at least two generations ago.'[160]

Virginia's argument, with its wealth of material drawn from her knowledge of 'the lives of the obscure', with its highlighting of the barriers preventing women taking up professions exclusively reserved for men and its mockery of the male predilection for ceremonial costume and regalia, can still be read with enjoyment. Virginia is always entertaining, especially at her most polemical. Progress has overtaken much but not all of it. Towards the end she acknowledges the growing menace of fascism as she reluctantly agrees to part with her final guinea to the cause sponsored by her correspondent but this danger is not what motivates her main thrust.

Three Guineas received a sympathetic review from Graham Greene in the *Spectator*, who thought that the only defect of 'this clear brilliant essay'[161] was when it touched on religion. He said she discussed Christianity 'only in terms of the Church of England' and he could not imagine even the most agnostic French woman agreeing with her view that God was a 'conception, of patriarchal origin, valid only for certain races, at certain stages and times.'[162]

Virginia was in two minds whether to send a copy of *Three Guineas* to Vita, who had not liked *The Years*, but did so adding 'Its only a piece of donkey-drudgery'.[163] Vita had recently been to see Virginia in London and the meeting had been so successful that Virginia had said to Leonard after she had disappeared in her 'sweeping black car' that Vita was the nicest person they knew. Her interest in Vita's lesbian circle had not diminished. Vita had made a friend of Edith Craig, the daughter of Ellen Terry, who lived with her female partner in a house at Smallhythe in Kent, of which the barn had been turned into a theatre where plays by women, and concerned with the problems facing women, were regularly performed. Virginia wished to investigate this set-up but so far had not been successful. 'No sign from Edie,' she told Vita. 'There's a fate against my joining. But I mean to...'[164] This pleasant exchange took a turn for the worse when Virginia received Vita's reaction to the new book. She had enjoyed the style but had disliked and disagreed with much of the argument: '...I question very much [she told Virginia] whether any Englishwoman feels that England is not her country because she will lose her nationality if she should happen to marry a foreigner... (p196). Again, on p194, you suggest that "fighting is a sex characteristic which she cannot share," but is it not true that many women are extremely bellicose and urge their men to fight? What about the white feather campaign in the last war? I am entirely in agreement with you that they ought not to be like that, but the fact remains they frequently are. The average woman admires what she considers to be the virile qualities.'[165] They never pulled their punches when criticising each other's work and their relationship continued as before.

Around this time death ended Virginia's relationships with other outstanding women who had played a significant part in her life. Janet Case, her classics teacher, had died the year before aged 70. She and her sister Emphie, whom Virginia visited at their house in the New Forest, were stalwart examples of educated women who had always had to earn their own living and had lived a hard-working spartan existence in consequence. Virginia's obituary appeared in *The Times* as 'by an Old Pupil'.

Then came the death of Ottoline Morrell on 21st April 1938, and again Virginia wrote an obituary for *The Times* that appeared under her own name a week later, in the early editions only for some obscure reason, in which she said: '...with what imperious directness, like that of an artist intolerant of the conventional and the humdrum, she singled out the people she admired for qualities she was often the first to detect and champion, and brought together at Bedford Square and then at Garsington, Prime Ministers and painters, Bishops and freethinkers, the famous and the obscure!'[166] And in May came the news that Ka Arnold-Foster, Ka Cox as she was when Virginia had first met her in the Cambridge circle of Rupert Brooke, had died aged 51. Virginia had not been in touch with her for a long time but it came as a great shock.

There were worrying doubts, too, about Leonard's state of health. He was diagnosed as having a kidney disorder and then as needing a prostate operation but after innumerable tests and X-rays the specialists decided, to Virginia's immense relief, that there was nothing wrong with him after all. For all her female friendships (Ethel, still in the ascendant, was 80 on 23rd April 1938), he remained the rock that gave Virginia's existence its stability. They decided that they both needed a holiday and in June they drove to the Isle of Skye. To Virginia it seemed like the South Seas: 'completely remote, surrounded by sea, people speaking Gaelic, no railways, no London papers, hardly any inhabitants,'[167] as she told Vanessa and congratulated her on Duncan's Scottish ancestry.

They returned to England via Kirkby Lonsdale where Margaret Llewelyn Davies's father John had been the rector for many years, and where she had first organised the Women's Cooperative Movement from its vicarage, and where one of Margaret's beloved Apostle Society brothers had drowned in a swimming accident. It 'seemed', Virginia told her, 'as lovely as any place we saw—I longed to take an old grey house I saw to let on the road. It was a perfect morning, after violent storms, and the moors looked magnificent, and the town so dignified, and an old woman said she remembered your father, and I could hardly bear to drive away.'[168]

They did drive away and it was back to work as soon as they were home. A mixture of altruism and loyalty to an old Bloomsbury friend made Virginia agree to write the biography of Roger Fry, her next professional task. It was an imposition that taxed all her self-discipline and tact in view of his private life; but she pressed on with it, frequently in blackest despair about the project, and by March 1940 she had a text to show Leonard. He did not like much of what he read and for once he spoke his mind. He thought her method was the wrong one, that of analysis not history. 'Austere repression,' he said. 'In fact dull to the outsider.' However, what mattered in the end was what Margery Fry thought of it. When her letter came Virginia breathed again. 'It's him,' Margery wrote, expressing her 'unbounded admiration' at the portrait of her brother.

Let us leap forward, for the moment, to August 1940 when *Roger Fry A Biography* was published at a time when World War Two was entering its second year and France had fallen. In his *New Statesman* review E M Forster said he viewed the book in the light of one of mankind's darkest hours when all that Fry stood for appeared to have failed. He concluded that: 'Mrs Woolf preaches best when she does not preach, and her accurate account of her friend's life, her careful analysis of his opinions, have as their overtone a noble and convincing defence of civilisation.'[169]

Unlike the polemic of *Three Guineas,* Virginia's analysis of a life dedicated to practising and promoting art, in painting, writing and lecturing, showed her at her most convincing about a writer of her own generation whose belief in the healing power of nature and renewal through art were similar to her own. A younger generation of art-lovers thought differently as Virginia discovered when she received a letter from Ben Nicolson, Vita's son, then aged 24, giving his reaction to the book. He said that it was plain from her biography that during the years leading to the World War Two, Roger Fry had been living in 'a fools paradise.' He had 'shut himself out from all disagreeable actualities and allowed the spirit of Nazism to grow without taking any steps to check it...'

Roused by that comment to white-hot indignation, Virginia replied at length in a letter written from Monk's House in August 1940[170] after an air-raid warning had sounded during the course of which she stopped writing to go out and watch the German bombers passing overhead on their way to Newhaven. She told Ben that Roger had faced death, insanity, disappointment in his career, among many other disagreeable actualities. (But they were not the disagreeable actualities that Ben meant. She is, whether consciously or not, missing the point.) And, anyway, she continued, what more could Roger have done to combat the spirit of Nazism than he had done by his lectures and writings? She became so angry that she wondered whether to send the letter, applying to Leonard for his opinion. He said calmly that it was difficult to see what anyone could have done to stop the rise of Nazism; and after that she decided she would send it.

Ben had helped Virginia with her research on the book, going through Roger's uncollected articles and lectures annotating them. The idea was for him to make another book out of these; but the project was abandoned when the war broke out and he obtained a commission in the intelligence corps. In a further letter, Ben said that his quarrel was 'not with art but with Bloomsbury'. They should have done more to educate the majority to become aware of what was happening in the world at large. He quoted an isolated remark of Roger's as typical of the Bloomsbury attitude: 'More and more I understand nothing of humanity in the mass'. Virginia riposted that that observation was simply one person's point of view; and not especially typical of Roger's outlook over the years. Moreover, she objected to Ben's use of the term Bloomsbury as if it represented a single, consistent attitude. She could not be held responsible for all of Roger's utterances, nor could the other members of Bloomsbury, and she pointed to Leonard's output. He, too, was Bloomsbury and 'he has spent half his life in writing books like International Government, like the Barbarians at the gates [sic], like Empire and Commerce, to prevent the growth of Nazism; and to create a League of Nations.' And Maynard Keynes was Bloomsbury. He wrote the *Economic Consequences of the Peace*, a work that warned the world of the folly of the Treaty of Versailles.[171]

Virginia bore no grudge against Ben. Indeed she admired the honesty and outspokenness he had shown in his dispute with his mother's old friend. Amicable relations were resumed when he came to visit the Woolfs during his leave. Seeing him in the winter of 1940, he seemed to Virginia to be 'an odd sample of the young man cut adrift'.[172] After the war Ben resumed his career as an art historian and became editor of the *Burlington Magazine*, the authoritative art journal that Roger had helped to found.

Finale

—A strong feeling of invasion in the air. Roads crowded with army wagons: soldiers. Just
back from half a day in London. Raid, unheard by us, started outside Wimbledon. A sudden
stagnation. People vanished. *Virginia's Diary for 13ᵗʰ September, 1940*

Finale

Sir (as he then was) Bruce Richmond's retirement before the war from *The Times Literary Supplement* was a landmark in Virginia's life, ending an association that had lasted for 30 years. She remembered how pleased she used to be when he rang almost every week to ask her to do a review. Leonard, picking up the phone, would shout: 'You're wanted by the Major Journal!' 'I learnt a lot of my craft of writing for him [Richmond]: how to compress; how to enliven; & also was made to read with a pen & notebook, seriously'[173] After the two *Common Readers*, her work as a literary journalist was reprinted in volumes such as *The Death of the Moth, The Moment, The Captain's Death Bed, Granite and Rainbow*, several published posthumously; and they have been followed by a scholarly *Collected Edition* of her essays where they may be read and studied as a whole in chronological order of their original publication.

Virginia did not write as many short stories as essays; even so there are enough of them to fill a stout volume, *The Complete Shorter Fiction of Virginia Woolf*. In her latter years Virginia was, for an appropriate fee, happy to respond to an inquiry for a story. When she was too busy to write one from scratch, she would ransack her stockpile of unpublished work to see if she had anything suitable. On a request from *Harper's Bazaar*, New York, while writing the Fry book, she found a piece she had written 20 years before called 'Lappin and Lapinova'. She 'rehashed' it, as she put it, and it appeared in April 1939. It turns on the giving of pet names to those we love, a practice to which, as we have seen, Virginia was especially prone. The

This portrait by Man Ray appeared in Time *magazine, 4ᵗʰ December, 1937*
Previuos pages: The docks and East End of London ablaze after an air raid, 1941

young wife pictures her husband as a rabbit. His pet name becomes her point of entry into a fantasy world to which she retreats to escape from the reality of a dismal marriage that collapses when, at the height of an emotional storm, he scorns the pet name that no longer seems valid.

Virginia's own emotional storms were mainly to do with her writing rather than Leonard's and her pet names. They came, too, from her tendency to overextend herself in congenial company. She loved parties. Leonard's invariable 'Virginia, it is time we went home' at 11pm meant Cinderella had to leave the ball. She always obeyed his curfew without demur. Then there was the ever-present danger that an adverse review could trigger deep depression. She wrote a long essay entitled 'Reviewing' in which she suggested the present system of reviewing should be scrapped and replaced by counselling sessions between novelists and critics. It was partly a joke but it was published as one of the Hogarth pamphlets, with a note by Leonard disagreeing with her conclusions.

In May 1939 the Woolfs felt they could no longer stand the noise from demolition work in progress next door to them in London and decided they must move. Their new address was 37 Mecklenburgh Square, to the east of Coram Fields, not all that far from Tavistock Square. To the usual upheaval was added the problem of installing the Hogarth Press there. This was in a London urgently preparing for war with air-raid shelters appearing all over the capital.

Of the Jewish artists and scientists who had taken refuge in Britain to escape Nazi persecution, the most eminent was Sigmund Freud, whom Leonard and Virginia met in Hampstead in January 1939. Freud had left Vienna in the summer of 1938 and was living in a large house at 20 Maresfield Gardens with some members of his family. Virginia had hardly read any Freud at this time, even though the Hogarth Press had published translations of his work by Lytton's brother, James Strachey. When later that year she did read him in large doses—'gulped' him, she said—the result was confusion. He reduced her mind to a 'whirlpool; & I daresay truly. If we're all instinct, the unconscious, whats all this about civilisation, the whole man, freedom &c? His savagery against God good. The falseness of loving one's neighbours. The conscience as censor. Hate…But I'm too mixed.'[174]

Sitting in his study at a table with statues from the flat in Vienna on it, she felt more like a patient than a guest. She saw him as: 'A screwed up shrunk very old man: with a monkeys light eyes, paralysed spasmodic movements, inarticulate: but alert. On Hitler. Generation before the poison will be worked out. About his books. Fame? I was infamous rather than famous. didn't make £50 by his first book. Difficult talk. An interview. Daughter [Anna Freud, the child psychologist] & Martin [one of Freud's sons] helped. Immense potential, I mean an old fire now flickering.'[175]

Leonard in his memoirs also recalled the meeting. For him '[Freud] had an aura, not of fame, but of greatness. The terrible cancer of the mouth which killed him only eight months later had already attacked him. It was not an easy interview. He was extraordinarily courteous in a formal old-fashioned way—for instance, almost ceremoniously he presented Virginia with a flower (a narcissus from the well-stocked garden). There was something about him as of a half-extinct volcano, something sombre, suppressed reserved. He gave me the feeling which only a very few people I have met gave me, a feeling of great gentleness, but behind the gentleness, great strength. The room in which he sat seemed very light, shining, clean, with a pleasant open view through the windows into a garden. His study was almost a museum, for there were all round a number of Egyptian antiquities which he had collected. He spoke about the Nazis. When Virginia said that we felt some guilt, that perhaps if we had not won the 1914 war there would have been no Nazis and no Hitler, he said, no, that was wrong; Hitler and the Nazis would have come and would have been much worse if Germany had won the war.'[176]

On Sunday 3rd September 1939 Leonard and Virginia were at Rodmell enjoying the fine weather. At 11.15am, they heard Chamberlain's broadcast when he informed the British people they were now at war as a consequence of Germany having

Leonard Woolf's immaculate garden at Monk's House.

ignored the British Government's ultimatum to withdraw its troops from Poland. Virginia's and Leonard's response was to make sure that Monk's House was completely blacked out at night. Virginia spent a couple of hours sewing curtains for this purpose and was glad of the task. Even she was unable to concentrate sufficiently to be able to read a book on that day. Evacuees—children from London's East End and their mothers—began to appear in the village to escape bombing raids on the capital, which were feared to be imminent. On the following Wednesday at 8.30 in the morning as she lay

in bed Virginia heard an air-raid warning, 'a warbling that gradually insinuates itself', but there was no raid.

What did Virginia look like at this period? If there was one thing she loathed more than having her portrait painted, it was having her photograph taken, but fortunately for us, she was unable to avoid this altogether. In November 1934 she had attended a private view in London of work by the Paris-based Jewish-American photographer and artist Man Ray. Exercising all his fabled charm with women, he succeeded in persuading her to sit for him. The result is a brilliant set of monochrome portraits. Her hair is swept back in a bun, the fine eyes stare out, the lips are emphasised by the lipstick he forced her to use. In one, where she is resting her arms on the back of a chair, we can see to the full the beauty of her hands, her long tapering fingers and the absence of a wedding ring.[177] Another Parisian photographer, Gisèle Freund, also approached Virginia more than once before the war, asking if she might add her to those writers and artists of whom she had done portraits, but Virginia always refused. In June 1939, one of Virginia's fervent admirers, Victoria Ocampo, a wealthy Argentinian lady who founded and published the literary review *Sur,* arrived one afternoon and, without warning Virginia in advance, brought Freund and all her equipment with her. Virginia was livid but submitted to the photographic ordeal and the result is another most revealing portrait. The visage has 'wanned' somewhat (as Hamlet said about the player-king) since the earlier ones and the faraway expression has become more distracted. She seems both aloof and full of anxiety.

During 1939 there were two more deaths of people in Virginia's family circle. One was that of Stella's widower Jack Hills. She thought that of all their 'youthful directors he was the most open minded, least repressive, could best have fitted in with later developments, had we not gone our ways—he to politics & sport, we to Bloomsbury.'[178] Leonard's mother died in July and was buried at the Jewish Cemetery on Balls Pond Road with *kaddish* (prayers for the dead) said for her in a service at the West London Synagogue.

Leonard had frequent meetings in London to discuss the war with Kingsley Martin, his editor at the *New Statesman.* In Sussex he was rejected for the Home Guard because of his nervous tremor. Instead he became an auxiliary fireman and when not on duty, or writing, he continued to work hard at his gardening. One of the delights of the garden at Monk's House was an immaculate bowling lawn. He and Virginia had become keen bowlers, competing against each other after dinner on summer evenings and against old friends who came to visit like William Plomer, the writer and publisher's literary adviser, who lived in Sussex and was a frequent guest. Locally Virginia did, as we have seen, play her part as a member of the Rodmell Women's Institute.

Virginia was close to her nephew Quentin and to her niece Angelica. Her first professional engagement as an actress was as a member of the chorus in a production of *Lysistrata* in Regent's Park, the Aristophanes comedy whose theme Virginia had, as we saw, made use of in an early story. At the age of 16 Angelica had been told by Vanessa who her real father was: not Clive Bell, as she had been brought up to believe, but Duncan Grant—a most bewildering revelation, as she later described in *Deceived by Kindness* (1984), after she had abandoned acting for painting, writing and marriage.

As soon as she was clear of work on Roger Fry, Virginia started in earnest on two writing projects dear to her heart. One was a novel with the working title of 'Pointz Hall' and the other was a history of England seen through its literature, a way of putting all those Hours in a Library (to borrow the title of Leslie's collections) into one huge comprehensive book. It never got written, in spite of her having done much research for it, but the novel was completed and was published after her death as *Between The Acts*. It is a book of fewer than 150 pages centred on an English country house. The way of life of the family who own the house and live there is gracious and well regulated, with a butler, a cook and a bevy of servants below stairs to look after them. In novels roughly contemporary, Henry Green's *Loving* and Evelyn Waugh's *Brideshead Revisited,* and indeed in *Orlando*, such houses are seen as idyllic havens, described with affection and nostalgia; here the idyll becomes rancid.

The conversation after dinner, on the glorious evening in June 1939 when the novel begins, is all about the cesspool. The barn where refreshment is to be served on the day of the pageant is crawling with insects and mice. The tea tastes like rust boiled in water and the cake is flyblown, though the visiting gentry pronounce it delicious. 'They had a duty to society,' Virginia tells us. The water in the fish pond is opaque over the mud. A snake in the pathway is trying to eat a toad and choking. Crushing it, Giles gets its blood over his white tennis shoes. Pointz is starved of sunlight having been built in a hollow facing north.

Isa, the poetry-loving wife and mother, has violently ambivalent feelings about her handsome husband and is attracted to a local gentleman farmer. Mrs Manresa, a sexy 45-year-old, who breezes in uninvited for lunch with her friend William Dodge, is attracted to Isa's husband, and so is William. In a conventional novel these amorous lusts would form the essence of the plot. Here they become incidental when the main narrative turns to the pageant to be performed on the terrace of the house during the afternoon.

The elaborate spectacle acted by local people, each one deftly characterised, has been written and rehearsed by an eccentric, masterful woman who lives in the village but as an outsider, belonging nowhere in the hierarchical ranks of its society. Her script to the accompaniment of music on a wind-up gramophone unfolds the story of England from the time of Chaucer to that day. (In 1935 there was a historical pageant performed at Abinger in Surrey where E M Forster lived; he wrote the speeches for it.) The family, their guests and their neighbours all become members of the audience, closely observed as they experience what is enacted before them, the work of art. The double time-scale, the progression of the centuries in the pageant in counterpoint with the 24 hours of the external action, reminds one of both *Mrs Dalloway* and *Orlando*. Within the pageant are playlets giving the flavour of the different periods, lively, skilful parodies. They are followed by the spectators' reactions.

Miss La Trobe, the pageant-mistress, with her anxiety and despair at the reception of her work, her refusal to confront the public directly or acknowledge the applause afterwards, is a memorable portrait of the Artist, an amalgam of Virginia herself, Ethel Smyth and Edith (Edie) Craig, whose Kentish barn auditorium Virginia had, presumably, by now visited.

If I had to choose only one of Virginia's novels to take with me on a desert island, I would choose *Between The Acts* over its more imposing siblings. Its ingenuity of construction would never cease to delight and at each re-reading I am sure I would discover fresh insights into the hidden lives of the characters. It fixes forever the England of the period between the coronation of George VI in 1937 and the outbreak of World War Two, the era of appeasement.

Most reviewers were lukewarm about the novel and several suggested the author would have drastically revised it had she lived. The exception was Edwin Muir in the *Listener* who said it was one of her 'most ambitious and perfect novels'. Time has tended to endorse that opinion.

Virginia's anxiety deepened in 1940 as the German armies overran Europe and France fell to them. She reckoned (probably rightly) that Leonard, a Jew and a promoter of the League of Nations, and she herself as his wife would be among the first to be taken away to the gas chambers were the Nazis to conquer Britain. Moreover, she believed they soon would, as did many others at that time without voicing their fears. She and Leonard discussed suicide and decided to do it together in the garage by inhaling fumes from their car with the engine running. He kept enough petrol in reserve for the purpose. They abandoned this plan when Adrian Stephen, Virginia's brother, now a practising psychoanalyst, provided them with a lethal dose of morphia to use instead.

As a prelude to the feared Nazi invasion came the German air assault, the Battle of Britain—and the Woolfs were in the flight-path of the Luftwaffe bombers. On 16th August 1940 Virginia wrote: 'They came very close. We lay down under the tree. The sound was like someone sawing in the air just above us. We lay flat on our faces, hands behind head. Don't close yr teeth said L. They seemed to be sawing at something stationary. Bombs shook the window of my lodge. Will it drop I asked? If so, we shall be broken together. I thought, I think, of nothingness— flatness, my mood being flat. Some fear I suppose. Shd we take Mabel [their maid] to garage. Too risky to cross the garden L. said. Then another came from Newhaven. Hum & saw & buzz all round us. A horse neighed on the marsh. Very sultry. Is it thunder? I said. No guns, said L. from Ringmer, from Charleston way. Then slowly the sound lessened. Mabel in kitchen said the windows shook. Air raid still on, distant planes.'[179]

A month later a bomb exploded in Mecklenburgh Square and their ceilings caved in, their china was smashed, their books damaged. Virginia wondered why they ever left Tavistock Square, but they would have been no better off staying there. It, too, was hit. In October she saw the room where she had written so many of her books with only one wall still standing; the rest was rubble. Vanessa's and Duncan Grant's studios in Fitzroy Street were bombed. The Hogarth Press moved under Lehmann's supervision to Letchworth in Hertfordshire.

Lehmann's *Penguin New Writing* now had a rival. Cyril Connolly's *Horizon* began to appear at the end of 1939. Stephen Spender, who was on Lehmann's board, was also helping Connolly and he asked Virginia to contribute to *Horizon,* but she never did. Those two journals and the back half of the *New Statesman* were avidly read by the many young men and women on active service who wished to keep in touch with the literary culture. David (Bunny) Garnett had been contributing the weekly Books in General article for the *New Statesman* but wartime duties at the Air Ministry forced him to give it up. The literary editor Raymond Mortimer offered the slot to Virginia who, though flattered, declined it. To the disquiet of Vanessa, Bunny was having an affair with Angelica, whom he married in 1942.

Leonard the fireman had to patrol the streets of Rodmell at night and learn how to operate a primitive pump. Apart from the Press, his responsibilities included those of secretary to the Labour Party Advisory Committee and chairman of the Fabian Society's International Bureau; but in spite of the privations of war, social life at Rodmell continued. One visitor was the novelist Enid Bagnold, who lived nearby at North End House, Rottingdean, with her husband Sir Roderick Jones, head of Reuters until 1941. Virginia had never warmed to her and thought of her merely as a second-rate friend of Vita's. Enid had written a bestseller *National Velvet* about a race-horse and her passion for horses was satisfied during the war when, with petrol severely rationed, she drove around Brighton in the

Victorian phaeton (a four-wheeled, horse-drawn open carriage) her husband had given her. She came in it to lunch at Monk's House when, as a favour to Vita, Virginia had invited her. She had promised Vita she would leave them alone together. Vita had replied that that would not be necessary as her friendship with Enid was purely platonic. Enid felt that at long last she was on the point of becoming a friend of Virginia's, but by then it was too late.

On 14th June 1940, the day the Germans entered Paris, Vita, Leonard and Virginia went to visit Penshurst Castle in Kent where Virginia had never been. It had the great interest for her of having been the dwelling of Sir Philip Sidney about whose prose romance *Arcadia* she had written a long, thoughtful essay. To visit it in the company of 'Orlando' was as good a way as any of spending that dreadful day.

Desmond MacCarthy, who had, as his main employment, been for many years the lead book-reviewer on the *Sunday Times*, visited Monk's House during the war with the philosopher G E Moore, hero of their youth. Virginia felt that at 65 some of the force had gone from Moore; but he remained a paragon of mental purity in Leonard's eyes. Another friend going back to Virginia's youth was Elizabeth Robins, the one-time Ibsenite actress, an acquaintance, as we saw, of Stella's. She lived as an American expatriate in Brighton where she shared a house in Montpelier Crescent with Octavia Wilberforce, a descendant of William Wilberforce, the campaigner against slavery. Octavia was thereby linked in her ancestry to Virginia through the Clapham Sect. She was an outstanding instance of someone who had repudiated her genteel upbringing and, in the face of fierce opposition from her family, became a doctor, encouraged and supported during her years of training by Robins.

Since 1923 Octavia had been a general practitioner with the Brighton house as her surgery; and she also ran a convalescent home for women, converted from a Sussex farmhouse belonging to Robins. When the Woolfs first knew Octavia, Robins was, as Leonard put it, 'already an elderly woman and a dedicated egoist, but she was still a fascinating as well as an exasperating egoist.'[180] She went back to her brother in America in 1940 and returned to England after the war. Octavia remained in Brighton and continued with her medical practice. She kept an eye on Virginia as a doctor as well as a friend. She made frequent visits to Monk's House, bringing with her welcome gifts of milk and cream. Despair over *Between The Acts* was bringing on a breakdown more severe than Virginia's usual reaction of disillusionment with the work she had just completed. When John Lehmann read the manuscript, he wrote to her about it enthusiastically but that did not make her feel any better. He wished to publish in the spring. She asked him to postpone publication until the autumn so that she could revise it.

One rainy day in March 1941 Virginia set out on her own for a walk and Leonard went to meet her. 'She came back across the meadows soaking wet, looking ill and shaken. She said that she had slipped and fallen into one of the dykes. At the time I did not definitely suspect anything, though I had an automatic feeling of desperate uneasiness.'[181] He persuaded her to go to Brighton and consult Octavia professionally which she did and afterwards seemed slightly better, but still in a state of deep depression. At this point Leonard should, as he afterwards admitted, have imposed a regime of perpetual surveillance and round-the-clock nursing, but he felt it might induce a repetition of the condition of hysterical madness that had occurred the year after they were married.

He did nothing but wait and observe her condition. On the morning of Friday 28th March, he was in the garden and thought she was in the house. At one o'clock he went in to lunch and found a letter for him on the sitting room mantelpiece that began: 'Dearest, I feel certain I am going mad again. I feel we can't go through another of those terrible times. And I shan't recover this time. I begin to hear voices, and I can't concentrate. So I am doing what seems the best thing to do. You have given me the greatest possible happiness. You have been in every way all that anyone could be. I don't think two people could have been happier till this terrible disease came. I can't fight any longer. I know that I am spoiling your life, that without me you could work. And you will I know...What I want to say is I owe all the happiness of my life to you...V.'[182]

Leonard went down to the river Ouse to search for her. Soon he found Virginia's walking stick on the bank. Three weeks later some children saw her body floating.

Had she not, for whatever reason (if that word is appropriate), drowned herself, she would undoubtedly have written more books; yet the immense amount of creative writing she did achieve, her lifetime of ceaseless effort at the task, have gained her a secure place among the immortals. Her precise placement within the ranks of the novelists of the 20th century is difficult to determine. She was a practitioner of the form at its most purely artistic. Her agenda as a novelist was never to try to change society, but to represent it as accurately as she possibly could through the command she had over the English language. Apart from her fiction, her Diary in its entirety would be enough to give her a permanent niche alongside Pepys and Boswell, to say nothing of her letters that are as complete a record of her time as those of her beloved Madame de Sévigné, or her essays covering so much of our literature, meditations to be put beside those of Lamb, Hazlitt and De Quincey. Her death was a shattering blow not just to her husband, friends and contemporaries, but also to a younger generation of writers who had fallen under her spell. The poet Sidney Keyes, then aged 19 and down from Oxford to serve in the army wrote an 'Elegy for Mrs Virginia Woolf' that began:

Unfortunate lady, where white crowfoot binds
Unheeded garlands, starred with crumpled flowers,
Lie low, sleep well, safe from the rabid winds
Of war and argument, our hierarchies and powers.

Two years later he was killed in action in Tunisia.

Footnotes

The following frequently cited works are abbreviated as follows:

BA: Leonard Woolf, *Beginning Again* (1964)

BB: Anthony Curtis (ed), *Before Bloomsbury: The 1890s Diaries of Three Kensington Ladies* (2002)

CH: *Virginia Woolf: The Critical Heritage* (eds R Majumdar and A McLaurin, 1975)

D: *The Diary of Virginia Woolf* (five volumes, ed Anne Olivier Bell, asst Andrew McNeillie, 1977-84)

ESS: *The Essays of Virginia Woolf* (six volumes, ed Andrew McNeillie, 1986)

L: *The Letters of Virginia Woolf* (six volumes, ed Nigel Nicolson and Joanne Trautmann, 1975-1980)

MOB: Virginia Woolf, *Moments of Being* (ed Jeanne Schulkind, revd ed 1985)

PA: Virginia Woolf, *A Passionate Apprentice: The Early Journals 1897-1909* (ed Mitchell A Leaska, 1990)

QB: Quentin Bell, *Virginia Woolf: A Biography* (two volumes, 1972)

All Woolf's novels are quoted from the nine-volume *Definitive Collected Edition of the Novels of Virginia Woolf*, with introductions by Quentin Bell and Angelica Garnett (1990)

[1] David Cecil, 'Two Twentieth Century Novelists' in *Poets and Storytellers* (1949)

[2] F R Leavis, 'After To the Lighthouse', *Scrutiny*, Vol 10, 1942

[3] Graham Greene, 'An English View of François Mauriac', *The Windmill*, 1946

[4] *Hyde Park Gate News*

[5] Quoted in QB 2, p128

[6] BB, p52

[7] MOB, p84

[8] MOB, p91

[9] QB 1, p45

[10] BB, p36

[11] VW, *The Voyage Out*, p16

[12] PA, p61

[13] PA, p105

[14] PA, p105

[15] PA, p116

[16] PA, p116

[17] PA, pp136 and 149

[18] L 1, p34

[19] L 1, p43

[20] 22 Hyde Park Gate in MOB, p177

[21] MOB, p69

[22] L 1, p130

[23] L 1, p133

[24] PA, p184

[25] L 1, p140

[26] QB 1, p90

[27] *Mrs Dalloway*, p83

[28] BB, p77

[29] *Sir Leslie Stephen's Mausoleum Book* (ed Alan Bell,1977) p104

[30] F W Maitland (ed), *The Life and Letters of Leslie Stephen* (1906), p474 ff

[31] L 1, p202

[32] L 1, p184

[33] L 1, p186

[34] PA, p217

[35] L 1, p313

[36] L 1, p251

[37] L 1, p266

[38] L 1, p268

[39] Quoted in W C Lubenow, *The Cambridge Apostles: 1820-1914* (1998)

[40] Paul Levy, *Moore: G E Moore and the Cambridge Apostles* (1979) pp65-66

[41] Michael Holroyd, *Lytton Strachey* (1994 edition) pp89-90

[42] L 1, p364

[43] QB 1, p207 and p209

[44] *Desmond MacCarthy: The Man & His Writings* (1984) from Introduction by David Cecil p15

[45] BB, p80

[46] VW, *Roger Fry: A Biography* (1940) p183

[47] L 1, p395

[48] L 1, p276

[49] VW, *The Voyage Out*, p72-3

[50] Christopher Hassall, *Rupert Brooke: A Biography* (1964) p280

[51] BA, p41

[52] L 1, p476

[53] BA, p28

[54] BA, pp30 and 31

[55] L 1, p485

[56] L 1, p496

[57] Frederic Spotts (ed), *Letters of Leonard Woolf* (1990) p170

[58] L 1, p501

[59] L 2, p3

[60] L 2, p6

[61] L 2, p108

[62] Matthew Sturgis, *Walter Sickert: A Life* (2005) p404; Richard Shone, *Bloomsbury Portraits* (1976) p66

[63] See Richard Shone, *The Art of Bloomsbury* (1999) p71

[64] D 1, p17

[65] L 2, p95

[66] CH, pp49, 50 and 51

[67] CH, p53

[68] CH, p55

[69] L 2, p150

[70] BA, p235

[71] L 2, p167

[72] CH, p10

[73] L 2, p144

[74] L 2, p159

[75] L 2, p174

[76] John Middleton Murry (ed), *The Letters of Katherine Mansfield* (1922) p72

[77] D 1, p94

[78] D 1, p165

[79] D 1, p174

[80] D 1, p179

[81] D 1, p216

[82] Osbert Sitwell, *Laughter in the Next Room* (1949) p18

[83] Osbert Sitwell, *Laughter in the Next Room* (1949) p23

[84] D 1, p202

[85] D 1, p259

[86] D 1, p269

[87] D 1, p286

[88] L 2, p390

[89] CH, p76

[90] CH, p79
[91] L 2, p295
[92] D 1, p316
[93] D 2, p339 ff
[94] CH, p93
[95] CH, p110
[96] CH, p112
[97] ESS 3, p421
[98] D 2, p178
[99] D 2, p206
[100] VW, *Mrs Dalloway*, p16
[101] VW, *Mrs Dalloway*, p17-18
[102] VW, *Mrs Dalloway*, p21
[103] CH, p159
[104] L 3, p129
[105] D 3, p18
[106] ESS 4, p160
[107] Edgell Rickword, *Essays & Opinions: 1921-31* (ed Alan Young, 1974) p201.
[108] L 1, 184
[109] VW, *The Years*, pp296-7
[110] 'Middlebrow' in Collected Essays 2, Hogarth Press pp196-7.
[111] VW, *Mrs Dalloway*, pp27 and 30
[112] L 3, p150
[113] D 3, p18
[114] CH, p193
[115] CH, pp200-1
[116] L 3, p297
[117] L 3, p108
[118] VW, *Orlando*, p3
[119] VW, *Orlando*, p5
[120] VW, *Orlando*, p7
[121] VW, *Orlando*, p87
[122] VW, *Orlando*, p128
[123] VW, *Orlando*, p98
[124] L 3, 541
[125] VW, *A Room of One's Own*, p10
[126] VW, *A Room of One's Own*, p16
[127] CH, p258
[128] CH, p259
[129] D 3, p292
[130] L 4, p140
[131] L 4, p140-1
[132] L 4, p160
[133] L 3, pp358-9
[134] VW, *Granite and Rainbow*, p18
[135] VW, *Granite and Rainbow*, pp18-19
[136] D 3, p190
[137] D 3, p257; D 3, p262
[138] D 3, p113
[139] VW, *The Waves*, p152
[140] CH, p266
[141] CH, p267; CH, p270
[142] CH, p275
[143] D 4, p26
[144] D 4, pp64-5
[145] D 4, p82
[146] John Lehmann, *Thrown to the Woolfs* (1978) p13
[147] D 4, p243
[148] D 4, p16
[149] CH, p299
[150] CH, p325
[151] VW, *To the Lighthouse*, p123
[152] CH, pp303-4
[153] CH, p312
[154] QB 2, p256
[155] Collected Essays 2, Hogarth Press p175
[156] CH, p377
[157] VW, *Three Guineas*, p109
[158] VW, *Three Guineas*, p110
[159] VW, *Three Guineas*, p110
[160] CH, p415

[161] CH, p407

[162] CH, p408

[163] L 6, p231

[164] L 6, p232

[165] Louise De Salvo and Mitchell A Leaska (ed), *The Letters of Vita Sackville-West to Virginia Woolf* (1984) p442

[166] D 5, p365

[167] L 6, p243

[168] L 6, p250

[169] CH, p425

[170] L 6, p413

[171] L 6, p420

[172] L 6, p449

[173] D 5, p145

[174] D 5, p250

[175] D 5, p202

[176] Leonard Woolf, *Downhill all the Way: An Autobiography of the Years 1919-1939* (1967), pp168-9

[177] See *Man Ray: Photographs* (1982)

[178] D 5, p198

[179] D 5, p311

[180] Leonard Woolf, *The Journey Not the Arrival Matters* (1969), p84

[181] Leonard Woolf, *The Journey Not the Arrival Matters* (1969), p91

[182] QB 2, p226

ACKNOWLEDGEMENTS

The author and publisher wish to express their thanks to the following for permission to quote from the works, letters and diaries of Virginia Woolf: The Society of Authors, Random House (U.K.), Harcourt Brace (U.S.) and to Henrietta Garnett for permission to quote from a letter by Vanessa Bell to Kitty Maxse.

The author and publisher also wish to express their thanks to the following sources of illustrative material and/or permission to reproduce it. akg-London, Charles Beresford Estate, Henrietta Garnett, Getty Images, Topham Picturepoint, Virginia Woolf Estate, The Society of Authors.

Selected Bibliography

Works by Virginia Woolf

The Voyage Out, 1915

Melymbrosia: an early version of The Voyage Out edited DeSalvo, 1982

The Mark on The Wall (one of *Two Stories* 'written and printed by Virginia Woolf and L S Woolf') 1917

Night and Day, 1919

Kew Gardens, a short story with woodcuts by Vanessa Bell, 1919

Monday or Tuesday, 1921

Jacob's Room, 1922

The Common Reader, 1925

Mrs Dalloway, 1925

To the Lighthouse, 1927

Orlando: A Biography, 1928

A Room of One's Own, 1929

The Waves, 1931

The Waves: The two holgraph drafts, edited Graham, 1976

The Common Reader: Second Series, 1932

Flush: A Biography, 1933

Letter to a Young Poet, 1933 (included in *The Hogarth Letters*, 1985)

Walter Sickert: A Conversation, 1934

The Years, 1937

The Pargiters: the novel-essay portion of The Years edited Leaska, 1978.

Between the Acts, 1941,

The Definitive Collected Edition of the Novels of Virginia Woolf edited Quentin Bell and Angelica Garnett, 1990 (nine volumes, 1990, quotations in this book are from this edition)

Three Guineas, 1938 (in one volume with *A Room With A View*,1984)

Roger Fry, 1940

The Death of the Moth, 1942

The Moment and Other Essays, 1947

The Captain's Death Bed and Other Essays, 1950

Collected Essays of Virginia Woolf edited by Leonard Woolf, four volumes, 1966-69

The Essays of Virginia Woolf, six volumes edited McNeillie, 1986-95

Granite and Rainbow, 1958

Mrs Dalloway's Party, 1973

Freshwater A Comedy, 1976

The Complete Shorter Fiction of Virginia Woolf edited Dick,1989

Moments of Being edited Schulkind, 1976, revised edition 1985

Hyde Park Gate News: The Stephen Family Newspaper edited Lowe, 2005

A Writer's Diary edited Leonard Woolf, 1953

The Diary of Virginia Woolf edited Olivier Bell and McNeillie in five volumes, 1977-84

A Passionate Apprentice: the early journals of Virginia Woolf edited Leaska, 1990

The Letters of Virginia Woolf in six volumes edited Nicolson and Trautmann, 1975-1980

Congenial Spirits: The Selected Letters of Virginia Woolf edited Trautmann Banks (contains letters not in the six

228

volumes) 1989
Virginia Woolf's reading notebooks edited Silver, 1983

First-hand sources

Virginia Woolf by Quentin Bell (two volumes 1972)
An Autobiography by Leonard Woolf in five volumes:
Sowing; Growing; Beginning Again; Downhill All the Way; The Journey Not the Arrival Matters, 1961-1967
Letters of Leonard Woolf edited Spotts, 1990
The Life and Letters of Leslie Stephen by F W Maitland, 1906
Sir Leslie Stephen's Mausoleum Book edited Alan Bell, 1977
Selected Letters of Leslie Stephen in two volumes edited Bicknell, 1996
Julia Duckworth Stephen: stories for children, essays for adults edited Gillespie and Steele, 1987
The Selected Lettters of Vanessa Bell 1879-1961 edited Mahler, 1993
Virginia Woolf and Lytton Strachey: Letters edited Leonard Woolf and James Strachey, 1956
The Letters of Lytton Strachey edited Levy, 2005
Carrington: Letters and Extracts from her Diaries chosen by David Garnett, 1970
Portrait of a Marriage by Nigel Nicolson, 1973
Letters of Vita Sackville-West to Virginia Woolf edited DeSalvo and Leaska, 1984
Old Friends by Clive Bell, 1988.
Deceived by Kindness: A Bloomsbury

Childhood by Angelica Garnett, 1982
Before Bloomsbury: The 1890s Diaries of Three Kensington Ladies, edited Anthony Curtis, 2002
Bloomsbury by Quentin Bell, 1986
Elders and Betters (Bloomsbury Recalled in the US) by Quentin Bell, 1995
A Boy at the Hogarth Press by Richard Kennedy, 1972
The Golden Echo by David Garnett, 1953
Thrown to the Woolfs by John Lehmann, 1978
Virginia Woolf and the Raverats edited Pryor, 2003

Works on members of Virginia's family and friends

Leslie Stephen the Godless Victorian by Noel Annan, 1984
Lytton Strachey: The New Biography by Michael Holroyd, 1994,(latest edition)
E M Forster: A life by P N Furbank, 1979
Vita: The Life of Vita Sackville-West by Victoria Glendinning
Vanessa Bell by Frances Spalding, 1983
John Maynard Keynes by Robert Skidelsky (*Hopes Betrayed 1883-1920,* 1983, and *The Economist as Saviour 1920-1937,* 1992)
Moore: G E Moore and the Cambridge Apostles by Paul Levy
The Cambridge Apostles 1820-1914 by W C Lubenow, 1998
Carrington by Gretchen Gerzina, 1989

Duncan Grant by Frances Spalding, 1970

Roger Fry by Frances Spalding, 1997

Ann Thackeray Ritchie by Winifred Gérin, 1983

Anny: a life of Anne Isabella Thackeray Ritchie by Henrietta Garnett, 2004

Bloomsbury Portraits, 1976, and *The Art of Bloomsbury,* 1999, by Richard Shone.

Victorian Bloomsbury and *Georgian Bloomsbury 1910-1914* by S P Rosenbaum, 1987 and 2003

Journey to the Frontier: two roads to the Spanish Civil War by Peter Stansky and William Abrahams, 1966 (for Julian Bell)

Spinsters of this Parish: the life and times of F. M. Mayor and Mary Sheepshanks by Sybil Oldfield, 1984

Rupert Brooke by Christopher Hassall, 1964

The Neo-Pagans by Paul Delaney, 1987

The Life of Katherine Mansfield by Anthony Alpers, 1980

Katherine Mansfield A Secret Life by Claire Tomalin, 1987

Ottoline by Sandra Jobson Darroch, 1976

Ottoline Morrell: Life on ther Grand Scale by Miranda Seymour, 1992 (revised 1998)

Bloomsbury and Beyond: the Friends and Enemies of Roy Campbell by Joseph Pearce, 2001

The Enemy a biography of Wyndham Lewis by Jeffrey Meyers, 1980

Enid Bagnold by Anne Sebba, 1986

Travel and photography

Travels with Virginia Woolf edited Morris, 1993

Virginia Woolf's London by Jean Moorcroft Wilson, 2000 (earlier title, *Virigina Woolf, life and London* in the *Bloomsbury Heritage* series published by Cecil Woolf, Leonard's nephew)

The Hidden Houses of Virginia Woolf and Vanessa Bell by Vanessa Curtis, 2005

Snapshots of Bloomsbury by Maggie Humm, 2006

A complete list of previous biographies and studies of Virginia Woolf may be consulted through any Public Library on-line catalogue or better still through the British Library Integrated Catalogue via the Internet on http://catalogue.bl.uk

Cast

Stephens, Duckworths and Bells

Leslie Stephen (1832–1904), VW's father, Victorian man of letters and editor, previously married to Harriet Marion (Minny) Thackeray (1840–1875) by whom he had a mentally retarded daughter, Laura (1870–1945).

Julia Stephen (1846–1895), VW's mother, previously married to lawyer Herbert Duckworth (1833–1870) by whom she had a daughter (Stella) and two sons (George and Gerald).

George Duckworth (1868–1934), VW's older stepbrother, private secretary to Sir Joseph Austen Chamberlain (1863–1937), Conservative Chancellor and Foreign Secretary.

Stella Duckworth (1869–1897), VW's beloved stepsister. She married J W (Jack) Hills (1867–1938), solicitor, later Conservative MP, in 1897, and died later that year.

Gerald Duckworth (1870–1937), VW's younger stepbrother. Founder of publishing house, Duckworth & Co, which published VW's two earliest novels.

Thoby Stephen (1880–1906), VW's older brother who died of typhoid fever. Model for Jacob in *Jacob's Room* and Percival in *The Waves*.

Vanessa Bell (1879–1961, born Stephen), VW's sister, artist who lived at Charleston in Sussex for much of the year. She married Clive Bell (1881–1964), art critic and author, in 1907. Mother of Julian (1908–1937), poet, killed in the Spanish Civil War; Quentin (1910–1996), potter, art historian, author, and Angelica, artist, (born 1918).

Adrian Stephen (1883–1948), VW's younger brother, psychiatrist. Married Karin Costelloe (1889–1953), younger daughter of American Mary Berenson (1864–1945), wife of art guru Bernard Berenson (1865–1959), sister of man of letters Logan Pearsall Smith (1865–1946).

(Sir) James Fitzjames Stephen (1829–1894), baronet, VW's eminent lawyer uncle, head of Stephen family.

Caroline Emelia Stephen (1834–1909), 'the Nun', VW's aunt, a devout Quaker who lived in Cambridge.

Katherine Stephen (1856–1924), Sir James's eldest daughter, Principal of Newnham College, Cambridge. James Kenneth Stephen (1859–1892), his mentally disturbed son, in love with Stella Duckworth.

VW's Vaughan and Fisher Cousins

Margaret Vaughan (1862–1929), 'Marny', daughter of Julia Stephen's sister Adeline (1837-1881) and Henry Halford Vaughan (1811–1885).

William Wyamar Vaughan (1865–1938), schoolmaster (headmaster of Rugby), married Margaret (Madge) Symonds (1869–1925) daughter of Victorian man of letters, John Addington Symonds (1840–1893), and model for Sally Seton in *Mrs Dalloway*.

Emma Vaughan (1874–1960), 'Toad', Marny's youngest sister.

Florence Fisher (1863–1920), daughter of Julia Stephen's sister Mary (1841–1916) and Herbert W Fisher (1825–1903). Florence married Frederick William Maitland, (1850–1906), legal historian and first biographer of Leslie Stephen.

Adeline Fisher (1870–1951), Florence's sister, married to composer Ralph Vaughan Williams (1872–1958).

Stephen neighbours and friends

(Lady) Anne Ritchie (1837–1919), novelist, Leslie Stephen's sister-in-law, daughter of novelist W M Thackeray (1811–1863). VW knew her as 'Aunt Anny'. Model for Mrs Hilbery in *Night and Day*.

Catherine (Kitty) Maxse (1867–1922, born Lushington), society hostess, married to Leopold James (Leo) Maxse (1864–1932), right-wing editor and journalist. Model for Clarissa Dalloway

and for Kitty Lasswade in *The Years*.

Margaret Massingberd (1869–1906, born Lushington), Kitty's younger sister, close friend of Stella.

Susan Lushington (1870–1953), Kitty's youngest sister. The Lushingtons were outstanding amateur musicians, frequent visitors to 22 Hyde Park Gate and guests at Talland House, St Ives.

Violet Dickinson (1865–1948), very tall, wealthy spinster, great-niece of novelist Emily Eden (sister to Lord Auckland, she accompanied him to India when he became Governor General of India). VW recovered from her first breakdown in 'ViDick's' country house at Welwyn, Hertfordshire.

Mary Sheepshanks (1872–1960), deputy principal of Morley College, Lambeth, adult education institution. Nicknamed by VW, who took classes there, 'the Sheep'.

Janet Case (1863–1937), Cambridge classical scholar and feminist who taught VW Greek and became lifelong friend.

Margaret Llewelyn Davies (1861–1944), general secretary of the Women's Cooperative Guild, for whom LW worked, and who became close friend of VW. Her father the Rev John Llewelyn

Davies (1826–1916) was a radical English clergyman, and her aunt, Emily Davies, one of the founders of Girton College, Cambridge.

Lady Eleanor (Nelly) Cecil (born Lambton, 1868–1959), wife of Robert, Viscount Cecil of Chelwood, son of Marquess of Salisbury, Conservative Prime Minister. Well-read, friend of VW and Vanessa; among the first to encourage them in their work.

Katherine, Countess of Cromer (born Thynne 1865–1933), married to Evelyn Baring, 1st Earl Cromer; Lady Beatrice Thynne (1867–1941) her sister. Friends of VW when young.

Cambridge

The Apostles, the name by which the Cambridge Conversazione Society, founded in 1820, is usually known. Their style of hard-hitting intellectual disputation was adopted by Bloomsbury. An asterisk has been put after the names of those below who were elected members of it.

Leonard Woolf * (1880–1969), Cambridge contemporary of VW's brother Thoby, at Trinity College. District officer in Ceylon (present-day Sri Lanka) for seven years before he married VW in 1912.

Lytton Strachey* (1880–1932), essayist and biographer, close friend of Thoby at Trinity.

James Strachey* (1887–1967), Lytton's younger brother, Cambridge contemporary of VW's brother Adrian. Married Alix Sargant-Florence in 1920. After working for his cousin St Loe Strachey, editor of *Spectator*, went to Vienna and was analysed by Freud, whose writing he translated and the Woolfs published.

Saxon Sydney-Turner* (1880–1962), member of Thoby's Cambridge circle. Passionate music-lover, especially of Wagner. Career as civil servant spent largely at the Treasury. Never married.

(Sir) Desmond MacCarthy* (1877–1952), literary and dramatic critic; famous for his conversation. Married Mary (Molly) Warre Cornish, author, daughter of Eton master, and founder of the Bloomsbury Memoir Club. Their only daughter Rachel MacCarthy married (Lord) David Cecil (1902–1986), Oxford don and biographer.

Roger Fry* (1866–1934), painter, art historian and critic, museum curator and organiser of the 1910 and 1912 Post-Impressionist Exhibitions in London.

E M (Morgan) Forster* (1879–1970), novelist, lifelong friend of LW and VW; Cambridge contemporary of

(Sir) Sydney Waterlow (1878–1944), diplomat and francophile, unsuccessful suitor of VW.

John Maynard Keynes* (1883–1946), economist and Cambridge don whose doctrine of 'full employment' was highly important for Britain. Married Lydia Lopokova (1892–1981), star of the Diaghilev Ballet Company in 1925. VW borrowed traits of Lydia's good nature for Rezia in *Mrs Dalloway*.

G E Moore* (1873–1958), Cambridge philosopher whose *Principia Ethica* has been called the Bible of Bloomsbury.

Artists, authors and patrons

Duncan Grant (1885–1978), painter, a cousin of Lytton Strachey, longtime partner of Vanessa Bell, and father of her daughter, Angelica.

David (Bunny) Garnett (1892–1981), novelist and critic, son of Russian translator Constance (1862–1946) and publisher's literary adviser, Edward Garnett (1868–1936). After the death of his first wife Ray (born Marshall) in 1940 he married Angelica in 1942.

Dora Carrington (1893–1932), painter, who devoted her life to looking after Lytton Strachey though married in 1921 to Ralph Partridge. Her fellow students at the Slade included the artist Mark Gertler (1891–1939) in love with her and

Barbara Hiles (later Bagenal) who worked for the Hogarth Press.

Rupert Brooke (1887–1915), poet of World War One, at one time in love with his Cambridge contemporary Katherine (Ka) Cox (1887–1938) who married William (Will) Arnold-Forster. VW knew Brooke and his set as 'the Neo-Pagans.'

Jacques Raverat (1885–1925), artist, one of the Neo-Pagans, Frenchman who grew up in England and who married Gwen (1885–1957, born Darwin), woodcut artist and author of Cambridge and Kensington memoir *Period Piece*.

Lady Ottoline Morrell (1873–1938), flamboyant society hostess, who took over Garsington Manor, near Oxford, where VW, LW and many other famous people were her guests. Married to Philip Morrell (1870–1943), Liberal MP and pacifist.

Lady Sibyl Colefax (1874–1950), society hostess, who became an interior decorator after her husband's death. Her regular guests ranged from VW and LW to the Duke and Duchess of Windsor.

Katherine Mansfield (1888–1923), New Zealand-born short story writer. Married to critic and editor J Middleton Murry (1889–1957). Died of TB.

T S Eliot (1888–1965), poet, dramatist, critic, and editor of the

Criterion, a literary quarterly. The Woolfs published his early work including *The Waste Land* at their Hogarth Press.

Wyndham Lewis (1884–1957), artist, novelist and critic who savagely attacked work of VW. Started and largely wrote a periodical he called *The Enemy*.

Arnold Bennett (1867–1931), novelist of the old school who as a regular reviewer launched the first attack on VW's method and work.

Hugh Walpole (1884–1941), novelist of the old school of whom VW was personally very fond.

Victoria (Vita) Sackville-West (1892–1962), novelist and poet, lesbian friend of VW, married to (Sir) Harold Nicolson (1886–1968), MP, biographer and critic. Mother of Ben Nicolson (1914–1978), art historian, and Nigel Nicolson (1917–2004), writer, publisher, MP, and co-editor of VW's letters.

Dame Ethel Smyth (1858–1944), composer and memoir writer, elderly lesbian and ebullient friend of VW with whom she was in love.

Ethel Sands (1873–1962), wealthy American-born painter and art patron. Pupil of artist Walter Sickert. Lived with her friend Nan Hudson (1869–1957), also an artist. Acquaintances of VW.

Elizabeth Robins (1862–1952), American actress who championed Ibsen in London in the 1890s. Friend originally of Stella Duckworth then, after settling in England and becoming a writer, friend in Sussex of VW and LW who published her.

Octavia Wilberforce (1888–1963), one of the first women doctors in England, lived with Robins and practised in Brighton. Attended Virginia during her final illness.

Dr F R and Q D (Queenie) Leavis (1895–1978 and 1906–1981), Cambridge academics who attacked VW and Bloomsbury in their influential critical journal, *Scrutiny*.

John Lehmann (1907–1987), poet and editor who became a partner of the Hogarth Press. His friends the poets Stephen Spender (1909–1995), W H Auden (1907–1973), Louis MacNeice (1907–1963) and the novelist Christopher Isherwood (1904 –1986) contributed to his *New Writing* collections.

Chronology

25 January 1882
Adeline Virginia Stephen born at 22 Hyde Park Gate, Kensington, to Julia Prinsep Duckworth (born Jackson) and Leslie Stephen.

1882-94
Virginia and her older sister Vanessa educated at home. In summer the Stephen family goes to Talland House, St Ives, Cornwall.

5 May 1895
Julia dies. Soon after, Virginia has a breakdown.

15 February 1897
Virginia resumes regular lessons.

10 April 1897
Her stepsister Stella Duckworth marries John (Jack) Waller Hills.

19 July 1897
Stella dies. Afterwards Kitty Maxse and Margaret Massingberd, Kensington neighbours and daughters of Julia's great friend, Jane Lushington, give Virginia and Vanessa support. Virginia has close friendships with her cousins Margaret and Emma Vaughan, their sister-in-law Margaret (Madge) Vaughan and with Violet Dickinson.

3 October 1899
Her older brother Thoby's first term begins at Trinity College, Cambridge. Among his contemporaries are Lytton Strachey, Saxon Sydney-Turner, Leonard Woolf and Clive Bell, future members of Bloomsbury circle. All except the last

are elected to the Apostles society and come under influence of philosopher G E Moore .

October 1900
Virginia goes to King's College, London.

26 June 1902
Leslie Stephen is knighted.

October 1902
Leslie has cancer. Operation in December by Sir Frederick Treves. Leslie finds solace in the company of Kitty Maxse, who 'mothers' Vanessa, now studying at the Royal Academy, and to a lesser extent Virginia.

14 November 1903
Leslie dictated his last entry to Virginia of his long letter (known as the *Mausoleum Book*) to his children begun after Julia died.

22 February 1904
Leslie dies.

April–May 1904
Virginia and Vanessa visit Florence and Paris.

May 1904
Virginia's second serious breakdown. Looked after at Violet Dickinson's house in Hertfordshire. Dr Savage prescribes rest from physical and mental exertion. The Duckworths and Stephens make plans to move to Bloomsbury.

October 1904
Virginia joins Vanessa, Thoby and their younger brother Adrian at 46 Gordon Square, Bloomsbury. She begins writing for periodical publications. Her

essay on 'Street Music' accepted by Leo Maxse (Kitty's husband) for publication in the *National Review*.

January 1905
Virginia arranges to give a weekly class at Morley College, Lambeth, with its deputy principal, Mary Sheepshanks, a feminist.

16 February 1905
Thoby's weekly evening At Home gatherings begin at Gordon Square. Several who attend are Cambridge Apostles.

March 1905
Virginia meets Bruce Richmond, editor of *The Times Literary Supplement*

10 March 1905
Virginia's first review (anonymous as always) in the *The Times Literary Supplement*

October 1905
Vanessa starts the Friday Club where artists meet regularly for discussion.

January 1906 onwards
Virginia takes classes at Morley, does regular reviewing, daily letter-writing and enjoys busy social life.

September 1906
Tour of Greece by Virginia, Vanessa and Violet. They join Thoby and Adrian at Olympia.

21 October 1906
All arrive back in London on November 1. Vanessa and Thoby have typhoid fever.

20 November 1906
Thoby dies.

November 1906
Vanessa slowly recovers; she and Clive Bell become engaged.

7 February 1907
Marriage of Vanessa and Clive at St Pancras Register Office.

10 April 1907
The Bells take over Gordon Square, Virginia and Adrian move to 29 Fitzroy Square.

October 1907
Virginia starts novel with title *Melymbrosia*, the earliest version of *The Voyage Out*.

4 February 1908
Vanessa gives birth to son, Julian. Virginia signed up to write a bi-monthly review-article for *The Cornhill* in tandem with Lady Eleanor (Nelly) Cecil.

3 September 1908
Virginia visits Italy with the Bells.

1 October
Her regular Thursday evening At Homes resume.

30 March 1909
Dines with Lady Ottoline Morrell.

10 February 1910
Participates in 'The Dreadnought Hoax'.

April onwards
Works for women's suffrage. Her health declines.

June-August 1910
Takes a rest cure at nursing home in Twickenham run by Miss Jean

Thomas, who becomes a friend.

8 November 1910
The First Post-Impressionist Exhibition, organised in London by Roger Fry, opens. The secretary is Desmond MacCarthy. Roger becomes Vanessa's lover.

January 1911
Virginia buys house at Firle, East Sussex, which she calls Little Talland House.

14–19 August 1911
Stays at The Old Vicarage, Grantchester, with Rupert Brooke. On August 27 to summer camp at Drewsteignton, Devon, where Bloomsbury people meet the Cambridge set Virginia calls the Neo-Pagans.

16–19 September 1911
Leonard Woolf on leave from Ceylon (Sri Lanka), where he has been working as a district officer for seven years. He and Marjorie Strachey, Lytton's sister, stay with Virginia at Firle.

October 1911
Virginia moves in Sussex from Firle to Asham House, Beddingham, and in London to 38 Brunswick Square. She, Adrian, the painter Duncan Grant (a cousin of Lytton Strachey), the economist John Maynard Keynes, and Leonard have rooms there and take meals together.

9 December 1911
Virginia rejects proposal of marriage from Sydney Waterlow.

11 January 1912
Leonard proposes to Virginia.

February 1912
Housewarming party at Asham. Virginia takes rest-cure at Miss Thomas's nursing home. Leonard and Ka Cox stay with her in April.

2 May 1912
Leonard resigns from Colonial Civil Service.

29 May 1912
Virginia accepts Leonard's proposal.

10 August 1912
Leonard and Virginia married at St Pancras Register Office.

18 August 1912
Honeymoon tour of France, Spain and Italy ending at Venice.

3 October 1912
Woolfs installed in 38 Brunswick Square. Leonard secretary of Fry's 2nd Post-Impressionist Exhibition.

Late October 1912
Woolfs move to rooms at 13 Clifford's Inn, adjoining Fleet Street.

January 1913
Virginia ill. Leonard sees doctors and discusses pros and cons of her trying to have a child.

9 March 1913
Manuscript of *The Voyage Out* given to Gerald Duckworth, head of his publishing firm, Duckworth & Co. Read by Edward Garnett, who recommends publication. This is delayed on account of Virginia's mental state.

March–December 1913
Virginia seriously ill for much of this period. Consensus of opinion against her attempting pregnancy. A suicide attempt by Virginia in September.

January 1914
Virginia resumes letter-writing and reading.

4 August 1914
War with Germany declared.

16 October 1914
Woolfs move to 17 The Green, Richmond.

January 1915
Virginia begins her adult Diary. Woolfs view Hogarth House and resolve to acquire it and install a printing press.

March 1915
Virginia becomes manic and violent; in nursing home while Leonard organises move to Hogarth House.

26 March 1915
The Voyage Out published

1 April 1915
Virginia brought to Hogarth House. Four nurses needed. Last one does not leave till November.

30 May 1916
Leonard examined by Army Medical Board and declared unfit because of congenital nervous tremor.

October 1916
Vanessa, in love with Duncan Grant, moves to farmhouse at Charleston in same part of Sussex as Asham.

December 1916
Rev John Llewelyn-Davies dies. Virginia cuts Kitty Maxse at his funeral.

24 April 1917
Printing Press installed at Hogarth House.

July 1917
Virginia's 'The Mark on the Wall' published as first publication of Woolfs' Hogarth Press with Leonard's 'Three Jews'.

17–19 November 1917
Ottoline and Philip Morell now have Garsington Manor, Oxfordshire. Woolfs' first visit coincides with furore over Sassoon's anti-war poems.

May 1918
Eminent Victorians by Lytton Strachey published.

June 1918
Katherine Mansfield's *Prelude* published by Woolfs.

25 December 1918
Daughter Angelica born to Vanessa and Duncan Grant at Charleston.

12 May 1919
Virginia's *Kew Gardens,* T S Eliot's *Poems* and Middleton Murry's *The Critic in Judgement* published by Woolfs.

1 September 1919
Woolfs move to Monk's House, Rodmell.

20 October 1919
Night and Day published by Duckworth.

4 March 1920
First meeting of Memoir Club.

April 1921
Monday or Tuesday published.

27–29 May 1922
Woolfs at Tidmarsh to visit Lytton and Carrington. Virginia meets Gerald Brenan.

8 October 1922
Virginia learns of Kitty Maxse's death by falling over banisters at her Kensington house.

27 October 1922
Jacob's Room published by Hogarth Press, as are all Virginia's works from now.

17 November 1922
Leonard fails to be elected to Parliament at General Election.

14 December 1922
Virginia meets Victoria Sackville-West.

9 January 1923
Katherine Mansfield dies.

August–September
Virginia writes satirical one-act play *Freshwater* and begins *Mrs Dalloway* under title *The Hours*.

March 1924
Woolfs move to 52 Tavistock Square for their London house.

30 October 1924
Essay *Mr Bennett and Mrs Brown* published in response to attack by Arnold Bennett.

23 April 1925
The Common Reader published.

14 May 1925
Mrs Dalloway published.

17–20 December 1925
Virginia stays with Vita at her house Long Barn in Kent.

5 May 1927
To The Lighthouse published.

11 October 1928
Orlando published.

20 October 1928 and following days
Virginia reads papers on women and fiction at Newnham and Girton Colleges, Cambridge.

24 October 1929
A Room of One's Own, a revised version of one of these papers, published.

21 January 1931
John Lehmann joins Hogarth Press.

8 October 1931
The Waves published.

21 January 1932
Lytton Strachey dies.

1 July 1932
A Letter to a Young Poet published.

31 August 1932
Lehmann leaves Hogarth Press.

13 October 1932
The Common Reader: Second Series published.

1933
Virginia starts work on a long essay-novel originally called *The Pargiters*.

5 October 1933
Flush published.

15 December 1933
Virginia meets Walter Sickert at Clive Bell's.

9 September 1934
Roger Fry dies.

20 October 1934
Walter Sickert: A Conversation (a pamphlet) published.

18 January 1935
Revised version of *Freshwater* performed in Vanessa's London studio.

July 1935
Lehmann resumes contact with Woolfs. Fry's sister Margery and mistress Helen Anrep try to persuade Virginia to write Roger's life.

15 March 1937
The Years (formerly *The Pargiters*) published to much acclaim.

18 July 1937
Julian Bell killed in Spain.

1938
Virginia working on biography of Roger Fry and planning new novel (*Pointz Hall*).

1 March 1938
John Lehmann buys Virginia's shareholding in Hogarth Press with aim of publishing his *New Writing* collections.

17 August 1939 and following
Woolfs and Hogarth Press move to 37 Mecklenburgh Square.

3 September 1939
World War Two begins.

27 April 1940
Virginia attacks work of younger poets in lecture to Workers' Educational Association in Brighton, afterwards published as *The Leaning Tower*.

25 July 1940
Roger Fry: a Biography published.

August 1940 and following months
Flight path of bombers is over Rodmell. Monk's House shaken by bomb blast. Woolfs' house at Mecklenburgh Square severely damaged in raid and 52 Tavistock Square shattered. Hogarth Press moves with Lehmann to Letchworth, Hertfordshire.

26 February 1941
Virginia finishes *Pointz Hall*, to be called *Between the Acts*.

18 March 1941
Virginia showing alarming signs of fresh onset of madness.

27 March 1941
Dr Octavia Wilberforce sees Virginia in Brighton.

28 March 1941
Virginia commits suicide by drowning in River Ouse and leaves letters for Leonard assuring him their marriage could not have been happier.

Index

160; Carrington and, 182; depicted in National Gallery, 188; perform VW's play, 188–9; attitudes criticised, 207; *see also* Memoir Club
'Blue and Green', 123
Bodenheim, Maxwell, 130
Bodkin, Maud, 189
Bomberg, David, 88
Booth, Charles, 28
Bosanquet, Theodora, 170
Boswell, James, 152, 223
Boxall, Miss Nellie, 160
Bradbrook, M C, 191
Bradley, F H, 65
Braque, Georges, 87
Brenan, Gerald, 133, 183
Brett, Dorothy, 89
Brighton, 29, 221–2
British Museum, 37
Brontë, Charlotte, 32
Brontë, Emily, 160
Brontë sisters, 50, 142
Brooke, Rupert, 16, 74–6, 81, 148, 204
Brooke, William, 16
Browne, Sir Thomas, 160
Browning, Robert, 186
Bullett, Gerald, 177
Bunin, Ivan, 132
Burgundy, 163
Burke, Edmund, 73
Burlington Magazine, 207
Burnham Wood, 43

C

Calcutta, 13
Calendar of Modern Letters, 143, 190
Cambridge, 16, 68, 185, 200; Duckworth brothers at, 10, 28; dons, 12, 113, 141; Union, 17; VW and Vanessa visit, 34; Trinity College, 35, 129, 167; friendships, 36, 42, 51, 53, 105, 125; Tripos, 49; Apostles Society, 63–5, 71, 75, 112, 150, 193, 205; Rupert Brooke's set, 74–5, 204; Heretics Society, 131; VW gives talk at, 167–8, 191; practical criticism, 190–1; literature teaching, 201–2
Cameron, Julia Margaret, 12–13, 188
Campbell, Mary, 157–60
Campbell, Roy, 157–60
Captain's Death, The, 211
Carrington, Dora, 89, 107, 111, 159; and Strachey, 103, 132, 181–3; death, 182–3, 193
Carrington, Samuel, 182
Case, Emphie, 71, 204
Case, Janet, 49, 71, 81, 109, 204
Cassell's Weekly, 130
Cassis, 171

Cecil, Lord David, 2, 52, 69, 131
Cecil, Lady Eleanor (Nelly), 52, 59, 69, 90, 93–4, 160
Cecil, Lord Robert, 52
Ceylon, 54, 65, 79–81, 86, 141
Cézanne, Paul, 68, 86, 88, 133
Chamberlain, Austen, 35
Chamberlain, Neville, 213
Chamson, André, 193
'Character in Fiction', 131
Charleston, 94, 113
Chaucer, Geoffrey, 141–3, 218
Chekhov, Anton, 93, 140, 142
Cheltenham, 32
Child, Harold, 115, 121
Chirol, Valentine, 51
Christianity, 203
Churchill, Winston, 104
Clapham Sect, 28, 221
Clifton College, 23, 35
Cocteau, Jean, 151
Cole, G D H, 120
Cole, Horace, 125
Cole, Margaret, 120
Colefax, Lady Sybil, 123, 148, 160, 162
Common Reader, The, 141–3, 152, 211
Comte, Auguste, 14
Connolly, Cyril, 220
Conrad, Joseph, 113, 142
Constant, Benjamin, 152
Constantinople, 56
Corby Castle, 32–3
Cornhill magazine, 59
Costelloe, Frank, 151
Costelloe, Karin, 75, 151
Costelloe, Ray, 75, 151
Coward, Noël, 199
Cox, Katherine (Ka), 74–6, 85, 88, 204
Craig, Edith, 203, 218
Craigie, Pearl (John Oliver Hobbes), 51
Creighton, Dr Mandell, 15
Criterion, 132, 135, 159
Cromer, Katie, 42, 52, 90

D

Daily News, 95
Darwin, Charles, 14, 75
Darwin, Frances, 75
Darwin, Sir George, 75
Davidson, Angus, 131, 141
Davies, Emily, 168
Davies, Sylvia, 26
Days circulating library, 89–90
de Charrière, Madame de, 152
de Polignac, Princesse, 151
De Quincey, Thomas, 160, 223
Death of the Moth, The, 211
Defoe, Daniel, 142, 160

245

249

ARTHUR ACKERMANN & SONS
A. BIDE LTD
157
SPEAIGHT
HOUSE AGENTS
JOHN BROADWO
SONS